LANGUAGE, BELIEF, AND METAPHYSICS

CONTEMPORARY PHILOSOPHIC THOUGHT

The International Philosophy Year Conferences At Brockport

LANGUAGE, BELIEF, AND METAPHYSICS

Edited by Howard E. Kiefer and Milton K. Munitz

STATE UNIVERSITY OF NEW YORK PRESS

ALBANY

PUBLISHED BY STATE UNIVERSITY OF NEW YORK PRESS
THURLOW TERRACE, ALBANY, NEW YORK 12201

© 1970 BY STATE UNIVERSITY OF NEW YORK,
ALBANY, NEW YORK. ALL RIGHTS RESERVED

LIBRARY OF CONGRESS CATALOG CARD NUMBER 69-14643
STANDARD BOOK NUMBER 87395-051-8
MANUFACTURED IN THE UNITED STATES OF AMERICA

DESIGNER: RHODA C. CURLEY

CONTENTS

vii

THE NATURE OF BELIEF

METAPHYSICS

ACKNOWLEDGMENTS

Fourteen international conferences on philosophy and related topics were held at the State University College at Brockport, New York, during the 1967–1968 academic year. Hundreds of scholars attended the conferences as participants and observers. Known as the International Philosophy Year, the program was supported by the United States Department of State, the National Endowment for the Humanities, Unesco, the Xerox Corporation, the International Business Machines Corporation, the Sperry and Hutchinson Foundation, Duryea Motors, the Brockport Student Government, the New York State Education Department, and the State University of New York. In addition, Mrs. John Dewey, widow of the late distinguished philosopher and scholar, generously provided Honors Scholarships for Brockport students through the John Dewey Foundation.

Contemporary Philosophic Thought is a four-volume anthology containing the major papers delivered at the conferences. Also included are some of the responses which were a regular part of the conference proceedings; space limitations did not permit the inclusion of more, much to the regret of the coeditors.

The International Philosophy Year was made possible through the encouragement and continuing support of President Albert W. Brown of the State University College of Arts and Science at Brockport, and Chancellor Samuel B. Gould of the State University of New York.

My friend and colleague, Milton K. Munitz, professor and department head of philosophy at New York University, served as Distinguished Visiting Professor of Philosophy at Brockport during the 1967–1968 academic year, and delivered the Brockport Lectures which are included in this anthology. Professor Munitz's immense scholarship, initiative, and creative participation in every aspect of the planning and execution of the program were indispensable, and I shall always remain in his debt. He consented to serve as coeditor of these four volumes, and assisted in the difficult task of arranging the wealth of materials produced during the conferences. In addition, he accepted editorial responsibility for Volumes 1 and 2 of this anthology.

Charles Frankel, professor of philosophy at Columbia University, was serving as United States Assistant Secretary of State for Educational and Cultural Affairs at the time the International Philosophy Year was in the planning stages, and he arranged for State Department support which enabled Professor Munitz and me to travel to Europe to make essential arrangements with Unesco and with a number of the distinguished European philosophers who later participated in the program. At Unesco headquarters in Paris, Director-General Dr. René Maheu graciously offered his support, and the support of the Division of Philosophy under Professor Jeanne Hersch, thus contributing in important ways to the international aspect of the entire program.

The National Endowment for the Humanities, under the direction of Barnaby C. Keeney, provided a grant which brought to the conferences a number of distinguished academicians and men active in public affairs, representing fields other than philosophy. This aspect of the total program contributed importantly to the effectiveness of the International Philosophy Year endeavor, and led to the establishment of the Center for Philosophic Exchange on the Brockport campus. The Center will continue the work of the International Philosophy Year on a long-term basis.

The New York Education Department provided a matching grant which permitted the making of twelve one-hour television tapes of informal discussions between major participants and Honors students in Philosophy. These television tapes were broadcast initially by Channel 21 of the National Education Television Network, and Channel 31 in New York has repeated the series on more than one occasion. The State Education Department continues to make the tapes available to universities and colleges, and to other interested groups, on application. In addition, television tapes were made of many of the major addresses, and of the discussions which followed, as time permitted.

Joseph Gilbert, assistant professor of philosophy at Brockport, acted as Assistant Director of the International Philosophy Year. His tireless concern with detail saved me from many errors, and his enthusiasm and devotion to the entire enterprise account in no small way for whatever success it enjoyed. He and I owe a special debt of gratitude to the other members of the Department of Philosophy at Brockport, and to

Mrs. Shirley Thomson, Anthony Gabrielli, and Henry Miller, who served as graduate assistants.

In addition to their formal participation in the program, many of the leading contributors permitted me to seek their advice on a number of matters. I am particularly grateful to Richard McKeon of the University of Chicago and to Sidney Hook of New York University, both of whom served as State University Professors in Residence during part of the period; Kai Nielsen of New York University, who participated on several occasions; Max Black of Cornell University; Charles Frankel of Columbia University; and my former teacher, Marvin Farber, of the State University of New York at Buffalo.

My secretary, Mrs. Elaine Taylor, cheerfully managed the ocean of correspondence and the arrangement details with her characteristic efficiency, earning the gratitude and respect of all of us.

This brief space does not permit me to name and duly thank all of those on whom I depended for assistance during the three-year period culminating in the publication of this anthology. But I must add that my deepest debt is to Mildred Crabtree Kiefer, who provided the indispensable love and encouragement which even a philosopher must require of his wife.

Howard E. Kiefer, Director
International Philosophy Year

INTRODUCTION

It is a commonplace that the contemporary philosophic scene—or, at least, a major segment of it, what goes by the name "analytic philosophy"—is dominated by a concern with language. Even where we find age-old questions being re-examined, the attention to matters of language in pursuit of these themes is an evident fact. Nowhere is this influence to be more clearly noted than in the study of logic. And this is no more than natural. For logic has as its concern, and as the etymology of the word itself confirms, an interest in probing the forms of discourse. It undertakes to make explicit and codify the rules and regulative standards for any thought that is to be judged sound. It is appropriate, therefore, in presenting to the reader the fruits of the year-long series of conferences at Brockport in the *International Philosophy Year* of 1967–1968, that we begin with a group of essays devoted to a study of the impact of language on philosophy.

In his paper on "Philosophical Progress in Language Theory," W. V. Quine surveys the field of contemporary scientific language-theory and argues that it exhibits a major shift in our understanding of empiricism. What he describes as the "externalization of empiricism" represents a change from the preoccupation of classical empiricists with internal mental phenomena—ideas, sense data and the like, to a concern with language as a social phenomenon, and as studied behaviorally in the external and publicly accessible world of human interactions. He examines some of the consequences and problems brought about by this shift from "ideas" to "verbal behavior." What, for example, are we now to say of the much-debated questions concerning meaningfulness and meaninglessness? And what are we now to make of traditional views about analyticity? Again, when one takes seriously this "behaviorizing of meaning," what pitfalls and problems confront those engaged in a program of radical translation from one natural language to another? His analysis of these themes recalls matters that occupied him in his *Word and Object,* in particular, questions about the "indeterminacy of translation" and the use of "analytical hypotheses" as ways of dealing with such problems of translation. The papers by Paul Ziff (on "The Logical Structure of English Sentences") and by Max Black (on "Logic and Ordinary Language") are both, in their own ways, concerned with a common theme, that of understanding the role of formal logic in its service of regulating discourse. What does such formalization come to? What are its limitations and its possible uses? Ziff examines some of the techniques and devices of modern formal logic, in particular the use of quantificational formulae. He raises the question as to how successful these are when offered as ways of regimenting the varied types of sentences and expressions to be found in a natural language such as English. Max Black re-examines the oft-repeated distinction between logical form and specific content and argues that the frequently glib and standard appeals to "form" are not as clarifying as they are sometimes thought to be. In his ruminative survey of these deep and fundamental matters in the philosophy of logic, he gives grounds for suggesting "that modern logic is neither a universal tool nor a panacea." Hilary Putnam's essay on "Is Semantics Possible?" examines what is meant by speaking of "natural kinds" as a putative theme of semantic theory. He criticizes certain traditional and current theories according to which we can find essential properties to define natural kinds and that can be specified in analytically true characterizations. What it is to be an "*x*" (say, a lemon), he argues, cannot be readily specified in such a way that it is applicable to all instances of *x*. In this connection, he offers a critique of Jerrold Katz's recent semantic theory, and offers some positive corrective suggestions of his own in dealing with natural-kind terms. Peter Strawson's paper on "The Asymmetry of Subjects and Predicates" undertakes to explore in depth a particular corner of logical theory. He starts with a point noted by Peter Geach and G. E. M. Anscombe according to which there is a basic difference or asymmetry between subjects and predicates as the major constituents of any proposition, when these are examined from a logical as distinct from a grammatical point of view. It is this: whereas predicates can be negated to form a new predicate, the names or other referring devices that serve as the logical subjects of a proposition cannot be negated. He calls this "the asymmetry thesis." He notes, in addition, a further asymmetry: that whereas we can, in a perfectly straightforward way, form compound predicates, we cannot form compound subjects. His paper is principally concerned with showing why these asymmetries do in fact hold, and in giving his reasons for sup-

porting this broadened "asymmetry thesis." His argument, as an exercise
in philosophical logic, recalls a number of broad philosophical distinctions between the particular and the general that he had considered at
length in his well-known *Individuals*.

The subject of "Belief" has come to acquire a centrality of interest
for philosophers, not unlike that long enjoyed by perception. Like perception, belief, while a familiar and pervasive aspect of human experience, is nevertheless one of the most difficult concepts to explicate.
Controversies and differences of approach are prominent features in the
literature of the subject. This is readily understandable when we come
to reflect upon the fact that the topic of belief, as is the case with so
many other fundamental concepts of philosophy, has the widest ramifications and repercussions. The stance we take with respect to it has the
most far-reaching effects. What, for example, are the similarities or differences between knowledge and belief? Approached psychologically, are
beliefs states of mind, occurrences, or dispositions? What similarities or
differences are there between believing *in* and believing *that*? What are
the connections between belief and faith? What connections are to be
traced between belief, propositions, and the concept of evidential support? These are but a few of the questions that readily present themselves for discussion, and that suggest by their scope and divergent directions of interest why the subject continues to engage the attention of
philosophers. The several papers on Belief in what follows deal with
some of the foregoing themes. Bernard Williams in his paper on "Deciding to Believe" begins by calling attention to certain familiar and elementary features that characterize belief. He points out that while there
are reasons why we might be prepared to ascribe to properly constituted
machines the having of beliefs, their being in what he calls "B-states"
(or having beliefs in a reduced sense), nevertheless there are ultimate
and irreducible differences between the sense in which we ascribe belief
to a *machine* and the sense in which we ascribe a belief to a *person*. He
points to the importance of such a simple fact as that we can say that a
person holds a belief *sincerely* or expresses his beliefs *insincerely*,
whereas these locutions are inappropriate in connection with machines.
Justus Hartnack in his discussion of "Logical Incongruities Between the
Concept of Knowledge and the Concept of Belief" surveys some elementary and important differences between what it means to say that a
person *knows* something and *believes* something. Arthur Danto in his
"Beliefs As Sentential States of Persons" undertakes to analyze belief in
terms of the central notion of a *sentential-state*. He proposes to view beliefs as internal states of a person, as something which characterize him
absolutely, rather than relationally. He suggests further how we may
make fruitful use of the notion of "quotations" in giving a characteriza-

tion of what it means to say that a person is in a sentential state. Finally, Wilfrid Sellars in his "Belief and the Expression of Belief" asks what it means to say, for example, "Jones believes that P." He shows how the notions of "settled dispositions," "thinking out loud," "questions whether-P," are all involved in a crucial way in explicating the concept of belief.

The field of metaphysics is represented in the present volume by two papers, those of Roderick M. Chisholm and Milton K. Munitz. Their themes, indicative of the kinds of perennial issues that belong to metaphysics, are respectively devoted to the problem of "Identity through Time" and "The Concept of the World." When we say that X is the same individual now that it was at an earlier time, what is to be understood by this claim? In what does the identity or sameness of X over a period of time consist? Chisholm, in dealing with this question, explores the basic differences which, in his judgment, hold for our views of physical objects as contrasted with persons. What does it mean to say that a physical object existing at one time is the same as or identical with that which existed at another time? And what does it mean to say that a person existing at one time is the same as or identical with that which existed at another time? Chisholm argues, in agreement with Bishop Butler, that the idea of identity (or "being the same") as used in connection with physical objects is only to be understood in a "loose or popular sense," whereas when used in connection with a person the same ideas are to be understood in a "strict and philosophical sense." Whereas, he maintains, some elements of convention or decision are appropriately invoked in our uttering judgments about the identity of physical objects which undergo significant changes or transformations, there is no comparable question of convention or decision in connection with such radical transformations or changes that might take place in the career of a person. The essay on "The Concept of the World" by Milton K. Munitz devotes itself to exploring what is sometimes called "the problem of Being" or the *Seinsfrage*. What does it mean to speak of "The World"? Can this term be assimilated to the way in which we would make reference to an individual, or, on the other hand, to a class or totality of some sort? Arguments are offered to show that neither of these familiar rubrics is adequate, and that the "logic" of this term is not readily assimilable to our conventional schema. More appropriately, but wholly guardedly, one might say of the world what in traditional theology has often been said about God—that as an ultimate "concept," it is at once fundamental for our total conceptual scheme, yet also indefinable. The proposal is made that the concept of the world is of something we can accordingly describe as being *transcendent*.

M. K. M.

PHILOSOPHY OF LANGUAGE

PHILOSOPHICAL PROGRESS IN LANGUAGE THEORY

W. V. Quine

Philosophy, or what appeals to me under that head, is continuous with science. It is a wing of science in which aspects of method are examined more deeply, or in a wider perspective than elsewhere. It is also a wing in which the objectives of a science receive more than average scrutiny, and the significance of the results receives special appreciation. The man who does this philosophical sort of work may be a philosopher in point of professional affiliation, but a philosopher with an interest in the special science concerned; or again, he may be an affiliate of the special science, but philosophical in attitude and motivation. Einstein was in this latter category. His empirical critique of the concept of simultaneity is a philosophical paradigm. Bohr's infusion of epistemology into quantum mechanics makes him another example. Further philosophical spirits in professional physics are the cosmologists, such as Bondi and Hoyle. For that matter, surely what has drawn most theoretical physicists to physics is a philosophical quest for the inner nature of reality.

Thus I picture the professional physicist and the professional philosopher as impelled alike, by philosophical curiosity, into physics and its philosophical wing. This picture strikes me as truer than the picture which depicts a general-utility philosophical reservoir as tapped now and again by physics or other sciences. True, empiricism and idealism are full-width philosophies, and Einstein and Bohr are sometimes regarded as funneling the one or the other into physics. On the other hand empiricism itself, surely, is no less justly seen as science's gift to philosophy. It is, at any rate, the separation that I am against. The relation between philosophy and science is not best seen even in terms of give and take. Philosophy, or what appeals to me under that head, is an aspect of science.

Rather than speak of applications of philosophy to a science, there-

3

fore, or even of progress in the philosophy of the science, I would speak of philosophical progress *in* the science. What I am to speak of more particularly is philosophical progress in language theory.

This progress is characterized, of course, by scrupulous empirical method. But we must notice in empiricism a curious opposition of currents which, in relation to language theory, can make all the difference between black and white. On the one hand, it is in the empiricist tradition to take subjective sense impressions as the starting point and to try to reduce all talk of external objects to this basis. On the other hand, the method of introspection is often condemned by empirical scientists as the very antithesis of empirical method.

This latter trend, the externalizing of empiricism, comes from a heightened appreciation of the role of language in knowledge. If I were to set an initial date, I might take 1786. That year saw the publication of a sort of declaration of independence. The author of the declaration was the philologist John Horne Tooke, who wrote in part as follows: "The greatest part of Mr. Locke's essay, that is, all which relates to what he calls the abstraction, complexity, generalization, relation, etc. of ideas, does indeed merely concern language." [1] With Tooke, and with his younger contemporary Jeremy Bentham, the theory of language was on its way to becoming independent of the theory of ideas. Ideas dropped to a subordinate status, as adjuncts of words. They stayed on as meanings or intensions or connotations of words.

Once the focus had shifted thus from ideas to language, the externalizing of empiricism was assured. For language, unlike the idea, is conspicuously external. Language is a social art, acquired on evidence of social usage.

The learning not just of language but of anything, at the level where learning is best understood, is of course external in one respect: it is a conditioning of responses to external stimulation. Even the old empiricists appreciated this point, in their way; *nihil in intellectu quod non prius in sensu*. But the learning of language, in particular, is an external affair also in a further respect—because of the social character of language. It is not just that we learn language by a conditioning of overt responses to external stimulation. The more special point is that verbal behavior is determined by what people can observe of one another's responses to what people can observe of one another's external stimulations. In learning language, all of us, from childhood on, are amateur students of behavior, and, simultaneously, subjects of amateur studies of behavior. Thus, consider the typical learning of a word, at its simplest: you are confronted by the object of the word in the presence of your teacher. Part of the plan is that he knows that you see the object and you know that he does. This feature is equally in point on the later occasion when the teacher approves or disapproves of your use of the word. The natural consequence is that the clearest words, or at least the words that are learned first and used most consistently, tend to be words not for sense impressions but for conspicuous external objects.

Thus it is that the declaration of independence precipitated a revolution, a Copernican flip. There are, we see, two factors: first, the philosophical shift of focus from idea to word; second, the linguistic fact that the words in sharpest focus are mainly words for external objects. For empiricism as thus reoriented, the focus of understanding is outside us. Our mental life settles into an inferential status. The internal looks now for its legitimation to external evidence. The ghost, in Ryle's phrase, is exorcised from the machine.[2] This is behaviorism. It has not become everyone's philosophy, nor even every empiricist's philosophy. The revolution has been, for empiricism, less a turning point than a splitting point.

Even those who have not embraced behaviorism as a philosophy are, however, obliged to adhere to behavioristic method within certain scientific pursuits; and language theory is such a pursuit. A scientist of language is, insofar, a behaviorist ex officio. Whatever the best eventual theory regarding the inner mechanism of language may turn out to be, it is bound to conform to the behavioral character of language learning: the dependence of verbal behavior on observation of verbal behavior. A language is mastered through social emulation and social feedback, and these controls ignore any idiosyncrasy in an individual's imagery or associations that is not discovered in his behavior. Minds are indifferent to language insofar as they differ privately from one another; that is, insofar as they are behaviorally inscrutable.

Thus, though a linguist may still esteem mental entities philosophically, they are pointless or pernicious in language theory. This point was emphasized by Dewey in the twenties, when he argued that there could not be, in any serious sense, a private language.[3] Wittgenstein also, years later, came to appreciate this point. Linguists have been conscious of it in increasing measure; Bloomfield to a considerable degree, Harris fully.

Earlier linguistic theory operated in an uncritical mentalism. An irresponsible semantics prevailed, in which words were related to ideas much as labels are related to the exhibits in a museum. To switch languages was to switch the labels. The uncritical mentalism and irresponsible semantics were, of course, philosophical too. I do not limit the role of philosophy in language theory to Tooke, Bentham, Dewey, and behaviorism; but I am speaking of philosophical *progress* in language theory.

It should be noted that the contrast between behaviorism and mentalism has little to do with the contrast in early empiricism between the learned and the innate. Any behaviorist account of the learning process is openly and emphatically committed to innate beginnings. The behaviorist recognizes the indispensability, for any kind of learning, of prior biases and affinities. Without these there could be no selective reinforcements or extinctions of responses, since all discriminable stimulations would count as equally dissimilar. There must be innate inequalities in our qualitative spacing, so to speak, of stimulations. This much applies to men and other animals equally, insofar as the conditioning of responses is to be possible at all.[4]

Moreover, it has long been recognized that our innate endowments for language learning go yet further than the mere spacing of qualities. Otherwise we should expect other animals to learn language; and also, as Chomsky has lately stressed, we should expect our own learning to take longer than it does. Two generations ago, the supplementary innate endowment that got the main credit was an instinct for mimicry. One generation ago, a babbling instinct moved to first place; the infant babbles at random and the parent reinforces these utterances selectively. Currently, the babbling instinct is losing favor and the instinct for mimicry is back in the ascendancy. I expect that both of these innate aids are there, and also of course the innate spacing of qualities, as well as some further innate apparatus which has not yet been identified.

Clearly the innate aids to language are extensive, whatever their details. I stress this because I have sensed of late a mistaken notion that there is a strain between behaviorism and innate dispositions. Nothing could be farther from the truth, since conditioning itself rests on innate spacing of qualities. I suppose the mistaken notion arises from first associating behaviorism with empiricism, which is right, and then associating empiricism with Locke's repudiation of innate ideas, which is as may be, and finally associating innate ideas with innate dispositions.

This chain of associations neglects the externalization of empiricism, which, I said earlier, makes all the difference between black and white. Before externalization, ideas were the stock in trade. Locke and his predecessors Hobbes and Gassendi, having to state empiricist standards in ideational terms, drew the line between ideas rooted in sensation and innate ideas; *nihil in intellectu quod non prius in sensu*. When empiricism is externalized, however, talk of ideas goes by the board. If any of it is to be dredged back up, it must be made sense of in terms of dispositions to overt behavior. It is this insistence on making sense in terms of dispositions to overt behavior that characterizes empiricism after externalization; and there is nothing unempirical, in this sense, about innate dispositions to overt behavior.

I spoke of the externalization of empiricism as a Copernican flip. For Dewey this subordination of idea to word was complete. *Verbum sapienti satis est.* "Meaning," Dewey wrote, [5] "is primarily a property of behavior." The reorientation may also be seen in the latter-day Wittgenstein. "The meaning of a word," Wittgenstein wrote,[6] "is its use in the language." I regret to say that the flip has not been so neat in all quarters. There has been reorientation by degrees. A usual latter-day posture is a posture with one foot in words and the other in ideas; and progress in such cases is to be seen only in the degree of shifting of weight from the one foot to the other.

One index of this shifting of weight is an increasingly critical attitude toward the old notion of analyticity: the notion that some truths are marked off from others as being true solely by virtue of meanings and independently of matters of fact. The more of one's weight one supports on the left or verbal foot, the less distinction remains between truth that is analytic and truth that is just generally believed. The distinction wavers as soon as we try to base it on verbal behavior. When you consider how the notion of analyticity has dominated empiricist philosophy, the shortcoming that vitiates the notion is ironical; for it is that the notion is just insufficiently empirical. If this seems paradoxical, however, the resolution of the paradox is not far to see. It is the externalization of empiricism that leaves the notion of analyticity without a foot to stand on. It is externalized empiricism, or behaviorism, that welcomes innate dispositions while looking askance at analyticity.

Analyticity was a philosophical notion. The critique of it is thus not a case of philosophy's impact on linguistics, but rather a backlash on philosophy. Still, it is philosophical progress in language theory.

A notion that has much in common with that of analyticity is the notion of meaninglessness. Both are prominent in philosophy; both are linguistic in the sense of purporting to apply to expressions; and both are challenged by the externalizing of empiricism. While the museum myth lasted, a meaningless expression could just be thought of as an unattached label. But when we try to infer meaninglessness from verbal behavior, we cannot easily distinguish it from mere extravagance. Carnap's example, "This stone is thinking about Vienna," and Russell's, "Quadruplicity drinks procrastination," were intended as neither true nor false but meaningless. On the strength of verbal behavior we could as well say that they are meaningful but just too extravagantly false to be worth denying.

In the heyday of the Vienna Circle, the notion of meaninglessness played a normative role. Metaphysics was denounced as meaningless. For this purpose a sentence was rated as meaningless if neither it nor its negation was either analytic or empirically verifiable. However, the notion of analyticity has its troubles, and the notion of verifiability has had, increasingly through the years, its troubles too.

The critique of metaphysics was not the only philosophical use of the notion of meaninglessness. Another philosophical use was in the deduction of the categories, modern style. Two expressions counted as belonging in the same category if and only if the result of putting the one for the other in a meaningful expression was never meaningless. Categories, in turn, had their use in Ryle's doctrine of category mistakes, and also in buttressing certain dubious doctrines such as that the verb "exist" differs in meaning according to whether it is applied to particulars or to universals.

Is the notion of meaninglessness, like that of analyticity, to be declared meaningless? Not exactly; this declaration would be false or meaningless. But what we can say of both notions is that no definitions of them are at hand which meet the demands of users of the terms and at the same time the demands of clarity.

Besides the philosophers' normative notion of meaningfulness there is the linguists' descriptive notion of meaningfulness: the notion of grammaticality. The foregoing definition of category, repeated now in terms of this descriptive notion of meaningfulness, gives a descriptive notion of category; and this is the notion of what linguists call a substitution class—the scientific successor of the notion of a part of speech. These linguistic notions of grammaticality and substitution class are likewise found to be less than firmly moored when we look to behavioral evidence.

To be ungrammatical is indeed simply to be foreign to the language. Yet the fact that a form is not heard in the community, and cannot by ordinary procedures be elicited, is not enough to brand the form as ungrammatical; for the Carnap and Russell examples, after all, are counted as grammatical, and reckoned to the language. How does the linguist settle how much unspoken nonsense of this sort to count within the language? Essentially just by rounding out the recorded or predicted corpus of actual utterances, letting in enough else to keep his description of the language conveniently simple and general. A prior and absolute standard of grammaticality in behavioral terms is not to be hoped for.

The externalizing of empiricism begets, we saw, a behaviorizing of meaning. This, for all its repercussions, is simply a proposal to approach semantical matters in the empirical spirit of natural science. An aid to taking this proposal seriously is the *Gedankenexperiment* of radical translation. Imagine yourself among savages, setting about to learn their language by unaided empirical inquiry, unaided by manuals or interpreters. You pick up a native expression which, by its circumstances, could mean "rabbit." You confirm this hypothesis by querying the expression on subsequent occasions and finding that natives give what you take to be assent to the query whenever a rabbit is pointed to, and dissent when anything else is pointed to. In principle any such findings would be equally compatible with some perverse alternative translations of the native expression. There is no distinction, after all, between pointing to a rabbit and pointing to a temporal stage of a rabbit, or to an undetached part of a rabbit. In principle there is no way of deciding among the translations "rabbit," "rabbit stage," "undetached rabbit part," except by questioning the natives in terms not yet translatable: terms hinging on singular and plural, sameness and difference. I have argued elsewhere [7] that the translation of this apparatus of singular and plural and of sameness and difference into the native language can itself be varied and juggled in compensatory ways, so as to accommodate the perverse choice "rabbit stage" or "undetached rabbit part" no less than the natural choice "rabbit."

In principle, thus, any of the above translations could be sustained —"rabbit" or a more perverse one—barring, of course, the imposition of some restraining principle. But in fact we would impose, however unconsciously, this restraining principle: Where there is choice, favor the short translation.

A lesson that can be learned at this point is a lesson in wariness toward what linguists call linguistic universals. Suppose a linguist were to propound, as a linguistic universal, a *law of Gestalt*. The law might say roughly that speakers of all languages tend to favor short expressions such as "rabbit" for enduring things that resemble one another and contrast with their surroundings in color and movement. It would be a plausible law, borne out by observation of languages and predictable anyway from common-sense psychology. But what a linguist unwary of his universals is apt to overlook is that observation of languages is here irrelevant. The law comes of our unconsciously imposed maxim of favoring short translations. Common-sense psychology is relevant only as jusifying this maxim and not as explaining an objective trend in linguistic behavior.

In the old days when the idea idea was supreme, there was a comfortable illusion of determinacy of translation. To understand a language was to get its labels on to the right ideas. We could make mistakes, but still was an objectively right answer to be found; and supposedly it always could be found, though the method was not spelled out—it was too intuitive for spelling out. As soon as we recognize that there is nothing in meaning that is not in behavior, on the other hand, we are bound to expect ultimate indeterminacies of translation. To settle such indeterminacies we resort, as in the rabbit example, to arbitrary choices or analogies or maxims unconsciously adopted. The more our translations depend on these self-imposed guides, the less can justly be said for linguistic universals. Is the subject-predicate structure a linguistic universal, or is it imposed? What supposed linguistic universals can withstand an audit of behavioral evidence?

The indeterminacy of translation clamors for exploration also apart from linguistic universals. Radical translation is a straightforward inductive enterprise only at the initial phase, where what we are construing are observation sentences. An observation sentence is an occasion sentence, that is, a sentence whose truth value varies from one occasion of utterance to another; but it is a special sort of occasion sentence, one whose truth value depends wholly on circumstances that are intersubjectively observable on the occasion of the utterance of the sentence. All speakers agree, nearly enough, in assenting to or dissenting from an observation sentence when they are given the same concurrent stimulations; this uniformity even constitutes a behavioral criterion distinguishing observation sentences from others. As soon as a field linguist has settled provisionally on what to take as native signs of assent and dissent, he is in a position to make tests and draw inductive conclusions as to the meanings of native observation sentences. He can settle inductively, to his satisfaction, what stimulations would prompt assent to the sentence and what stimulations would prompt dissent; and that, for an observation sentence, is meaning enough. He is in a position at that point to translate the observation sentence into English, though only holophrastically; that is, without imputing any relevance to the individual English words beyond the observable situation that they combine to report. He may translate it as "that is a rabbit" so long as this sentence is taken only as keyed to the presence of rabbits and hence of rabbit stages and rabbit parts. He cannot, without exceeding his evidence, impute to the native sentence, or to any segment of it, the distinctive significance of "rabbit" as against "rabbit stage" or "rabbit part."

The great subsequent strides which are needed in order to translate the native language depend heavily on what I call analytical hypotheses. These may begin as exploratory equations between segments of native observation sentences and English words; equations whose only justification is that they make the translations of whole observation sentences come out verifiably. Some analytical hypotheses may be guided by maxims such as what I called the law of *Gestalt*; this maxim would favor "rabbit" over "rabbit stage" and "rabbit part" at one point. Other analytical hypotheses will recommend themselves on the score of simplicity, or perhaps just because they occurred to us first. Some of them will be more devious than mere equations between native segments and English words. One thing they will all lack, in any event, is strict inevitability. They bridge indeterminacy of translation. The only constraint to which they are subject, apart from simplicity and other maxims, is the requirement that the yielded translations turn out right when they can be objectively checked. Observation sentences are not the only check points; something can be done with other occasion sentences, and scattered confirmations are possible in certain other quarters. I have developed these matters somewhat more fully elsewhere.[8] But the fact remains that the possible check points are far more meager than a man with both feet planted in the realm or slough of ideas is apt to have imagined.

One outlying point where fresh evidence is available is negation as an operation on sentences; for, we have in terms of assent and dissent an obvious semantic criterion of negation. A stimulation should prompt assent to the negation of a sentence if and only if it prompts dissent from the sentence itself, and a stimulation should prompt dissent from the negation if and only if it prompts assent to the sentence itself. If we assume as before that our linguist has settled on what to take as native signs of assent and dissent, then, adopting the semantic criterion of negation that I just stated, the linguist can make tests and settle by induction to his satisfaction whether to construe some particular native vocable or construction as negation. A favorable outcome would not mean, of course, that he should always translate that native vocable or construction into English as "not"; for "not," in its irregularity, does not perfectly fit our semantic criterion of negation. A favorable outcome would, however, reveal the full meaning of the native vocable or construction in question, and it would reveal it as genuine logical negation.

I must stress the difference between the familiar inconclusiveness of induction and the indeterminacy of translation. The linguist could of course be wrong about the stimulus conditions of a native observation sentence, since any induction from limited instances is fallible. He could be wrong also, and for the same reason, in identifying negation. But in these cases there is a fact of the matter, something to be wrong about; the linguist could even be proved wrong by a later counter-instance. What I am calling indeterminacy of translation, on the other hand, is indeterminacy in principle and in the face of all possible data; indeterminacy relative to the totality of behavioral dispositions, sampled and unsampled. It is indeterminacy to be settled only by the free adoption, however unconscious, of analytical hypotheses of translation. That it is a matter of indeterminacy in principle, and not just of inscrutability in practice, cannot be appreciated until we give up the gallery myth and fully recognize that there is nothing in meaning that is not in behavior.

Once this move is made and indeterminacy is recognized, a new line of inquiry opens up: the comparison of degrees of indeterminacy.[9] Observation sentences are wholly determinate, and so is negation; determinate, that is, to within simple induction, and recognition of native signs of assent and dissent. A notable construction that is just less than wholly determinate is the logical operation of conjunction of sentences.

A partial semantic criterion of conjunction is obvious, on the analogy of what we had for negation: namely, a stimulation should prompt assent to the conjunction if and only if it prompts assent to each of the conjoined sentences. On the dissent side, however, there is a gap.[10] Certainly a stimulation should prompt dissent from the conjunction *if* it prompts dissent from a component; but not *only if*. For instance, lacking information, you may not be prepared to dissent from the statement that I was born in Pittsburgh, nor to dissent from the statement that I was born in Detroit; but still you will dissent from the conjunction of the two. In general, when a speaker is unprepared to assent to each component of a conjunction *and* unprepared to dissent from either component, there is no telling whether he will dissent from the conjunction or just leave it open. It all depends on the example and the special circumstances.

We see that the linguist can satisfy himself, by straightforward induction from tests, that a given native vocable or construction does three quarters of the job of conjunction. He will probably then construe it forthwith as conjunction, and translate it in most positions as "and," though allowing of course, here as in the case of "not," for minor English deviations from the strict truth function in question. This step is a sensible one, but it is an analytical hypothesis. Conceivably it might even be revoked in the face of conflict with some system of additional analytical hypotheses which work out more simply in other quarters. Conceivably the linguist might decide on such grounds to construe the native vocable or construction in question not quite as conjunction after all, but as some non-truth-functional operation that deviates from conjunction in certain cases where the speaker is unprepared to dissent from either component and unprepared to assent to both.

In conjunction, then, we have considerable determinacy but some residual dependence on analytical hypotheses. Alternation is exactly parallel, except that its blind quarter comes where the speaker is unprepared to dissent from both components and unprepared to assent to either. In these cases he may assent to the alternation or he may just leave it open, depending on special circumstances. Not being prepared to say that I was born in Pittsburgh, and not being prepared to say that I was born in Detroit, you may or may not be prepared to say that I was born in either Pittsburgh or Detroit.

There is a kind of quantification, or quasi-quantification, which has been espoused by Leśniewski and Ruth Marcus and which I call *substitutional* quantification. It, again, will be found to show the same partial determinacy of translation and the same partial indeterminacy as do conjunction and alternation. The idea of substitutional quantification is that a quantification of this sort, if existential, counts as true just in case a true sentence can be got by dropping the quantifier and substituting some expression for the variable. Similarly a universal quantification of this sort counts as false just in case a false sentence can be got by dropping the quantifier and substituting for the variable. It is evident how, up to a point, we can determine whether certain vocables and constructions of the native language play the role of substitutional quantification. In the case of existential quantification we demand that the native be prepared to dissent from his analogue of a quantification, whatever it is, if and only if prepared to dissent from his analogue of every substitution instance. Also we demand that he be prepared to assent to the quantification if prepared to assent to a substitution instance. If, but not only if; there is a blind quarter here corresponding to that in the case of alternation. A man may have reason to affirm an existential quantification, even of the substitutional kind, with or without being prepared to affirm any specific substitution instance. Thus existential quantification of the substitutional kind is, like conjunction and alternation, covered three quarters of the way by semantical criteria of translation, and left open in the remaining quarter for indirect evidence or analytical hypotheses. It is obvious that similar remarks apply to universal quantification of the substitutional kind.[11]

I spoke of substitutional quantification as only a quasi-quantification for two reasons. One reason is that what pass for its variables need not stand in referential positions, such as are appropriate to names; they can stand in for expressions of any sort. The other reason is that even when its variables do take the positions of names, the quantifications in their substitutional interpretation fail to quantify over nameless objects. For these two reasons, substitutional quantification must not be confused with real or referential or objectual quantification. It is this latter sort of quantification that is the primary channel of objective reference and of ontic commitment, once a theory is regimented along the lines of modern logic.

From the point of view of radical translation and indeterminacy, objectual quantification is worse off than substitutional quantification. For we cannot identify such quantification, in the native language, without also getting clear on what to count in the native language as names and what to count as singular terms and, to some extent, what to count them as referring to. I have argued that this sort of thing cannot, in an objective sense, be known; it has to be settled by analytical hypotheses, even when the terms are so-called observation terms. The rabbit example is a case in point; for I urged that whereas a native observation sentence may be translatable holophrastically as "that is a rabbit," without resort to analytical hypotheses, still any construing of its segments as terms does require such resort.

The simple classical forms of categorical proposition—"All S is P," "Some S is P," and two more—are in the same boat with objectual quantification: they depend utterly on the identifying of terms, and hence on analytical hypotheses. It is curious that these ancient and simple-minded categorical forms should be more parochial, more subject to indeterminacy of translation and more dependent on analytical hypotheses, than the new-fangled substitutional quasi-quantification of Leśniewski and Ruth Marcus.

We have been seeing that the abandonment of the gallery myth, in favor of recognizing that there is nothing in meaning that is not in behavior, has fundamental and far-reaching consequences in the theory of translation. It has yet more. It throws general doubt upon imputations of strange doctrines to benighted peoples, insofar as these imputations are predicated on native testimony rather than on nonlinguistic practices; for, as soon as we consider method, we have to recognize that the linguist has no access to native meanings apart from what he can glean from the observed circumstances of utterances. The analytical hypotheses that he contrives are subject to no further check, except that native utterances not conveniently linked to observable circumstances should still turn out on the whole to be plausible messages.

An extreme example of the unwarranted imputation of strange doctrines is one that I have used repeatedly: the notion of a prelogical culture, where self-contradictions are knowingly accepted as true. Any appearance in native discourse of wanton self-contradiction is evidence of wanton mis-translation. Surely, if the linguist is to be guided by anything but caprice in settling upon translation of logical particles, a prime criterion is bound to be the superficial consistency of native discourse. Insofar as the linguist is guided by the semantical criteria noted earlier for negation, conjunction, alternation, and substitutional quantification, this assurance is even built in.

When a doctrine imputed to the natives is somewhat less absurd than overt contradiction, its imputation is correspondingly less conclusive evidence of bad translation; but a tension between implausibility of native doctrine and plausibility of translation remains evident, as long as we keep method in mind. The less plausible a story appears in translation, the less plausible the manual of translation.

There is something that has come to be known as the Whorf hypothesis, after the late Benjamin Lee Whorf. It is not so much an articulated hypothesis as a domain of speculation. The general idea is that the speakers of a language radically different from ours will be found to differ radically from us in their ways of thinking and of looking upon the world. The idea is plausible, but one has second thoughts when one reflects again on method and recalls that implausibility of native doctrine systematically detracts from plausibility of translation.

The dissenting conclusion for us to draw, however, is not that the natives see things as we do after all, but only that the issue is elusive. How we depict the native's view of the world depends on how we construe his words and grammar, and how we construe his words and grammar depends on what we take to be his view of the world.

If we find a language hard to translate, if we find very little word-by-word isomorphism with genuine and idiomatic English, then we already have right there, in a featureless sort of way, a kind of measure of remoteness. So far so good. If, however, as a second step a translation into funny or compromise English is undertaken in order to reveal the exotic native *Weltanschauung*, then no conclusion deserves to be drawn until some methodological account is taken of how the English compromise was struck. What evidence allowed certain elements of good English to weather the stresses of translation while other elements of good English gave way to those stresses? The temptation at this point, which Whorf himself admirably resisted, is to cast methodological nicety to the winds and to wallow in an unstructured intercultural impressionism.

My position is not that alien cultures are inscrutable. Much can be determined about a culture by leaving language alone and observing nonverbal customs and taboos and artifacts. Much also can be determined, beyond peradventure, with help of language. We can construe observation sentences, after all, on an objective behavioral basis; and we can note, in particular, just which ranges of stimulations are packaged under the shortest observation sentences in a given language. Languages may be expected to differ, in this matter of short observation sentences, in ways that reflect palpable differences in material culture. Also there is, as already noted, a general and undirected measure of remoteness of one language from another in the sheer degree of difficulty of intertranslation, the degree of elaborateness of the interlinguistic manual. Per-

haps this rough index of distance can be resolved into dimensional components sometime, and a body of post-Whorf hypotheses worthy of the
name of hypothesis may come after. A proper awareness of the purely
behavioral nature of meaning, at any rate, is a safeguard against nonsense in this domain and a precondition of responsible theory.

The crucial point, both as it touches the notion of a prelogical culture and as it touches the Whorf hypothesis, is that homeliness of content is itself partial evidence of fair translation. The thrust of translation
is homeward. Translation with exotic intent, translation with an interest
or acquiescence in the bizarre, suffers from built-in stresses and must be
approached with circumspection.

When the field linguist begins his project of breaking into a strange
language, he is methodologically bound to trust in the homeliness of the
native mind. The linguist has to assume that the native will see the
main distinctions that we do, and that he will tell the truth. The linguist is bound to assume that the sentence which the natives persist in affirming or assenting to, when rabbits appear, is a sentence which in all
sincerity announces rabbits rather than wolves. The alternative, indeed,
that natives almost always lyingly or deludedly announce rabbits as
wolves, reduces to nonsense when we reflect that there is nothing in
meaning that is not in behavior.

Eventually, of course, the linguist drops his initially indispensable
assumption that natives tell the truth. He does not go on forever modifying his growing theory of the native language so as to accommodate
each succeeding affirmation as true. Just where the linguist reaches that
critical stage or age of discretion where he can make bold to give the native the lie, is a nice question.

The linguist does not summarily stop modifying his theory of the
language just when he starts imputing falsity. It is a question rather of
ratio. Even we in our own language will still occasionally decide that our
compatriot is using a word strangely, rather than impute to him some
excessively silly belief about the world; and when we so decide we are
modifying our theory about his idiolect of English.

How do we decide whether to change our theory of a man's language or to impute falsity to his statement? The basis for the decision is
most evident when we consider the case of our English-speaking friend.
What we ordinarily base such a decision on is a swift and unpretentious
speculation in the psychology of learning. Our friend has said something
which, if we take his words our way, would betray an unaccountable failure on his part to have learned something that was long staring us all in
the face. We decide, however swiftly and tacitly, that his failure to have

learned our use of some key word of his sentence would present less of a challenge to psychology.

The same, surely, is true of the linguist. Whether he should change his mind about the native language in the face of unexpected native testimony on some topic, or should rather just count the testimony factually false, is a question to be settled by weighing probabilities regarding native psychology. If the new quirk which the linguist would have to introduce into his theory of the native language in order to make the native's statement come out true is a quirk that would make the language pretty queer from the point of view of a theory of language learning, and if on the other hand the native could quite plausibly have made an adequate mistake of observation or judgment about the subject matter of his statement, then the theory of the language should stand and the native's statement should be accounted false. In this way many of the linguist's decisions are bound to turn, if often unconsciously, on practical psychology.

The point has its peculiarly philosophical bearing too, especially in connection with the Oxford philosophy of ordinary language. Thus take the question of the truth of religious tenets. Since meaning is use, the statements that are characteristically agreed upon by the spokesmen of religion must be true. For, various key words such as "God" and "grace" turn up mainly in the statements of those spokesmen; these statements exhaust most of the use of those words. The statements that are generally agreed upon by religious spokesmen are then true and even analytic, that is, true by virtue of the meanings of words. This is a facile defense of religion, too facile ever to be welcomed by believers, who rightly find no comfort in a religious tenet with so trivial a basis as this. It is less interesting as a defense of religion than as a challenge to ordinary-language philosophy.

The answer lies, again, in psychology. If we master the religious vocabulary sufficiently to join substantive issue with religious speakers, we do so not just by taking their statements as true, but by reconstructing in some measure the psychology of their belief. There need be nothing unbehavioristic about their psychology or our reconstruction of it, and therefore nothing unbehavioristic about our approach to meaning. What saves the consensus of religious speakers from being trivially true is not a failure of the behavioral theory of meaning, but just that meaning in all its behaviorality can call, in an extremity, for a lot of behavioral psychology.

On reflection it is evident that some offhand psychological judgment is involved generally in determinations of meaning. When the linguist first broaches the jungle language by inductively determining the stimulations appropriate to some native observation sentence, he is already involved in psychology; he is conjecturing that the native's sense of similarity, his associations and his cut-off points on the score of similarity, are like ours. He is assuming that the native will not tend to group certain white rabbits primarily with certain wolves while dissociating them from other rabbits.

The sort of psychology that figures in translation in such cases is psychology at such a common-sense level that it passes unnoticed. But there is a place also, in translation, for more sophisticated psychology: for psycholinguistics of a profundity not yet achieved. If we had a deep understanding of the inner mechanisms of language learning and of the innate aptitudes behind it, we might use this knowledge to narrow our choice among sets of analytical hypotheses which are on a par from the point of view of verbal behavior. We might find that one choice somehow simulated universal language-learning mechanisms better than another. Such a development would not refute the indeterminacy of translation, but it would afford superior ways of accommodating it.

NOTES

1. John Horne Tooke, ῎Επεα πτεροέντα; or, the Diversions of Purley. 2 Vols. (London, 1786, 1805, 1829). First American edition, 1806, p. 32.
2. Gilbert Ryle, The Concept of Mind (Hutchinson's University Library, London, 1949).
3. John Dewey, Experience and Nature (W. W. Norton, New York, 1925), pp. 170, 178, 185.
4. See my Word and Object (M.I.T. Press, Cambridge, 1960), pp. 83 ff.
5. Experience and Nature (W. W. Norton, New York, 1925, 1929), p. 179.
6. Ludwig Wittgenstein, Philosophical Investigations (Blackwell, Oxford, 1953), p. 14.
7. Word and Object, pp. 51 ff.
8. Word and Object, pp. 46–51, 57–73.
9. I am indebted here to a suggestion of Dreben's.
10. In Word and Object, p. 58, I missed this point.
11. For more on these and related matters, see my essay "Existence and quantification" in J. Margolis, ed., Fact and Existence (Blackwell, Oxford, 1969).

For helpful criticism of the first draft of the present paper I am grateful to Burton Dreben.

COMMENTS ON QUINE'S PAPER

Max Black

I cannot do justice in a short time to Professor Quine's rich and far-ranging paper. I shall, therefore, confine myself to saying a few things about some of the points which most interested me, choosing especially those that I may have misunderstood.

Let me start with Quine's preliminary remarks concerning the relations between philosophy and science. He has told us that philosophy "is continuous with science"; he also said philosophy is both a wing of science and an aspect of it. Quine's topography of the scientific mansion is somewhat confusing. I presume each branch of science has its own "wing," with still another, for the philosophy of probability and induction, to serve them all. Should there perhaps also be a place, however humble, for art and the humanities? The intended design is hard to grasp.

Again, it seems to me somewhat difficult to think of a "part" of science as "continuous" with the whole. Even if philosophy were continuous with science, it might be clearly distinguishable from it. Continuity is, of course compatible with striking difference—as, say, red is continuous with yellow, but different from it.

Altogether, I am not clear about how Quine conceives of philosophy. I conjecture that he is really thinking of it as a part of science. He says, for example, that "philosophical progress in language theory" must use "scrupulous empirical method." Well, much depends on how one understands empirical method or the science to which it ministers. If by science Quine means something like *episteme*, or *Wissenschaft* in the German sense, then there is no reason to disagree. Philosophy does aim at knowledge, among other things, and can be so far "scientific." But if Quine means science in the special sense of the word that has been current for only a century, his claim is less plausible. I recall that the great Lord Rutherford once defined science as "physics—and stamp collecting." And I think this is how Quine, too, really thinks of science. For him, it seems fair to say, science is or ought to be modeled on physics.

Consider how Quine uses "behavior." The word is not intended to apply to such obvious examples as smiling, gritting one's teeth, recognizing another person, or being angry—all of which might reasonably be called examples of "observable behavior." Such ordinary-language descriptions could, however, have no role in physics. For Quine, as for other behaviorists, "behavior" is typically the kind of thing that could be recorded and classified by some inanimate physical instrument.

I may be wrong about this. One thing that leads me to suspect so is Quine's surprising apposition of physics with "a philosophical quest for the inner nature of reality." That sounds astonishingly metaphysical for a radical empiricist.

At any rate, it seems clear to me that Quine is not practising science in this paper. Whatever else he may be doing, he is offering a persuasive definition of "science"—and I wonder whether we *should* be persuaded that all the questions arising in connection with a science can be assimilated under "empirical methods." My own opinion is that in this paper Quine is not even trying to be severely "empirical," but is rather offering us a kind of picture or perspective. Whether to accept the picture or not seems to me not really a straightforwardly scientific question.

I shall turn now to the central theme of the "externalizing of empiricism," as Quine has called it. I remind you that he describes this as "a shift of focus from ideas to words," with a heightened appreciation of the relation of the "linguistic fact that the words in sharpest focus are mainly words for external objects." For empiricism thus rejuvenated, Quine says, "Our mental life settles into an inferential status." And, finally, "This is behaviorism."

Let me say, first, that I was a little surprised to see Horne Tooke and Bentham so prominently featured. These two writers, whatever their merits, have had negligible influence on the development of linguistics. On the other hand, outstanding linguists like De Saussure and Sapir have rarely been behaviorists or radical empiricists, but often some kind of unsystematic idealists.

But after all, I suspect, Quine is not offering us serious historical remarks. He *is* presenting a specific conception of language learning: words as learned in the presence of the object, of the word, and of the teacher. This is, of course, a drastically over-simplified picture. Taken quite literally, the recommended picture of learning to speak would be something like this: another person exclaims "rabbit" when a rabbit appears; hearing the word so used in such episodes, a bystander then learns the meaning of "rabbit" by induction. But this kind of episode, if it ever occurs, is surely exceptional. If one is really to learn any language or any part of it, one has to know a good deal about the teaching situation and has to assume that one's partner shares this knowledge. Indeed, Quine himself brings this out in a number of remarks. "Part of the plan is that he, the teacher, knows that you see the object and you know that he does." Quite so. But now we are a long way away from the simple stimulus-response paradigm. The stimulus, if it is still to be called that, must now include the relevant background knowledge. And similarly for the case of the field-linguist, trying to learn from native informants what they mean when they use certain words. What puzzles me is that, according to the view under discussion, the "externalization of empiricism," it is supposed to follow that mental life is an inference—"our mental life settles into an inferential status." And so a good empiricist is advised to reject "mental entities" as "pointless or pernicious." We are, indeed, picturesquely warned against "the slough of ideas."

I am puzzled on two counts. First, why the inference, if it occurs, should cast doubt upon the status of the thing inferred: you can hardly infer to something unless it exists. Even in the case of learning the meaning of "cat," as Quine emphasizes, inference is present, on his principles. Why should he not say, therefore, that the existence of cats is as much a matter of inference as the existence of minds and warn us against the "slough" occupied by felines? On the other hand, if he really means that references to *my own* pains, thoughts, and so on, are based upon inference, then, so far as I can see, he is plainly wrong. When I say that I can feel my thumb now, I am certainly not inferring, and yet I am clearly talking about something which, in Quine's terminology, is part of my mental life. (Perhaps he means that only references to the mental occurrences of *others* involve inference, which would, of course, be much more plausible.)

I shall turn now to Quine's defense of behaviorism. Quine has told us that the scientific linguist must be a behaviorist. The linguist may admit "innate beginnings"—indeed, "Any behaviorist account of the learning process is openly and emphatically committed to innate beginnings" (surely an over-statement?). But any talk of ideas must "make sense" in terms of dispositions to overt behavior.

Is this properly described as behaviorism? It looks as if Quine is implying that any view that focuses upon words rather than ideas and infers mental events from outward manifestations should count as behaviorist. Of course you might call it that. But the position is compatible with extreme forms of philosophical dualism. A man might be a dualist, and still say that difficulty of access to other minds forces him to "focus" upon the observable gestures, words, etc.: such a man might even claim to *infer* the existence of other "mental contents." This would fit, as far as I can see, Quine's specification of behaviorism, odd as it would be to apply the label in such a case.

I wonder whether Quine is not conflating two things in what I will call nonbehaviorism. On the one hand, a denial of behaviorism (i.e. what he calls "mentalism,") and on the other hand something that he calls "the gallery myth," namely, the view that a word, roughly speaking, is just a tag or a label for an idea. But a nonbehaviorist need not believe in the "gallery myth." He can adopt any view whatsoever, as far as I can see, about the relationships between ideas and their expression—even, the implausible view that only entire sentences have meaning (without one-to-one correspondence between words and "ideas")—and *still* be a nonbehaviorist.

If a definition is desired, I would suggest that a nonbehaviorist might be identified as somebody who thinks that there is at least one bit of mental life which is not *logically* connected with any observable expression. I do not know whether this would satisfy Quine.

Finally, I want to remind you of Quine's provocative remark that ideas must be dispositions to overt behavior. I wonder why he insists upon the *"must."* Would he allow that when I use the word *horse*, say, I do in some sense or other have a corresponding idea? But if so, what is the corresponding disposition? So far as I can see, there is no detectable simple disposition connecting the idea of horse with the utterance of "horse." The nearest I could get to it would be something like the following: There is a disposition (if you want to talk in that way) such that if I have the idea or concept of a horse, and think I see a horse, and intend to reveal my putative knowledge by a verbal sign, then I will say "horse" and not something else. That is a pretty complex disposition, involving reference, knowledge, observation, and intention, all of which are on the face of it "mental." If these in turn are to be treated as dispositional, we would have a very complex analysis, with second and perhaps third order dispositions involved. I wonder whether this really is good empiricism, conforming to the reiterated slogan that all meaning must be in behavior?

Finally, I would like to make some brief comments about Quine's provocative thesis of the radical indeterminacy of translation. A *Gedankenexperiment*, as Ernst Mach among others taught us, can be extremely illuminating: and Quine's attention to the situation of a hapless linguist, bereft of all previous knowledge and starting from scratch in the native society, is stimulating and helpful. Quine's analysis leads him to claim an indeterminacy *in principle*, as to the question, for example, whether a particular word, "gavagai" (the invented word used in his book) really means *rabbit*. The do-it-himself linguist hears the word "gavagai," and has any amount of access to native speakers' utterances and responses, but in spite of all that, does not know and will never know whether the word means rabbit, rabbit-stage, or rabbit-part (or any of an indefinite number of other things that an ingenious philosopher might imagine). This is an indeterminacy "in principle"—no further observations could remove it or have any tendency to so do. If it were just a matter of knowing with less than absolute certainty, the indeterminacy would be philosophically as uninteresting as the unreliability of weather reports. But Quine really does claim, quite explicitly, that none of us know or ever can know what the native speakers mean. He is advocating an extreme form of skepticism—which makes his position, of course, all the more interesting.

I wonder whether the position of our frustrated linguist is radically different from that of any child, faced with the task of learning his first language? If we are to think in terms of deliberately simplified models, why should we not say that the child learner is in the same position as the linguist faced with the foreign culture? The child has no language yet, so he cannot use the reports of other children, or get any information at second hand: he, too, is reduced to observation and induction. Unless there is some radical difference between the position of the child and that of the linguist, the same conclusion ought to follow in both cases. To wit, that the child is, *in principle*, unable to determine whether father and mother mean a rabbit when they say "rabbit," or mean something else; and no amount of further experience, induction, hypothesizing, and so on, can ever relieve this ignorance.

Furthermore, I wonder now whether this same line of argument does not also apply as between adult and adult. Does Quine mean rabbit when he says "rabbit"? How am I to find out? Suppose that when he says "rabbit" he means rabbit-stage: then I suppose when he says "rabbit stage," he means "rabbit-stage stage," and similarily when he says "rabbit part" he means "rabbit-stage part." Unless I have overlooked something, it would seem to me that there is no way, on Quine's view, for me to find out; I am doomed to remain eternally ignorant. Quine thinks of this situation as an indeterminacy between different hypotheses. But here an application of the principle of verifiability seems to be in order. If no conceivable experience could really assure me (or even make it more likely than not) that Quine, or my father, or the Swahili, really do mean material objects when they use certain words, I am inclined to think that something has gone wrong in our description; that we think we are offering different hypotheses, but are in fact not doing so. I confess that I find Quine's indeterminacy incredible. I am convinced that I do know that Quine has the concept of a material object, part of my evidence being the way he is holding his pencil right now, and what he is doing with it. It seems to me that this, plus a great deal more about him, is conclusive evidence that he really does possess the concept. I am confident that if he were to tell me that something was a pencil he really would be meaning a pencil and nothing else. If we cannot know this much, but must accept Quine's radical skepticism, then linguistics would in my judgment be impossible. But of course this is not a refutation of Quine's arguments, which deserve more careful and extended examination than I have been able to supply.

THE LOGICAL STRUCTURE OF
ENGLISH SENTENCES

Paul Ziff

A sentence of English, of a natural language, has a logical structure, but what its structure is is not always evident. And if it is not, it may be desirable to scan the sentence from a formal point of view, thus, in effect, to attempt a schematic representation of the English sentence as a sentence of a formal logic, the sentences of which bare their structure to the eye.

That a formal logic is of utility in connection with the logical analysis of a discourse is not to be doubted. A formal logic is an instrument for mapping a conceptual scheme, thus a device for subverting any plotted logical confusion. But any map must be read aright if it is to be of utility, and any map may be misread, and misreadings may give rise to misgivings about the value of the mapping enterprise. It is with such misreadings and misgivings that we shall be concerned here.

An uninterpreted formal system may be taken to be a finite collection of expressions of some appropriate sort together with various precise rules for their manipulation.[1] One can also think of such a system as constituted simply by various rules for the production of expressions of some appropriate sort together with precise rules for their manipulation. (Thus the formal system presented on pp. 56–68 of the volume of *The Journal of Symbolic Logic*, 5 (1940), in the library at Chicago Circle may then be said to be identical with the formal system presented on pp. 56–68 of the volume of *The Journal of Symbolic Logic*, 5 (1940), in the library at Princeton in that each is in accordance with precisely the same rules.)

To provide an interpretation of a formal system is then to supply further rules that serve to establish relations between expressions of the formal system and various things or various matters. If a system admits

25

of the principal interpretation required here, it is a logistic system. A formal logic is here construed as an interpreted formal logistic system. The principal interpretation required is that the well-formed formulas of the system be interpreted in such a way that their interpretations are, or are somehow associated with, what is true or what is false.

Different interpretations of the underlying formalisms can yield different logics. To illustrate: let "$p \supset p$" be a well formed formula of an uninterpreted logistic calculus C. In providing an interpretation for C, we may let the letter "p" be a variable for propositions that are either true or false; [2] or we may let "p" be a variable for sentences that are either true or false,[3] in which case "$\supset$" may then be construed as a syntactic constant representing the result of a specific operation over a pair of sentences to yield a single compound sentence; or we may let "p" be a place holder for an arbitrary sentence, a dummy of a sort, in which case "$\supset$" need not be construed syntactically but may be interpreted as a sentence connective.[4] If C contains quantifiers, expressions of the form "(p)" or "$(\exists p)$," then in case "p" is construed simply as a dummy sentence, the quantifiers can be construed simply as asides to the effect either that it does or that it does not matter which sentence "p" is a dummy for.

To provide a formal logical analysis of an English sentence, one may attempt to pair off the sentence with an expression of a formal logic. If the logistic system has been interpreted in terms of propositions, we shall have to suppose that the English sentence expresses a proposition and we shall have to find a proposition of the formal logic to pair off with it. If the system has been interpreted in terms of sentences, then we need not suppose that the sentence of English expresses a proposition, but we shall still have to find a sentence of the logic to pair off with it and we shall have to suppose that sentences may be either true or false.

Neither of these alternatives is particularly palatable. That declarative sentences of English express propositions is somewhat dubious; that such sentences are literally either true or false is even more dubious. The obvious difficulty is that declarative sentences of English are not invariant either with respect to the expression of propositions or with respect to truth. If a sentence in one discourse is deemed to express a proposition, or to be true, another token of the same type (or if you prefer, another replica) in another discourse may express a radically different proposition, or may be false or even neither true nor false. For example, think of "He is hungry" said in reference to George, who is hungry, in reference to Josef, who is not, and displayed (or voiced) here by way of an example. The proposition varies, the truth of what is said varies, but the logical structure of the sentence has presumably remained invariant.

This situation can, however, readily be remedied by supplementing our sentential interpretation of the formal system. Thus we further interpret the sentences of the logistic system as representatives of (or metonyms for) statements that are either true or false. I shall, however, in the interests of brevity, speak of sentences as true or false (and of predicates as true or not true of something), but this is to be understood as follows. To say that a sentence is true (or false), for example, to say that "It is raining" is true (or false), is to say that the sentence token displayed (or voiced) here represents a sentence token that may be uttered in some appropriate way under some appropriate conditions such that in uttering it the person uttering it is making a true (or a false) statement. It is to be further understood that though in fact the sentence token displayed (or voiced) here—the one about the weather —can equally well represent many different sentence tokens, some of which may be employed in making true statements and some in making false statements, if the sentence is here said to be true, it is to be taken as representing only those tokens such that the utterance of the tokens does not exemplify an instance of semantic deviation and does constitute the making of a true statement. But rather than, say, all this every time, I shall simply speak of a sentence as being true or false.

To provide a logical analysis of a sentence of English one can attempt to pair off the English sentence with a sentence of a formal logic. The second member of such a pair can be thought of as a representation of the English sentence in the formal system. For example, to let "p" stand in place of an arbitrary declarative sentence is not to assign much content to "p," but such a representation is all that is required for the purposes of sentential logic. A consequence of this is that a representation of an English sentence in a sentential logic is essentially schematic in character; thus a representation of "If it doesn't rain then it will snow" is "$-r \supset s$": this suffices to display a logical structure of the English sentence even though it conveys little of its content. Such a representation then constitutes a (partial) logical analysis of the English sentence.

Insofar as there are different formal systems, each of which under an appropriate interpretation qualifies as a formal logic, it is evident that there can be no unique formal logical analysis of an English sentence. In consequence, such a sentence cannot have a unique formal logical structure. The best that one could hope is that a sentence have a unique formal logical structure relative to L, where L is some formal logic.

For example, let L_1 be a classical sentential logic and L_2 an intuitionistic sentential logic. For the sake of definiteness, let L_1 be the logic determined by axioms 1–7, 8°, and L_2 the logic determined by axioms 1–7, 8^I, in Kleene's *Introduction to Metamathematics*, sections 19, 23. Axiom 8° is "$-p \supset p$" and axiom 8^I is "$-p \supset (p \supset q)$." Consider the representation of "If it doesn't rain then it will snow" in L_1 and in L_2. Represented in L_1, the sentence takes the form "$-r \supset s$"; represented in L_2, the sentence takes the form "$-r \supset s$." At a glance it may seem as though the structures thus assigned to the sentence were one and the same. But that would be an illusion fostered by the notation. The symbols "$-$" and "$\supset$" in L_1 cannot be identified with the corresponding symbols in L_2. The symbols "$-$," "$\supset$," "V" and "$\cdot$" of L_1 are interdefinable; the corresponding symbols of L_2 are not. From "$-r \supset s$" in L_1 one can infer "$-s \supset r$": no such inference is possible in L_2.

Another example: let L_1 and L_2 be equivalent sentential logics differing only in that L_1 has a constant "f" but "$-$" does not appear as a primitive improper symbol, whereas L_2 has no constant and "$-$" is a primitive. The representation of "If it doesn't rain then it will snow" in L_1 takes the form "$-r \supset s$," and in L_2 it takes the form "$-r \supset s$." Here, unlike the previous example, owing to the fact that L_1 and L_2 are equivalent, there is no inferential difference between the two representations. Nonetheless, the English sentence has been assigned two different though equivalent structures, for in L_1, on the elimination of abbreviations, "$-r \supset s$" takes on the form of "$(r \supset f) \supset s$." (An analogue: the structure of $a + [b + c]$ differs from that of $[a + b] + c$, but that difference makes no difference in ordinary arithmetic.)

To represent an English sentence in a sentential logic is not much of a problem though the inefficacy of such a representation in revealing the logical structure of the sentence in question is, on occasion, not to be doubted. For example, the discourse "George ate: he ate and he ate and he ate and he ate" would seem to have the structure "$p \cdot p \cdot p \cdot p \cdot p$," which is equivalent to "p." But from the English discourse one can infer that George ate a great deal, not so from its logical representation. Again, from "It snowed and it snowed and it snowed" one can infer that it snowed a great deal, but not so from its logical representation. The reason for this lacuna in sentential logic is not hard to discern: the repetitive use of a verb in a discourse is equivalent to an adverbial modification of the verb. Sentential logic is not equipped to cope with adverbial modifiers. (Nor, for that matter, is quantificational logic, as we shall see.)

Matters become more complex, however, when one considers the representation of sentences in a first order quantificational logic. Consider the sentence "Something is grey." In a standard first order logic this sentence would take the form of "$(\exists x)[Fx]$." Here it is necessary to consider what interpretation is being put on the formalism, thus what sort of logic one is working with.

We have assumed that the principal interpretation of a logistic system here is such that the well-formed formulas of the system are interpreted as sentences that are either true or false. If this is so, it must be allowed for by the interpretations assigned to the variables and constants of the system. This is usually accomplished by letting "x" be a variable for individuals and letting the predicate (or predicative expression) "Fx" denote what is called "the class that is the extension of the predicate." Given such an interpretation, sentences of the form "$(x)[Fx \supset Fx]$" prove to be logically true, and a sentence of the form "$(\exists x)[Fx]$" is true just in case there is something belonging to the class in question. But such an interpretation of the formalism poses philosophic problems, in particular, both so-called "ontological" problems and semantic problems.

First, to interpret "Fx" as denoting the class that is the extension of the predicate is to suggest or to seem to suggest that there are such things as classes that have an independent existence, that exist apart from a system of logic or apart from a language; thus it is to go along with what is currently known as a "Platonistic ontology." One who would be skeptical of such views should then be somewhat reluctant to employ such a logic. But secondly, and more importantly, to accept the representation as adequate is to accept the view, indeed a semantic theory, to the effect that the predicative expression "is grey" denotes a class. I, for one, have strong feelings of no enthusiasm for such a theory. Fortunately there are viable alternatives.

One can alter the interpretation of the formalism. Thus we can let "x" be a variable for individuals while stipulating that "Fx" is to stand in place of an arbitrary predicative expression; we further stipulate that a sentence of the form "$(\exists x)[Fx]$" is true just in case "Fx" is true of at least one individual. Thus rather than saying that "Fx" denotes something, we say it is true or false of something. (Here Quine has pointed the way in his many fine essays on these and related topics.)

A representation of "Something is grey" will then take the form "$(\exists x)[Gx]$," where "Gx" stands in place of the open sentence "x is grey." A representation of "Something is amiss" would then seem to take the form "$(\exists x)[Ax]$." On the intended interpretation, a sentence of that form is true just in case the predicate "Ax," that is, "x is amiss," is true of at least one individual. Since there is no individual that the predicate is true of, the sentence must be false, which is of course absurd, for here one could truly say that something is amiss. But to suppose that when one says that something is amiss one is saying that some individual is amiss is equally absurd. If we are to represent such sentences of English in our formal logic, the logic will have to permit such a representation. This means that the interpretation of the formalism must be adapted to that purpose. In consequence, perhaps we cannot simply let "x" be a variable for individuals. Or can we?

What we have touched upon here is not simply an anomalous sentence but a fertile field of discourse. Quine has said "The quantifier '$(\exists x)$' means 'there is an entity x such that,' and the quantifier '(x)' means 'every entity x is such that'." [5] This is of course to presuppose that "x" has been interpreted as a variable for individuals, or entities, or objects. A first order quantificational logic, so understood, would then seem to be a logic for those who would speak only of objects and object to any other way of speaking. Yet there are other sensible ways of speaking, which is not to say that there is an entity x such that x is a way of speaking.

To say "There was an annular eclipse" is not to say that there was some individual or entity or object such that it was an annular eclipse. Eclipses are not entities but events. "Eclipses exist" is a deviant sentence, which is not to deny that eclipses occur. "There was a shot; whenever there is a shot, there is a reason to be wary: therefore there was a reason to be wary." This would seem to be a reasonable piece of reasoning. But neither a shot nor a reason to be wary can reasonably be characterized as an individual or an entity or an object, and a reason to be wary cannot reasonably be characterized as an event. Then there are such sentences as "There is something wrong with the view," "There is a time to speak and a time to be silent," and there is also no need to multiply examples beyond necessity.

I have said that a formal logic is an instrument for mapping a conceptual scheme. In constructing a map one inevitably adopts one form of projection or another, and one uses materials adequate to the purpose. On my map of the States, Arizona is red and the city of Phoenix is a deep red dot. But the state of Arizona is certainly not red, nor is it any other color, nor is Phoenix a dot. Better then to print a map of no color at all. But this would mean no map. Best learn to read the map.

What the ultimate constituents of the universe may be, may be a matter for a cosmologist to ponder but it need not exercise the talents of a logician concerned with the analysis of reasoning. We need not insist that "$(\exists x)$" is to mean "there is an entity x such that": we could with equal grace and greater ease read it simply as "there is an x such that." But then what is "x" a variable for? (This is like asking what color the map shall be, for it must be some color.) So let "x" be a variable for individuals or entities or objects, whatever you like; and one will have to read the quantifier to mean "there is an individual (or entity or object) x such that." This need not occasion a resolute obmutescence: then to say "There is an entity x such that Fx" is merely to adopt a logician's *façon de parler*.

The exigencies of a formal approach inevitably necessitate some blinking here and there. But it need not matter. A logician can close his eyes to the difference between an adjective and a noun phrase and no harm need be done. Thus a representation of "Something is grey" and of "Something is a map" will take the form of "$(\exists x)[Gx]$" and of "$(\exists x)[Mx]$," which means that both sentences have been assigned the same structure. (The difference in letters, "M" in place of "G," marks a difference in predicates, not a difference in structure.) But there does seem to be a difference in logical structure between these two English sentences, a difference that arises from and is owing to the fact that "grey" is a predicate adjective whereas "a map" is a noun phrase. And this difference appears to give rise to an inferential difference: to be a map is *ipso facto* to be an entity of some sort, but to be grey is not *ipso facto* to be an entity of some sort. The sentence "Something is grey" is, I think, the sentence *par excellence* for logical parsing. But the undeniable difference between "grey" and "a map" makes no difference here. For if the predicate "x is grey" is true of at least one individual, then that which it is true of is bound to be an entity of some sort. Thus even though to be grey is not *ipso facto* to be an entity, anything that is grey is an entity (as much as anything that is "a so-and-so" is, as "a sky full of larks"). Thus there is no reason to insist that the logic show a difference between "Something is grey" and "Something is a map."

Blinking is one thing, but blindness is another. Consider the sentence "Something moves slowly"; one could represent this sentence as of the form "$(\exists x)[Sx]$", where "Sx" stands in place of "x moves slowly." Such an analysis would fail to assign structure to "moves slowly." In consequence, it would serve to block any attempt to account for the obvious truth of such a sentence as "If a man moves slowly and another moves quickly then at least two men move." One might attempt to cope with the matter by representing the sentence as of the form "$(\exists x)[Sx \cdot (z)[Sz \supset Mz]]$," where "$Sx$" stands in place of "$x$

moves slowly" and "*Mz*" stands in place of "*z* moves." But this would mean that the sentence "Something moves slowly" would be assigned the same structure as "Something moves slowly and if anything moves slowly then it moves": that the logical structures of these two English sentences are identical is hardly credible. So long as "*Sx*" stands in place of "*x* moves slowly," the logical structure of the sentence appears to be simply that of "$(\exists x)[Sx]$"; any supplementary clause would then serve to express an inference based on an analysis of the predicate "*Sx*."

It is fairly clear, I think, that the problem posed by the sentence "Something moves slowly" is a general problem. It is occasioned by the fact that familiar quantificational logics are not equipped to cope with adverbs in any simple way. The basic form of sentences in a quantificational logic is "$(\exists x)[Fx]$," and the simplest way to understand such an expression is to think of the letter "*F*" as standing in place of a predicate adjective. The task of logical analysis, with respect to a familiar quantificational logic, is to make out that every expression is either the name of an individual or a predicate adjective at heart. And even the names of individuals need not appear in the final analysis. To put "$(\exists x)$" before "*Fx*," thus to write "$(\exists x)[Fx]$", is simply a way of indicating that "*Fx*" does not always convert to a false closed sentence.

Adverbs in general, however, are not adjectives at heart. (The contrary is more often the case. "Utter" in "He is an utter fool," "fast" in "He is a fast runner," "perfect" in "He is a perfect stranger," are adverbs in adjective's clothing.) Adverbs and adverbial objects operate on verbs, as does "slowly" in "He ran slowly." Since the conspicuous operation in quantificational logic is that of predication, if one is to cope with the problems posed by adverbs, the only device available is to construe adverbial modification as an instance of predication. Thus one must cast "slowly" in the guise of "is slow," which means conjuring up an entity to fill the bill in "*x* is slow."

Since our logic requires us to conjure up entities, if we are to cope with adverbs, let us do so and see what they are like. Let us suppose that, among the things that can be values of our variables for individuals, we shall count such things as a run that was slow. One could then represent the sentence "Something ran slowly" as "$(\exists x)(\exists y)[Pxy \cdot Ry \cdot Sy]$," where "*Pxy*" stands for "*x* performed *y*," "*Ry*" for "*y* was a run," and "*Sy*" for "*y* was slow." This is to construe running as a relation between a person and a run he performs. In this case such an analysis is readily seen to be essentially a *façon de parler*. We are not required to suppose that somehow runs have an existence of their own apart from things that run.

Yet I am inclined to think that such an analysis is on a par with an analysis of "George is thinking of Josef" in terms of a relation between George and a thought, or an analysis of "George thinks that Josef is dead" in terms of a relation between George and a propositional function in intension.[6] Both the phrases "of Josef" and "that Josef is dead" are best seen as adverbial objects modifying the associated verbs. And of course the point in question is obvious in connection with one reading of the sentence "George is hunting unicorns." "Unicorn" is then best seen as an adverbial object modifying the verb "hunting." In this case we can make that point clear by placing the adverbial object before the verb and so saying "George is unicorn hunting." Analogously we might say "George is of-Josef-thinking" and "George that-Josef-is-dead-thinks."

Another quite different move can be made to cope with adverbs. It too calls for conjuration. Following Reichenbach's lead, one can leap to a higher logic, introduce the letter "f" as a variable for properties, and then solve the problem in a trice.[7] If something moves then it has one of the properties we may speak of as "motion properties." And to move slowly is then a matter of this property having the property of being slow. So we may represent "Something moves slowly" as "$(\exists x)(\exists f)[fx \cdot Mf \cdot Sf]$." Or as a variation on the theme, we can conjure up classes and class membership instead of invoking properties, in which case "Something moves slowly" takes on the guise of "$(\exists x)(\exists \sigma)[x\epsilon\sigma \cdot \sigma\epsilon M \cdot \sigma\epsilon S]$." The reference to properties or classes here is best seen as no more than a logician's device for sliding smoothly from "slowly" to "slow." Yet it seems that such fictive entities are all too often supposed to have some independent reality.

Frege's famous analysis of "x is an ancestor of y" takes the form of "$(\sigma)[y\epsilon\sigma \cdot (z)(w)[w\epsilon\sigma \cdot Fzw \cdot \supset z\epsilon\sigma] \cdot \supset \cdot x\epsilon\sigma]$." Here there is explicit quantification over classes. (As it so happens in this particular case, it has proven possible to avoid such quantification by adopting Goodman's ingenious devices in his calculus of individuals. But as Goodman points out, the method does not work for the general case; in particular it does not yield an analysis of the ancestral of every two-place predicate of individuals.[8]) But it is not difficult to see that the difficulties faced in an analysis of "x is an ancestor of y" are of a piece with those encountered in connection with adverbs in general. That George is an ancestor of Josef can, at least in part, be expressed by saying "George is ancestrally related to Josef" (though this perhaps fails to make clear who is the ancestor of whom). To say that something moves slowly is to say how it moves. Just so, to say that George is ancestrally related to Josef is to say how he is related. And one could also say "George is related to Josef, ancestorwise" (which could be a way of saying that they have a common ancestor): the colloquial affix "—wise" here serves to mark the noun "ancestor" as an adverbial object.

Adverbs and adverbial objects are not the only source of special entities to be encountered in the course of logical analysis. Prepositional phrases make their own contribution: "George came after Josef in ancestral succession," "George came in a hurry and Josef left in a hurry, so both were in a hurry," and so forth. But the greatest share of all is undoubtedly contributed by nominalizations: a nominalization is at once the *bête noir* of a Nominalist and the pet of a Platonist.

The nominalizations of English that are particularly pertinent here are those dealing with predicate adjectives, for all such nominalizations can readily be seen to be intimately related to adverbial modifications. Consider the compound sentence "If the house is grey and being grey is dull then there is something dull about the house." The expression "being grey" can be viewed as the product of a nominalizing transformation of the predicate adjective "grey." By such an operation, the expression is converted to a noun phrase and thus rendered available for predication. If we try to indicate, in the notation of quantificational logic, the structure of such a sentence, we seem compelled to conjure up a special entity, the abstract entity supposedly denoted by the expression "being grey." For it clearly will not do to translate the sentence as "$(x)[Hx \cdot Gx \cdot \supset \cdot Dx]$," where "$Hx$" stands in place of "$x$ is a house," "Gx" in place of "x is grey," and "Dx" in place of "x is dull." That is not what we were saying: there may be something dull about the house even though the house is not dull.

Here it may be said that since the English sentence seems to say something about an abstract entity, the property of being grey, there is no reason to balk at a translation of the sentence that employs quantification over predicate letters, or that calls for properties as values of its variables. But there is no good reason to suppose that the English sentence makes reference to any abstract entity. For there is no good reason to suppose that such a nominalization as "being grey" must be construed as a referring expression. To say that being grey is dull is not to say that there is some entity, namely the property of being grey, and that entity is dull. To say that being grey is dull is to say that if anything is grey then, not it is dull *simpliciter* but, it is dull in respect of color, or it is dull to a certain degree, perhaps a slight and discountable degree, or it is somewhat or partially dull. And here evidently these various prepositional phrases all play the role of adverbial modifiers.

Again, consider the sentence "Tardiness is reprehensible": the word "tardiness" can be viewed as the product of a distinct morphologically productive process, a nominalizing transformation of the predicate adjective "tardy." By affixing "-ness," the adjective "tardy" is converted to a noun and thus rendered available for predication. To say that tardiness is reprehensible is again not to make reference to any supposed abstract entity: it is a way of saying, not that if anyone is tardy then he is reprehensible, which would be somewhat harsh, but rather that if anyone is tardy then he is *prima facie* reprehensible, which is compatible with not being reprehensible at all, for he may have an excuse that gets him off. Here again one is evidently dealing with an adverbial modification.

Quine has said "To paraphrase a sentence into the canonical notation of quantification is, first and foremost, to make its ontic content explicit, quantification being a device for talking in general of objects." [9] And he has said that "To decline to explain oneself in terms of quantification, or in terms of those special idioms of ordinary language by which quantification is directly explained, is simply to decline to disclose one's referential intent." [10] But I conclude that the invitation to produce such a paraphrase is a gambit to be played with considerable care and, on occasion, to be declined.

A quantificational logic is a remarkably rigid device for plotting our discourse in terms of what can be said about discrete objects. It stands to English as a mercator projection does to a globe; it is not better, but perhaps not worse, than that. If one is to represent the various sentences of English in a quantificational logic then inevitably one is compelled to perform feats of conjuration, to produce abstract and special entities. And that may be not a matter of making "ontic content explicit" but unhappily of creating the illusion of content. For there is no good reason to credit the existence of such entities apart from the particular system of logic which evokes them. They are best seen as devices, devised to flatten the path from the sphere of natural language to the plane of logic: not entities from some Platonic realm of being, but simply isoglosses drawn by a logistic cartographer concerned to plot a plausible course through our conceptual labyrinth.

NOTES

1. See, for example, P. Cohen, *Set Theory and the Continuum Hypothesis* (New York, W. A. Benjamin, Inc., 1966), 3.

2. As in A. Church, *Introduction to Mathematical Logic* (Princeton, Princeton University Press, 1956).

3. As in A. Tarski, *Introduction to Logic* (New York, Oxford University Press, 1941).

4. As in W. V. O. Quine, *Mathematical Logic* (New York, Norton, 1940), though Quine does not there actually present a formal uninterpreted calculus.

5. "On Universals," *The Journal of Symbolic Logic*, 12 (1947), 75.

6. Church's view; see his review in *The Journal of Symbolic Logic* 5 (1940), 163.

7. See H. Reichenbach, *Elements of Symbolic Logic* (New York, The Macmillan Co., 1947), 301 ff.

8. See N. Goodman, *The Structure of Appearance* (Cambridge, Harvard University Press, 1951), 40.

9. W. V. O. Quine, *Word and Object* (New York, John Wiley & Sons, 1960), 242.

10. *Op. cit.*, 243.

LOGIC AND ORDINARY LANGUAGE

Max Black

I don't know whether it will be a relief or a disappointment to know that I don't propose to argue a thesis or even to refute anybody. I thought, considering the amount of disputation that occurs in some of these papers, it might be a welcome change if, instead of trying to answer questions, I were simply to raise them. I shall try to do so with the hope that they may lead to a full and fruitful discussion.

The sort of questions I would like to raise are the following: What are the peculiar and distinctive features of modern logic? How far are these features products of the accidents of historical development, or how far do they reflect the lasting aims and character of the discipline of logic? What adjustments and accommodations, if any, need to be made when modern logic is applied to the analysis and evaluation (or criticism) of arguments expressed in natural language? Is modern logic in its canonical form adequate to the task of the criticism of informal arguments? If not, do we need certain extensions of modern logic, or do we perhaps need certain allied, supplementary but distinctive, techniques and disciplines, *or* interpretations, or whatever you like to call them?

By modern logic I mean, of course, the dominant contemporary formulations of logic, and especially in the first instance, the so-called propositional calculus together with quantification theory (the functional or predicate calculus)—in short, the subject that has launched a thousand textbooks. I shall leave set theory out of the picture, and I won't even raise the controversial question as to whether set theory should count as part of logic. I am not particularly happy about the term "modern logic," with its misleading implications, and perhaps a better name might be "basic logic," suggesting that it, or something *like* it, must be taken into account in all reasoning, no matter what supplementary corrections, additions, or refinements may seem appropriate.

Language must come into our discussion, I assume, because the units of reasoning, whatever they are, must be expressed in words or in substitute symbols. Here, you will notice, I am at one with Professor Quine. Without commitment to being either a behaviorist or a non-behaviorist, it does seem plain to me that for the evaluation and criticism of arguments, we must have something linguistic or symbolic before us, and that nothing else will do. As to ordinary language, that is involved because I shall be interested in those thoughts, assertions, and suppositions which are a general concern to human beings and are prior to all the specialized questions that arise in the various arts, disciplines, and sciences.

The topic seems to me important, if only because there always has been, and there still is, a strong connection between the logical and what people call the rational. Thus any conclusion one draws concerning the proper limits of logic reacts in turn upon one's conception concerning the rational or the reasonable.

Let me give you one or two examples of what I mean here. You will recall Francis Bacon, at the dawn of modern science, tried very hard to develop what he called a *novum organon*, a new logic, because he believed that the restrictions of his time to Aristotelian logic meant that a great deal of scientific method simply had to be relegated to the realm of what simply happens, without any criterion of validity. Or to take an example in the opposite sense, you will be familiar with Sir Karl Popper's well-known and somewhat paradoxical views about science, to the effect that in science we can never achieve knowledge, that we refute rather than establish, and so on. I believe these views are due to a rather strict and narrow conception of what logic is. He will accept a deductive refutation, but he doesn't like the idea of something that might perhaps be called logic, which will give us canons of certification or confirmation rather than "tight" proof. In general, it seems to me that an excessively strict and narrow view of logic is a kind of logical puritanism; it encourages skepticism and irrationality about everything that is left outside the logical pale. And so it seems to me that rather large issues turn upon the decisions in question.

Any choice concerning the limits of the term "logic," will be embarrassed by the historical fact that the term "logic," together with its synonyms in other languages, and its occasional substitute, "dialectica," has had an extraordinarily checkered career, comparable perhaps only to that of the term "philosophy." At various times logic has been declared to be a science, an art, an auxiliary instrument (that is to say an *organon*); it has been regarded as factual or positive or categorical, or, on the other hand, as normative. Its subject matter has been supposed to be the "nature of things," and so to belong to ontology; or to be the rules of language, *scientia sermocinalis;* the connection of concepts, regarded sometimes as objective, sometimes as not; the laws of thought, in some psychological sense and so on. In fact, one is almost tempted to say that logic has meant almost anything that anybody has wanted it to mean. And this might suggest that our range of choice, at this present moment, is very wide indeed.

Nevertheless, one can discern a common thread in this semantical history that was supplied in a reasonably satisfactory way at the very beginning of the subject by Aristotle's own definition. You will remember that in the *Topics* he said, or rather said in the corresponding Greek: "Reasoning is an argument in which certain things being laid down, something other than these necessarily comes about." And again very much in the same vein in the *Prior Analytics:* a syllogism (by which he meant what we would call an argument, I think) is discourse—*logos,* ". . . in which, certain things being stated, something other than what is stated follows of necessity from their being so." He adds, interestingly, at that point, that the premises "produce the consequence without any further term." That is to say, the premises suffice to produce that necessary consequence.

This suggests to me that an altogether appropriate preliminary definition of logic would be something like the science of necessary connection. Or perhaps even, less technically, the science of reasons, or even the science of what makes a reason a reason. I don't regard this as a very satisfactory formula, but it can serve as a pointer that perhaps might satisfy not only Aristotle, but, without their really knowing it, nearly all those who have ever been interested in logic. I won't elaborate upon that now.

The proposal that logic be construed as the science of necessary connection does, of course, imply that such a science is possible. That is to say, knowledge about what I am here calling necessary connection can ideally be obtained. This implication can very well be questioned.

Let me cite a quotation that seems to tell against this proposal. It runs as follows:

There are philosophers of ordinary language who have grown so inured to the philosophical terms *entails* and *inconsistent,* as to look upon them, perhaps, as ordinary language. But the reader without such benefits of use and custom is apt to feel somewhat the kind of insecurity over these motions that many engineers must have felt when callow over derivatives and differentials. At the risk of seeming unteachable, I go on record as one such reader.

I am confident that one person, Professor Quine, will recognize the statement, since he himself wrote it, in *Mind*, in 1953. I wonder, and this is a supplementary question, whether he can be right about this. The analogy he draws is with a technical notion, the notion of a derivative—or the differential—and of course there, before any explicit satisfactory definition is given, one may very well feel insecurity. But when I am talking about necessary connection, I believe I am not talking about anything recondite or technical.

The use of the term *entails* by certain English philosophers, I think, gives Professor Quine a handle. But what I am thinking of is something very familiar indeed, something that is expressed in ordinary language by such words as "therefore," "hence," "because," and "thus," all of which are marks of what I am calling necessary connection. I don't think that anybody need feel insecure about these things if he understands what I am saying when I say: "If it snows very heavily tomorrow, I shall stay in Brockport. *Therefore*, I hope that it will not snow tomorrow." If you understand that, I think you understand sufficiently for a start, the notion of necessary connection.

In fact I wonder, if I may digress for a moment, about the doubts that some philosophers express concerning not only the notion of necessary connection, but also about such allied notions as analytic, synthetic, and so on. I suspect that sometimes there is a sort of *docta ignorantia* here—a learned, acquired incapacity to see what really lies under one's nose. One reason for this may be a very general and tempting confusion between the use and the analysis of a term. I would be very embarrassed indeed to have to analyse the meaning of the "therefore" in my statement above; yet I think this kind of analysis is an important but extremely difficult task. This confession, however, is compatible with my belief that I am able to use the term "therefore" and to use it sufficiently correctly.

Thus I take as the starting point that we do in fact, in ordinary language, before we invent the technical dialects, often have occasion to make the illative step—to use and use correctly such words as "therefore" and its substitutes, and that there is an authentic question for science to determine: what are the rules, the correct rules, for the use of this kind of word? Let us call this kind of logic, assuming that it exists, *exact logic*.

The first point I would like to make about exact logic is that if it really is to be a science, and I think this point is obvious (you must excuse me for making it), it should consist of what are or what at least purport to be truths. That is to say it must be a doctrine. No knowledge can come from playing games, whether with marks on paper or with anything else. If there is to be a logic in this sense, then there will have to be authentic assertions, presented with whatever justification can be supplied in defense of those assertions. This will mean, in addition, that an exact logic, so conceived, will have to be as clear as possible about its subject matter. It will be committed to telling us what it is talking about, or to put it another way, it will have to tell us what the entities are about which it is making those assertions. So long as there is unclarity about what the assertions of logic are concerned with, there will be corresponding unclarity about the putative truth-value of the assertions.

Negatively, exact logic will not be committed, as far as I can see, to the use of any special method, mathematical or any other. In particular, it will not be committed to the use of special symbols, however useful, or to the use of what is called formalistic method, however convenient that may be.

In the light of what I've been saying, let us quickly take a look at some familiar features of modern logic. Modern logic, I take it, is and intends to be, a science, and like other sciences it is highly selective in its choice of subject matter. It is, to a certain extent, reconstructive, somewhat in the sense in which Carnap has used that expression. Also, like mathematics, but not like sciences in general, it is particularly concerned (or is said to be particularly concerned) with form, and again it is particularly concerned with using a formalistic method.

I will comment briefly on each of these four points. First, with regard to the selection of the subject matter, it is well known, of course, that modern logic in its canonical form is largely restricted to the logical constants "not," "and," and "all." This is a remarkably elegant choice of primitives, but it may raise doubts as to the adequacy of the subject so developed to the aims of logic as I have construed them. In particular, we notice that, at any rate until quite recent times, modal concepts have been excluded for the most part from modern logic on principle.

Perhaps the same might be said about concepts in the general area of probability. It is quite characteristic that when a logician like Carnap turns his attention to problems of induction, he tries to operate with exactly the same apparatus. He is very reluctant to make any radical change.

Next, with regard to reconstruction or idealization—and again I am sure I am telling you what you know all too well already—it is generally accepted that the entities logic is concerned with, are, have to be, independent of context: they have to be timeless, and they have to be what is called "extensional." In particular, as we know, the basic "if-then" connection itself is a trimmed, transformed version of the "if-then" that occurs in ordinary life. We don't have the primitive "if-then" that we use in ordinary language; we have what has been called material or Philonian implication.

All of this is familiar and need not cause concern. As for the traditional emphasis upon form, here I confess I am somewhat less happy. Every schoolboy, to echo Macaulay, is supposed to know that logic studies form and not matter. In the latest edition of the *Encyclopedia Britannica*, an article on logic written by Alonzo Church begins: "Logic is the systematic study of the structure of propositions and of the general conditions of valid inference by a method which abstracts from the content or matter of the propositions and deals only with their logical form." Thus he builds right into the definition of logic that it must be concerned with form and not with matter. He goes on to say something that puzzles me a great deal: "This distinction between form and matter is made whenever we distinguish between the logical soundness or validity of a piece of reasoning, and the truth of the premises from which it proceeds, and in this sense is familiar in every day usage." He seems to be saying that at the very moment at which I ask simply whether a conclusion follows from the premises, without raising the question whether the premises are true or false, I am recognizing a distinction between form and matter. I must say I just don't follow him. But I will also confess that the more I have thought about what logicians, and for that matter mathematicians too, mean by form when they say that logic and mathematics deal with form and not with content, the more puzzled I have become.

It is perfectly clear that this language arises from a very primitive distinction between a stuff and a shape. The etymology of the word "form" actually shows that. I suppose, at the tangible level, where we distinguish between the clay of which a pot is made and its shape, we do have a pretty clear and distinct idea of what the difference is. But if you try to extend this by analogy and to give some nonmetaphorical characterization of the distinction in general between form and matter, the task becomes extremely difficult. There is, for one thing, a serious risk of confusing logical form with the visual form of the token used for symbolizing a particular argument.

If you ask somebody, who is not too sophisticated, to explain what he means by the logical form of an argument, he will put up a diagram, and let's take a very crude one:

$$\text{All } A \text{ are } B$$
$$\text{All } B \text{ are } C$$
$$\therefore \text{ All } A \text{ are } C$$

Then he will say: "Well, you see that the A occurs there and there; the

B occurs there and there; the *C* occurs there and there; while the same *All—All* occur there; the same *are—are* occur there; and that shows the logical form of that particular argument." Of course, what he is drawing attention to is a visual pattern. He might just as well have drawn something like this: $+ \, ^\circ + \, ^\circ$ and said: "Look, you see the cross there and the cross there, a circle there and a circle there?" Then he would certainly be showing us visual form, and here too, I think, he is showing visual form. We are a long way away from having the logical form identified.

I suspect that the only reputable way to explain what is meant by logical form is by drawing a contrast between constants and variables. But if this is so, and I can think of no other way of responsibly explaining what logical form is, it seems to me we have the embarrassment of explaining why the logical constants should be called constants. Why do we say that these particular words—"all," "are," "no," "if," and so on— with a definite meaning, are to count as showing some aspects of the logical form, while the other words must be replaced by variables, by place holders?

For the medievals, who had rather strict and firm ideas about the relation between symbols, or words, and reality, there was an answer. They said that the subject and the predicate referred to the world, more or less directly, while the remaining words, those we nowadays call "logical constants" had only an auxiliary function. Thus the medievals had a picture of some words pointing out to the world, and other words, as it were, pointing laterally inside language.

I cannot see that we can today reasonably sustain that kind of imagery. If we take the simple sentence, "All the objects in my pocket are coins," it seems to me that the whole sentence does refer, in some way, to what is happening in my pocket, and that there isn't any good way of distinguishing the function of referring, or pointing, or denoting of the thing as a whole, as between words like "all" and words like "objects," "in," or "pocket." When I say "all the objects," I think I am pointing to some feature of the pocket; and in this respect, "all" looks as material as "objects in my pocket."

No doubt, distinctions must be drawn. I am not pretending that the many, many occasions on which logicians and mathematicians have insisted upon the form that is involved in logic and mathematics have involved only empty noise, but I really don't in the end understand what the metaphor comes to. This seems to me a problem that eminently deserves further work. I am inclined to think that the famous concern with form goes back in the end to Aristotle. Once the metaphors are stripped away, and once the form is no longer regarded as something substantial that could be seen, then that metaphor reduces to little more than a claim of very high generality.

On the last point, the formalistic method, or what might perhaps be called the deliberate abdication of meaning in the technical treatment of logical systems, all that needs to be pointed out here is that this seems to be a question of useful technique. It does not seem to be in any way implied by the basic aims of logic. In any case the process of formalization can never be completed. There will have to be in logic itself, or at least in the meta-language of logic, words that are not being used with abdication of meaning, and in particular, we shall have to use something like the logical constants ourselves in stating the principles of logic.

Very likely, my brief account of the character of modern logic is unsatisfactory. But perhaps I have said enough to remind us that modern logic is in some ways a very peculiar subject. Its great and undoubted successes are probably due, in part, to these peculiarities. I think that if the problems of logic had been approached, as it were, in full generality, without the particular restrictions that have occurred in the career of logic, its course would have been by no means as spectacular and as brilliantly successful as it has been. On the other hand, I cannot see that any of the specific features I have mentioned are *essentially* connected with the aim of exact logic, considered as a science of necessary connection.

On the issue of selectivity, it seems to me by no means certain, that, for example, a notion like entailment cannot be formally treated. To be sure, a lot of people have tried and haven't succeeded. But I can see no reason in principle why a calculus which would necessarily be less tidy than the calculus of material implication, should not be, in the end, devised for entailment. Nor is it clear that modal concepts must be excluded from the scope of logic. Most important of all, I think serious argument is needed to show, as Church seems to think, that all reasoning must be—has to be—reconstructable in wholly formal systems

I would like to suggest an analogy here. Modern logic might be compared to universal physics—to a science that undertakes to deal with the common properties of all matter. But this ambitious aim is certainly comparable with the development of special branches of physics, such as chemistry, that are concerned with a department, and not with the entire subject-matter. Why shouldn't there be something similar in the case of inference? Why shouldn't there be a general and universal logic, something like what we have already, or perhaps an extension of it, and at the same time, side by side with that, special logics dealing with departments?

I am thinking, for example, of the new investigations into what is sometimes called the logic of belief, the logic of time, or the logic of other special terms. One would obtain a calculus in which the term "belief" or "believes" occurs as a constant, while apart from that, there would be only variables. Should we or should we not call the rules for transitions containing that term and related terms a part of logic, or not? And if not, why not? I am not in the least proposing that we should abandon the methods that have been so productive in modern logic, but I think it would be quite as foolish to suppose that the technical convenience of modern logic must have some profound philosophical significance. Something I might call the lamp post or street light principle is suggested by the story of the drunk who was found looking for his key under the lamp post. When the bystander asked, "What are you doing, looking for your key? I suppose you dropped it there," he replied, "Oh, no, it's just lighter here." I think the approach of logicians to problems of actual reasoning sometimes exemplifies this same principle. They use modern logic because it's lighter there and, sure enough, it is. But the key that is missing may very well be in another place. In short, provoked by Professor Quine's question about science—what else is there?—I'm trying to strike a blow against what I would call logicolatry, or the superstitious veneration of logic in the special form that it has now achieved.

I turn now to the use of logic for the criticism of reasoning, and I am going to ignore the successes of modern logic in the domain of its least controversial applicability; I mean through rendering manipulable the structure of mathematical systems, construction of axiom systems, or the well-known and remarkable meta-mathematical investigations. I don't in the least undervalue these, of course, but I want to concentrate on something else: on what people have, I think, rather ill-advisedly, come to call "ordinary language." This is an unfortunate label because it suggests that there is something properly called extraordinary language, whereas the intended contrast is not between two kinds of language at all. I don't know that there is any extraordinary English; there just is English.

The intended contrast, I think, or the one that might be useful to intend, is between the speech—the used language of people about their ordinary business, the *Umgangsprache*—and the invented technical terms and ideographies of specialists. More specifically, the contrast is between the so-called ideal language of logicians and ordinary discourse.

The question I am raising here is the following: Is modern logic an organon for science and mathematics alone, or is it also the basis for a *logica utens* for informal discourse? (And I am assuming that logic that is not interested in application is on its way to degenerate into a logomachy, a sort of idle strife about logic itself.)

This kind of question about whether and to what extent logic can be helpful in the criticism of ordinary discourse at the outset requires a distinction between what a particular speaker means in a particular setting on a particular occasion, and, on the other hand, something more abstract, something like Frege's *Gedanke*, a shareable thought which can be abstracted somehow from the particular episode for the sake of examination and criticism by anybody. I shall refer to these two as the *illative act*, something that is actually going on in a particular situation, and the *abstracted argument*. As most linguists nowadays do, I believe that the starting and the ending points must be the illative episode. That is to say, in the end what interests us is criticizing a particular instance of discourse, not a particular bit of language, and the route through the language is for the sake of final return to the illative episode.

If we look at illative acts or episodes with an unbiased eye, we shall find all kinds of awkward obstacles to the application of modern logic. I shall mention some of them—they are not all equally important or obstinate. One is the presence in authentic full-blooded discourse of nonverbal indications of meaning. I think people forget how much of the actual transmission of meaning, especially in genuine speech, but even by transfer in writing, depends not upon the use of words at all, but upon gesture and a number of other things.

A second obstacle is that it seems to be characteristic of natural, used, languages that a tremendous amount that counts in the communication is not rendered explicit, so that we are constantly faced with the problem of how to deal with what is certainly in some sense communicated, though it cannot be identified in the sound waves or in the marks on paper.

I think the point is familiar, but allow me to give you one or two more examples. Toynbee once said, in this country I believe, "No annihilation without representation." I don't think what he intended was particularly mysterious, but it was certainly interestingly complex and witty. I do not suppose that a philosopher seriously arguing would be well-advised to use a rhetorical device of this complexity. But this example illustrates quite well what happens in simple situations—and what happens is far more than we always are willing to credit.

Here is another example that I have taken from a novel. A husband and wife are in a restaurant, and the wife says of the waiter to the husband: "He's terribly inefficient." The husband replies, "All the same, I think you should tip him." He is responding here to something that is certainly a deviant meaning of the utterance, but is closer to the meaning intended in that particular occasion than any formal paraphrase of the words used could be.

A third obstacle is something I would want to distinguish from the implications of an utterance, as something like the presuppositions of the utterance, in a sense a good deal broader than the one that Strawson used. If I ask, "How soon will this meeting end?," I am, in a familiar way, presupposing a tremendous amount of commonplace shared information. I am presupposing that you know what a meeting is, that there is such a thing as a meeting going on, that meetings, happily, do come to an end, and so on. All of this, while it lurks below the surface, is effective and must be taken into account.

We have to rely a good deal upon the setting and the context of the utterance, and here again in a rather different way, we are dealing with nonverbal factors. We assume certain broad understandings which identify, perhaps even constitute, the kind of games we are involved in. When a philosopher says, "I don't understand what so-and-so is saying," we know very well that he doesn't mean that he doesn't understand, and that this is one of the polite and useful conventions of the philosophical game. If we were to retort, as Moore did on a famous occasion, "You don't understand—how disgraceful!," that would be witty, but perhaps beside the point.

More seriously, there is a factor which doesn't enter into logic at all, namely the kind of thing that some linguists call the pregnancy with which terms and utterances are used. If I say, "The sky is white," I am implying the contrast with other things I might have said. How emphatic is the contrast? Do I mean "white, really white," so that a gray sky won't count, or am I using "white" properly, but rather loosely, in the sense in which a sky that on other occasions could be called gray will still count as white? If I'm using the "white" pieces on the chess board, "white" there may cover green, gray, a great many colors. All of this is consistent with a perfectly correct use of the term "white" and is something for whose control there are, as far as I can see, no formal rules.

I think this kind of thing, which no doubt is familiar, is taken much too lightly by people who are criticizing arguments. If you offer anything except a very trivial argument to a philosopher or to a logician, he will at once get out his stock of XYZ's and parentheses and capital letters, and start giving you a little bit of modern logic. I have yet to find any very interesting case where this was of much interest as a criticism of an authentic philosophical argument. To put it another way, I doubt very much whether what goes wrong with philosophical arguments is often formal fallacy.

We are still left with the question of whether these questions—the correctness or the soundness of a piece of reasoning—should be counted as part of the work of the logician or should be turned over to somebody else. If they are to be turned over to somebody else, I would like to know who is going to do it. I don't want to suggest that the complexity of authentic discourse is unmanageable; quite the contrary. The transition from the illative episode to the shareable argument can be made: we can paraphrase, we can bring out into the open the assumptions and the presuppositions, we can reduce reliance upon the context and the uptake of the speaker, we can highlight the behavior of crucial words. All this might be called, in a certain sense, formalizing the argument, not in the logician's sense of formalizing, but rather, perhaps, in the lawyer's sense of getting everything down on paper. It is unwieldly and time consuming, but it may be extremely illuminating. And as part of this process of formalizing in this popular sense, we shall reveal a number of things that look *somewhat like* the kinds of things that logicians worry about. But, what seems to me quite certain is that we shall also turn up a very large variety of uncanonical forms in the process.

I have already mentioned non-Philonian implications. We shall certainly stumble against intentional occurrences of propositional constituents. We shall run into the kind of problem that Professor Ziff has discussed—behavior of adverbs, and of many other things. Especially, I believe, we shall run into problems which one may call logical or not, which seem in some way to be connected with the rules of the language and which I would, therefore, assign to what I would like to call philosophical grammar.

Let me present two very simple illustrations: 1. This is a white elephant, and, 2. this is a small elephant. Superficially, we have similar forms here, but from "this is a white elephant" we can pass to "this is white"; we cannot similarly pass from "this is a small elephant" to "this is small." Therefore, there is a lack of parallelism.

Should we count this kind of point as belonging to logic or not? I would suggest that it would be reasonable to do so, although we are not dealing, to be sure, with the very general features that logicians are most concerned about. I would be inclined to say that if somebody argued by analogy that since something is a small elephant that same thing is something small, he would be committing an error in reasoning. If my wife sent me out to buy her something small and I came back with a small elephant, I think she would have grounds for complaint.

Much more could undoubtedly be said, but I hope I have said enough to stimulate discussion. I have been arguing for a view that is, perhaps, obvious and already accepted; namely, that modern logic, for all of its extraordinary merits, is neither a universal tool nor a panacea. If I had more time, I would argue the need of what Locke long ago called "another sort of logic and critique"; that is to say, a discipline dealing with the kinds of questions that arise in some of the instances that I have presented to you. I think this kind of work, which has already begun, is important: it will call for the combined work of linguists, of philosophers, of logicians, perhaps of other specialists. It does not, perhaps, matter very much whether you call it philosophical grammar or logic, provided that you work towards it.

IS SEMANTICS POSSIBLE?*

Hilary Putnam

In the last decade enormous progress seems to have been made in the syntactic theory of natural languages, largely as a result of the work of linguists influenced by Noam Chomsky and Zellig Harris. Comparable progress seems *not* to have been made in the semantic theory of natural languages, and perhaps it is time to ask why this should be the case. Why is the theory of meaning so *hard*?

The meaning of common nouns. To get some idea of the difficulties, let us look at some of the problems that come up in connection with general names. General names are of many kinds. Some, like *bachelor* admit of an explicit definition straight off ("man who has never been married"); but the overwhelming majority do not. Some are derived by transformations from verbal forms, e.g., *hunter = one who hunts.* An important class, philosophically as well as linguistically, is the class of general names associated with *natural kinds*—that is, with classes of things that we regard as of explanatory importance; classes whose normal distinguishing characteristics are "held together" or even explained by deep-lying mechanisms. *Gold, lemon, tiger, acid*, are examples of such nouns. I want to begin this paper by suggesting that (1) *traditional* theories of meaning radically falsify the properties of such words; (2) logicians like Carnap do little more than formalize these traditional theories, inadequacies and all; (3) such semantic theories as that produced by Jerrold Katz and his co-workers likewise share all the defects of the traditional theory. In Austin's happy phrase, what we have been given by philosophers, logicians, and "semantic theorists" alike, is a "myth-eaten description."

* While responsibility for the views expressed here is, of course, solely mine, they doubtless reflect the influence of two men who have profoundly affected my attitude towards the problems of language: Paul Ziff and Richard Boyd. I owe them both a debt of gratitude for their insight, their infectious enthusiasm, and for many happy hours of philosophical conversation.

On the traditional view, the meaning of, say, "lemon," is given by specifying a conjunction of *properties*. For each of these properties, the statement "lemons have the property P" is an analytic truth; and if P_1, P_2, ... P_n are all of the properties in the conjunction, then "anything with all of the properties P_1, . . . , P_n is a lemon" is likewise an analytic truth.

In one sense, this is trivially correct. If we are allowed to invent unanalyzable properties *ad hoc*, then we can find a single property— not even a conjunction—the possession of which is a necessary and sufficient condition for being a lemon, or being gold, or whatever. Namely, we just postulate *the property of being a lemon*, or *the property of being gold*, or whatever may be needed. If we require that the properties P_1, P_2, . . . , P_n *not* be of this *ad hoc* character, however, then the situation is very different. Indeed, with any natural understanding of the term "property," it is just *false* that to say that something belongs to a natural kind is just to ascribe to it a conjunction of properties.

To see why it is false, let us look at the term "lemon." The supposed "defining characteristics" of lemons are: yellow color, tart taste, a certain kind of peel, etc. Why is the term "lemon" *not* definable by simply conjoining these "defining characteristics"?

The most obvious difficulty is that a natural kind may have *abnormal members*. A green lemon is still a lemon—even if, owing to some abnormality, it *never* turns yellow. A three-legged tiger is still a tiger. Gold in the gaseous state is still gold. It is only normal lemons that are yellow, tart, etc.; only normal tigers that are four-legged; only gold under normal conditions that is hard, white or yellow, etc.

To meet this difficulty, let us try the following definition: X is a *lemon* $= df$; X belongs to a natural kind whose normal members have yellow peel, tart taste, etc.

There is, of course, a problem with the "etc." There is also a problem with "tart taste"—shouldn't it be *lemon* taste? But let us waive these difficulties, at least for the time being. Let us instead focus on the two notions that have come up with this attempted definition: the notions *natural kind* and *normal member*.

A natural kind *term* (to shift attention, for the moment, from natural kinds to their preferred designations) is a term that plays a special kind of role. If I describe something as a *lemon*, or as an *acid*, I indicate that it is likely to have certain characteristics (yellow peel, or sour taste in dilute water solution, as the case may be); but I also indicate that the presence of those characteristics, if they are present, is likely to be accounted for by some "essential nature" which the thing shares with other members of the natural kind. What the essential nature is is not a matter of language analysis but of scientific theory construction; today we would say it was chromosome structure, in the case of lemons, and being a proton-donor, in the case of acids. Thus it is tempting to say that a natural kind term is simply a term that plays a certain kind of role in scientific or pre-scientific theory: the role, roughly, of pointing to common "essential features" or "mechanisms" beyond and below the obvious "distinguishing characteristics." But this is vague, and likely to remain so. Meta-science is today in its infancy: and terms like "natural kind," and "normal member," are in the same boat as the more familiar meta-scientific terms "theory" and "explanation," as far as resisting a speedy and definitive analysis is concerned.

Even if we *could* define "natural kind"—say, "a natural kind is a class which is the extension of a term *P* which plays such-and-such a methodological role in some well-confirmed theory"—the definition would obviously embody a theory of the world, at least in part. It is not *analytic* that natural kinds are classes which play certain kinds of roles in theories; what *really* distinguishes the classes we count as natural kinds is itself a matter of (high level and very abstract) scientific investigation and not just meaning analysis.

That the proposed definition of "lemon" uses terms which themselves resist definition is not a fatal objection however. Let us pause to note, therefore, that if it is correct (and we shall soon show that even it is radically oversimplified), then the traditional idea of the force of general terms is badly mistaken. To say that something is a lemon is, on the above definition, to say that it belongs to a natural kind whose normal members have certain properties; but not to say that it necessarily has those properties itself. There are no *analytic* truths of the form *every lemon has* P. What has happened is this: the traditional theory has taken an account which is correct for the "one-criterion" concepts (i.e., for such concepts as "bachelor" and "vixen"), and made it a general account of the meaning of general names. A theory which correctly describes the behavior of perhaps three hundred words has been asserted to correctly describe the behavior of the tens of thousands of general names.

It is also important to note the following: if the above definition is correct, then knowledge of the properties that a thing has (in any natural and non "ad hoc" sense of property) is not enough to determine, in any mechanical or algorithmic way, whether or not it is a lemon (or an acid, or whatever). For even if I have a description in, say, the language of particle physics, of what are in fact the chromosomal properties of a fruit, I may not be able to tell that it is a lemon because I have not developed the theory according to which (1) those physical-chemical characteristics are the chromosomal structure-features (I may not even have the notion "chromosome"; and (2) I may not have discovered that chromosomal structure is the *essential* property of lemons. Meaning does not determine extension, in the sense that given the meaning and a list of all the "properties" of a thing (in any particular sense of "property," one can simply *read off* whether the thing is a lemon (or acid, or whatever). Even given the meaning, whether something is a lemon or not is, or at least sometimes is, or at least may sometimes be, a matter of what is the best conceptual scheme, the best theory, the best scheme of "natural kinds." (This is, of course, one reason for the failure of phenomenalistic translation schemes.)

These consequences of the proposed definition are, I believe, correct, even though the proposed definition is itself still badly oversimplified. Is it a necessary truth that the "normal" lemons, as we think of them (the tart yellow ones) are really normal members of their species? Is it logically impossible that we should have mistaken what are really very atypical lemons (perhaps diseased ones) for normal lemons? On the above definition, if there is no natural kind whose normal members are yellow, tart, etc., then even these tart, yellow, thick-peeled fruits that I make lemonade from are *not literally lemons*. But this is absurd. It is clear that they are lemons, although it is not analytic that they are *normal* lemons. Moreover, if the color of lemons changed—say, as the result of some gasses getting into the earth's atmosphere and reacting with the pigment in the peel of lemons—we would not say that lemons had ceased to exist, although a natural kind whose normal members were *yellow* and had the other characteristics of lemons *would* have ceased to exist. Thus the above definition is correct to the extent that what it says *isn't* analytic indeed isn't; but it is incorrect in that what would be analytic if it were correct isn't. We have loosened up the logic of the natural kind terms, in comparison with the "conjunction of properties" model; but we have still not loosened it up enough.

Two cases have just been considered: (1) the normal members of the natural kind in question may not really be the ones we *think* are normal; (2) the characteristics of the natural kind may change with time, possibly owing to a change in the conditions, without the "essence" changing so much that we want to stop using the same word. In the first case (normal lemons are blue, but we haven't seen any normal lemons), our theory of the natural kind is false; but at least there is a natural kind about which we have a false theory, and that is why we can still apply the term. In the second case, our theory was at least once true; but it has ceased to be true, although the natural kind has not ceased to exist, which is why we can still apply the term.

Let us attempt to cover both these kinds of cases by modifying our definition as follows:

X is a *lemon* = *df* X belongs to a natural kind whose . . . (as before) OR X belongs to a natural kind whose normal members used to . . . (as before) OR X belongs to a natural kind whose normal members were formerly believed to, or are now incorrectly believed to . . . (as before).

Nontechnically, the trouble with this "definition" is that it is slightly crazy. Even if we waive the requirement of sanity (and, indeed, it is all too customary in philosophy to waive any such requirement), it still doesn't work. Suppose, for example, that some tens of thousands of years ago lemons were unknown, but a few atypical oranges were known. Suppose these atypical oranges had exactly the properties of peel, color, etc., that lemons have: indeed, we may suppose that only a biologist could tell that they were really queer oranges and not normal lemons. Suppose that the people living at that time took them to be normal members of a species, and thus thought that oranges have exactly the properties that lemons in fact do have. Then all now existing oranges would be lemons, according to the above definition, since they belong to a species (a natural kind) of which it was once believed that the normal members have the characteristics of yellow peel, lemon taste, etc.

Rather than try to complicate the definition still further, in the fashion of system-building philosophers, let us simply observe what has gone wrong. It is true—and this is what the new definition tries to reflect—that one possible use of a natural kind term is the following: to refer to a thing which belongs to a natural kind which does *not* fit the "theory" associated with the natural kind term, but which was believed to fit that theory (and, in fact, to be *the* natural kind which fit the theory) when the theory had not yet been falsified. Even if cats turn out to be robots remotely controlled from Mars we will still call them "cats"; even if it turns out that the stripes on tigers are painted on to deceive us, we will still call them "tigers"; even if normal lemons are blue (we have been buying and raising very atypical lemons, but don't know it), they are still lemons (and so are the yellow ones.) Not only will we still *call* them "cats," they are cats; not only will we still call them "tigers," they are tigers; not only will we still call them "lemons," they are lemons. But the fact that a term has several possible uses does not make it a disjunctive term; the mistake is in trying to represent the complex behavior of a natural kind word in something as simple as an analytic definition.

To say that an analytic definition is too simple a means of representation is not to say that no representation is possible. Indeed, a very simple representation is possible, *viz.*:

> *lemon*: natural kind word   associated characteristics:
>   yellow peel, tart taste, etc.

To fill this out, a lot more should be said about the linguistic behavior of natural kind words; but no more need be said about *lemon*.

Katz's theory of meaning. Carnap's view of meaning in natural language is this: we divide up logical space into "logically possible worlds." (That this may be highly language-relative, and that it may presuppose the very analytic-synthetic distinction he hopes to find by his quasi-operational procedure are objections he does not discuss.) The informant is asked whether or not he would say that something is the case in each logically possible world: the assumption being that (1) each logically possible world can be described clearly enough for the informant to tell; and (2) that the informant can say that the sentence in question is *true/false/not clearly either* just on the basis of the description of the logically possible world and the meaning (or "intension") he assigns to the sentence in question. The latter assumption is false, as we have just seen, for just the reason that the traditional theory of meaning is false: even if I know the "logically possible world" you have in mind, deciding whether or not something is, for example, a lemon, may require deciding what the best *theory* is; and this is not something to be determined by asking an informant yes/no questions in a rented office. This is not to say that "lemon" has no meaning, of course: it is to say that meaning is not *that* simply connected with extension, even with "extension in logically possible worlds."

Carnap is not my main stalking-horse, however. The theory I want to focus on is the "semantic theory" recently propounded by Jerrold Katz and his co-workers. In main outlines this theory is as follows:

(1) Each word has its meaning characterized by a string of "semantic markers."

(2) These markers stand for "concepts" ("concepts" are themselves brain processes in Katz' philosophy of language; but I shall ignore this *jeu d'esprit* here.) Examples of such concepts are: *unmarried, animate, seal.*

(3) Each such concept (concept for which a semantic marker is introduced) is a "linguistic universal," and stands for an *innate* notion —one in some sense-or-other "built into" the human brain.

(4) There are recursive rules—and this is the "scientific" core or

Katz' "semantic theory"—whereby the "readings" of whole sentences (these being likewise strings of markers) are derived from the meanings of the individual words and the deep structure (in the sense of transformational grammar) of the sentence.

(5) The scheme as a whole is said to be justified in what is said to be the manner of a scientific theory—by its ability to explain such things as our intuitions that certain sentences have more than one meaning, or that certain sentences are queer.

(6) Analyticity relations are also supposed to be able to be read off from the theory: for example, from the fact that the markers associated with "unmarried" occur in connection with "bachelor," one can see that "all bachelors are unmarried" is analytic; and from the fact that the markers associated with "animal" occur in connection with "cat," one can see (allegedly) that "all cats are animals" is analytic.

There are internal inconsistencies in this scheme which are apparent at once. For example, "seal" is given as an example of a "linguistic universal" (at least, "seal" occurs as part of the "distinguisher" in one reading for "bachelor"—the variant reading: *young male fur seal*, in one of Katz' examples); but in no theory of human evolution is contact with seals universal. Indeed, even contact with *clothing*, or with *furniture*, or with *agriculture* is by no means universal. Thus we must take it that Katz means that whenever such terms occur they could be further analyzed into concepts which really are so primitive that a case could be made for their universality. Needless to say, this program has never been carried out, and he himself constantly ignores it in giving examples. But the point of greatest interest to us is that this scheme is an unsophisticated translation into "mathematical" language of precisely the traditional theory that it has been our concern to criticize! Indeed, as far as general names are concerned, the only change is that whereas in the traditional account each general name was associated with a list of properties, in Katz' account each general name is associated with a list of *concepts*. It follows that each counterexample to the traditional theory is at once a counterexample also to Katz' theory. For example, if Katz lists the concept "yellow" under the noun "lemon," then he will be committed to "all lemons are yellow"; if he lists the concept "striped" under the noun "tiger," then he will be committed to the analyticity of "all tigers are striped"; and so on. Indeed, although Katz denies that his "semantic markers" are themselves *words*, it is clear that they can be regarded as a kind of artificial language. Therefore, what Katz is saying is that:

(1) A mechanical scheme can be given for translating any natural

language into this artificial "marker language" (and this scheme is just what Katz' "semantic theory" is).

(2) The string of markers associated with a word has exactly the meaning of the word.

If (1) and (2) were true, we would at once deduce that there exists a possible language—a "marker language"—with the property that every word that human beings have invented or could invent has an analytic definition in that language. But this is something that we have every reason to disbelieve! In fact: (1) We have just seen that if our account of "natural kind" words is correct, then none of these words has an analytic definition. In particular, a natural kind word will be analytically translatable into marker language only in the special case in which a marker happens to have been introduced with that exact meaning. (2) There are many words for which we haven't the foggiest notion what an analytic definition would even look like. What would an analytic definition of "mammoth" look like? (Would Katz say that it is analytic that mammoths are extinct? Or that they have a certain kind of molar? These are the items mentioned in the dictionary!) To say that a word is the name of an extinct species of elephant is to exactly communicate the use of that word; but it certainly isn't an analytic definition (i.e., an analytically necessary and sufficient condition). (3) *Theoretical terms* in science have no analytic definitions, for reasons familiar to every reader of recent philosophy of science; yet these are surely items (and not atypical items) in the vocabulary of natural languages.

We have now seen, I believe, one reason for the recent lack of progress in semantic theory: you may dress up traditional mistakes in modern dress by talking of "recursive rules" and "linguistic universals," but they remain the traditional mistakes. The problem in semantic theory is to get away from the picture of the meaning of a word as something like a *list of concepts*; not to formalize that misguided picture.

Quine's pessimism. Quine has long expressed a profound pessimism about the very possibility of such a subject as "semantic theory." Certainly we cannot assume that *there is* a scientific subject to be constructed here just because ordinary people have occasion to use the word "meaning" from time to time; that would be like concluding that there must be a scientific subject to be constructed which will deal with "causation" just because ordinary people have occasion to use the word "cause" from time to time. In one sense, *all* of science is a theory of causation; but not in the sense that it uses the word *cause*. Similarly, any successful and developed theory of language-use will in one sense be a theory of meaning; but not necessarily in the sense that it will employ any such notion as the "meaning" of a word or of an utterance. Elementary as this point is, it seems to be constantly overlooked in the social sciences, and people seem constantly to expect that psychology, for example, must talk of "dislike," "attraction," "belief," etc., simply because ordinary men use these words in psychological description.

Quine's pessimism cannot, then, be simply dismissed; and as far as the utility of the traditional notion of "meaning" is concerned, Quine may well turn out to be right. But we are still left with the task of trying to say what are the real problems in the area of language-use, and of trying to erect a conceptual framework within which we can begin to try to solve them.

Let us return to our example of the natural-kind words. It is a fact, and one whose importance to this subject I want to bring out, that the use of words can be taught. If someone does not know the meaning of "lemon," I can somehow convey it to him. I am going to suggest that in this simple phenomenon lies the problem, and hence the *raison d'être*, of "semantic theory."

How do I convey the meaning of the word "lemon"? Very likely, I show the man a lemon. Very well, let us change the example. How do I convey the meaning of the word "tiger"? *I tell him what a tiger is.*

It is easy to see that Quine's own theoretical scheme (in *Word and Object*) will not handle this case very well. Quine's basic notion is the notion of *stimulus meaning* (roughly this is the set of nerve-ending stimulations which will "prompt assent" to *tiger*). But: (1) it is very unlikely that I convey exactly the stimulus-meaning that "tiger" has in my idiolect; and (2) in any case I don't convey it directly, i.e., by describing it. In fact, I couldn't describe it. Quine also works with the idea of *accepted sentences*; thus he might try to handle this case somewhat as follows: "the hearer, in your example already shares a great deal of language with you; otherwise you couldn't tell him what a tiger is. When you 'tell him what a tiger is,' you simply tell him certain sentences that you accept. Once he knows what sentences you accept, naturally he is able to use the word, at least observation words."

Let us, however, refine this last counter somewhat. If conveying the meaning of the word "tiger" involved conveying the totality of accepted scientific theory about tigers, or even the totality of what I believe about tigers, then it would be an impossible task. It is true that when I tell someone what a tiger is I "simply tell him certain sentences"—though not necessarily sentences I *accept*, except as descriptions of linguistically stereotypical tigers. But the point is, *which* sentences?

In the special case of such words as "tiger" and "lemon," we proposed an answer earlier in this paper. The answer runs as follows: there is somehow associated with the word "tiger" a *theory;* not the actual theory we believe about tigers, which is very complex, but an oversimplified theory which describes a, so to speak, tiger *stereotype.* It describes, in the language we used earlier, a *normal member* of the natural kind. It is not necessary that we believe this theory, though in the case of "tiger" we do. But it is necessary that we be aware that *this* theory is associated with the word: if our stereotype of a tiger ever changes, then the word "tiger" will have changed its meaning. If, to change the example, lemons all turn blue, the word "lemon" will not immediately change its meaning. When I first say, with surprise, "lemons have all turned blue," lemon will still mean what it means now—which is to say that "lemon" will still be associated with the stereotype *yellow lemon,* even though I will be using the word to deny that lemons (even normal lemons) are in fact yellow. I can refer to a natural kind by a term which is "loaded" with a theory which is known not to be any longer true of that natural kind, just because it will be clear to everyone that what I intend is to refer to *that* kind, and not to assert the theory. But, of course, if lemons really did turn blue (and stayed that way) then in time "lemon" would come to have a meaning with the following representation:

> *lemon:* natural kind word   associated characteristics:
> *blue* peel, tart taste, etc.

Then "lemon" would have changed its meaning.

To sum this up: there are a few facts about "lemon" or "tiger" (I shall refer to them as *core facts*) such that one can convey the use of "lemon" or "tiger" by simply conveying those facts. More precisely, one can frequently convey the approximate use; and still more precisely, one cannot convey the approximate use *unless* one gets the core facts across.

Let me emphasize that this has the status of an empirical hypothesis. The hypothesis is that there are, in connection with almost any word (not just "natural kind" words), certain core facts such that (1) one cannot convey the normal use of the word (to the satisfaction of native speakers) without conveying those core facts, and (2) in the case of many words and many speakers, conveying those core facts is sufficient to convey at least an approximation to the normal use. In the case of a natural kind word, the core facts are that a normal member of the kind has certain characteristics, or that this idea is at least the stereotype associated with the word.

If this hypothesis is false, then I think that Quine's pessimism is probably justified. But if this hypothesis is right, then I think it is clear what the problem of the theory of meaning is, regardless of whether or not one chooses to call it "theory of *meaning*": the question is to explore and explain this empirical phenomenon. Questions which naturally arise are: What different kinds of words are associated with what different kinds of core facts? and By what mechanism does it happen that just conveying a small set of core facts brings it about that the hearer is able to imitate the normal use of a word?

Wittgensteinians, whose fondness for the expression "form of life" appears to be directly proportional to its degree of preposterousness in a given context, say that acquiring the customary use of such a word as "tiger" is coming to share a form of life. What they miss, or at any rate fail to emphasize, is that while the acquired disposition may be sufficiently complex and sufficiently interlinked with other complex dispositions to warrant special mention (though hardly the overblown phrase "form of life"), what *triggers* the disposition is often highly discrete—e.g., a simple lexical definition frequently succeeds in conveying a pretty good idea of how a word is used. To be sure, as Wittgenstein emphasizes, this is only possible because we have a shared human nature, and because we have shared an acculturation process—there has to be a great deal of stage-setting before one can read a lexical definition and guess how a word is used. But in the process of "debunking" this fact—the fact that something as simple as a lexical definition *can* convey the use of a word—they forget to be impressed by it. To be sure there is a great deal of stage-setting, but it is rarely stage-setting specifically designed to enable one to learn the use of *this* word. The fact that one *can* acquire the use of an indefinite number of new words, and on the basis of simple "statements of what they mean," is an amazing fact: it is *the* fact, I repeat, on which semantic theory rests.

Sometimes it is said that the key problem in semantics is: how do we come to understand a new sentence? I would suggest that this is a far simpler (though not unimportant) problem. How logical words, for example, can be used to build up complex sentences out of simpler ones is easy to describe, at least in principle (of course, natural language analogues of logical words are far less tidy than the logical words of the mathematical logician), and it is also easy to say how the truth-conditions, etc., of the complex sentences are related to the truth-conditions of the sentences from which they were derived. This much *is* a matter of finding a structure of recursive rules with a suitable relation to the transformational grammar of the language in question. I would suggest that the question, How do we come to understand a new *word?*, has far more to do with the whole phenomenon of giving definitions and writing dictionaries than the former question. And it is this phenomenon—the phenomenon of writing (and needing) dictionaries—that gives rise to the whole idea of "semantic theory."

Kinds of core facts. Let us now look a little more closely at the kind of information that one conveys when one conveys the meaning of a word. I have said that in the case of a "natural kind" word one conveys the associated *stereotype*: the associated idea of the characteristics of a normal member of the kind. But this is not, in general, enough; one must also convey the extension, one must indicate *which* kind the stereotype is supposed to "fit."

From the point of view of any traditional meaning theory, be it Plato's or Frege's or Carnap's or Katz', this is just nonsense. How can I "convey" the extension of, say, "tiger"? Am I supposed to give you all the tigers in the world (heaven forfend!). I can convey the extension of a term only by giving a description of that extension; and then that description must be a "part of the meaning," or else my definition will not be a meaning-statement at all. To say: "I gave him certain conditions associated with the word, *and* I gave him the extension" (as if that weren't just giving *further* conditions) can only be nonsense.

The mistake of the traditional theorist lies in his attachment to the word "meaning." If giving the meaning is *giving* the *meaning*, then it is giving a definite thing; but giving the meaning isn't, as we shall see in a moment, giving some one definite thing. To drop the word "meaning," which is here extremely misleading: there is no *one* set of facts which has to be conveyed to convey the normal use of a word; and taking account of this requires a complication in our notion of "core facts."

That the same stereotype might be associated with different kinds seems odd if the kind word one has in mind is "tiger"; but change the example to, say, "aluminum" and it will not seem odd at all. About all *I* know about aluminum is that it is a light metal, that it makes durable pots and pans, and that it doesn't appear to rust (although it does occasionally discolor). For all I know, every one of these characteristics may also fit molybdenum.

Suppose now that a colony of English-speaking Earthlings is leaving in a spaceship for a distant planet. When they arrive on their distant planet, they discover that no one remembers the atomic weight (or any other defining characteristic) of aluminum, nor the atomic weight (or other characteristic) of molybdenum. There is some aluminum in the spacecraft, and some molybdenum. Let us suppose that they guess which is which, and they guess wrong. Henceforth, they use "aluminum" as the name for molybdenum, and "molybdenum" as the name for aluminum. It is clear that "aluminum" has a different meaning in this community than in ours: in fact, it means *molybdenum*. Yet how can this be? Didn't they possess the normal "linguistic competence"? Didn't they all "know the meaning of the word 'aluminum' "?

Let us duck this question for a moment. If I want to make sure that the word "aluminum" will continue to be used in what counts as a "normal" way by the colonists in my example, it will suffice to give them some test for aluminum (or just to give them a carefully labelled sample, and let them discover a test, if they are clever enough). Once they know how to *tell* aluminum from other metals, they will go on using the word with the correct extension as well as the correct "intension" (i.e., the correct stereotype). But notice: it does not matter *which* test we give the colonists. The test isn't part of the meaning; but that there be some test or other (or something, e.g., a sample, from which one might be derived), is necessary to preservation of "the normal usage." Meaning indeed determines extension; but only because extension (fixed by *some* test or other) is, in some cases, "part of the meaning."

There are two further refinements here: if we give them a test, they mustn't make it part of the *stereotype—that would be a change of meaning. (Thus it's better if they don't all *know* the test; as long as only experts do, and the average speaker "asks an expert" in case of doubt, the criteria mentioned in the test can't infect the stereotype.) Asking an expert is enough of a test for the normal speaker; that's why we don't give a test in an ordinary context.

We can now modify our account of the "core facts" in the case of a natural kind word as follows: (1) The core facts are the stereotype *and the extension.* (2) Nothing normally need be said about the extension, however, since the hearer knows that he can always consult an expert if any question comes up. (3) In special cases—such as the case of colonists—there may be danger that the word will get attached to the wrong natural kind, even though the right stereotype is associated with it. In such cases, one must give some way of getting the extension right, but no one *particular* way is necessary.

In the case of "lemon" or "tiger" a similar problem comes up. It is logically possible (although empirically unlikely, perhaps) that a species of fruit biologically unrelated to lemons might be indistinguishable from lemons in taste and appearance. In such a case, there would be two possibilities: (1) to call them *lemons,* and thus let "lemon" be a word for any one of a number of natural kinds; or (2) to say that they are not lemons (which is what, I suspect, biologists would decide to do.) In the latter case, the problems are exactly the same as with *aluminum:* to be sure one has the "normal usage" or "customary meaning" or whatever, one has to be sure one has the right extension.

The problem: that giving the extension is part of giving the meaning arises also in the case of names of sensible qualities, e.g., colors.

Here, however, it is normal to give the extension by giving a sample, so that the person learning the word learns to recognize the quality in the normal way. Frequently it has been regarded as a defect of *dictionaries* that they are "cluttered up" with color samples, and with stray pieces of empirical information (e.g., the atomic weight of aluminum), not sharply distinguished from "purely linguistic" information. The burden of the present discussion is that this is no defect at all, but essential to the function of conveying the core facts in each case.

Still other kinds of words may be mentioned in passing. In the case of "one-criterion" words (words which possess an analytical necessary and sufficient condition) it is obvious why the core fact is just the analytical necessary and sufficient condition e.g. "man who has never been married," in the case of "bachelor"). In the case of "cluster" words (e.g., the name of a disease which is known not to have any one underlying cause), it is obvious why the core facts are just the typical symptoms or elements of the cluster; and so on. Given the *function* of a kind of word, it is not difficult to explain why certain facts function as core facts for conveying the use of words of that kind.

The possibility of semantics. Why, then, is semantics so hard? In terms of the foregoing, I want to suggest that semantics is a typical social science. The sloppiness, the lack of precise theories and laws, the lack of mathematical rigor, are all characteristic of the social sciences today. A general and precise theory which answers the questions (1) why do words have the different sorts of functions they do? and (2) exactly how does conveying core facts enable one to learn the use of a word? is not to be expected until one has a general and precise model of a language-user; and that is still a long way off. But the fact that Utopia is a long way off does not mean that daily life should come to a screeching halt. There is plenty for us to investigate, in our sloppy and impressionistic fashion, and there are plenty of real results to be obtained. The first step is to free ourselves from the oversimplifications foisted upon us by the tradition, and to see where the real problems lie. I hope this paper has been a contribution to that first step.

REPLY TO PUTNAM'S
"IS SEMANTICS POSSIBLE?"

Paul G. Morrison

On Putnam's view, the test of a semantic theory is its capacity for explaining how the meaning of words is taught and learned. He is especially concerned with the meaning of words that name classes whose normal characteristics are held together by deep-lying mechanisms which resist clear description in the present stage of meta-science. He calls these classes *natural kinds,* and as far as I can tell, construes the normal characteristics of a natural kind as manifest observation properties of its typical members. Since these properties are jointly sufficient to discriminate normal members of the kind, the idea that conveys them is called the *stereotype* of the natural kind in question.

The traditional theory of meaning, on Putnam's account—the semantic theory which pictures the meaning of a word as something like a list of concepts or properties comprehended by its stereotype—flunks its test, because, among other things, it affords no criterion for identifying the abnormal members of a natural kind. The theories of Carnap and Katz concerning the semantics of natural languages are allegedly committed, at least indirectly, to this traditional theory, and so, themselves, purportedly prove inadequate.

Putnam's own approach, however, presumably avoids the deficiency just mentioned by postulating that for each common noun associated with a natural kind there is a set of *core facts*—a composite of the stereotypic idea and a disjunction of test procedures any of which would enable at least some native speakers to tell whether the corresponding natural-kind name would apply in individual cases, normal or abnormal. Putnam refers to the stereotypic idea as an *intension,* and to any particular one of the test procedures as an *extension.* The core facts, then, are a composite of an idea and a test procedure — of the intension and extension of the natural-kind name.

In contrast to the traditionalist's concept list, the core facts enable native speakers to teach or to learn *the* correct natural kind to be associated with a given common noun. Recognizing and applying this insight will hopefully help us to make the first step toward formulating a general and precise model of a language user; and this is an indispensable prerequisite for a viable semantic theory of natural language.

So much for my résumé of Putnam's position. I now turn to my critique.

At one point, Putnam concedes that theoretical terms in science are typical items in the vocabulary of the natural languages. I gather, then, that any established technical term in the scientist's working vocabulary also belongs to the natural language which he speaks. With this in mind, I should like to examine the make-up of the core facts concerning a peculiar but very extensive class of compounds studied by organic chemists. I refer to the scores of substances, so well-known to chemistry majors, which, under ordinary conditions, are odorless, tasteless white powders of fairly comparable grain size. If Putnam will admit these to be natural kinds, we then have a profusion of natural kinds whose respective sets of core facts differ only in the extensional tests appropriate to their identification. For every one of these compounds will have the same stereotype as every other. The idea of an odorless, tasteless white powder clearly constitutes only one stereotype, no matter how many samples of chemically different substances exemplify it. But this uniformity makes the stereotype almost irrelevant in the discrimination of the natural kinds in question.

Each of these compounds also has both an empirical and a molecular formula, neither of which gives much of an indication as to how its samples may be synthesized, how their properties distinguish them from samples of other compounds, how they are apt to behave in various chemical reactions, or what chemical products they will help to generate. On the other hand, the *structural* formulas of these compounds, which reveal both the arrangement of their atoms and the way in which the atoms are connected in a single molecule, do afford detailed prognostics of this sort. In fact, various subgroupings of symbols within a structural formula typically alert the skilled reader to the dispositional properties of the compound, matching fairly closely, perhaps, the extensional tests that contribute to the core meaning in Putnam's sense.

What then, in this instance, has happened to the contrast between the property lists of the rejected traditional theory and the core facts of the preferred theory? Since stereotype in these cases does not help (ask any student who has been given a white powder to identify by a deadline) and since a trained chemist can almost read off dispositional properties from symbol groups in a structural formula, the core facts will then virtually amount to a finite property list.

It is my belief that Putnam's position can be made plausible only through his judicious choice of examples. Of course, he may reply that my own selection is farfetched. But it is he who introduces the notion of scientific expertise as an indispensable feature of his characterization of core facts. Notice the lengths to which he must go to set up possibilities of faulty identification involving a hybrid of mundane natural kinds with scientific natural kinds.

In one case, he must postulate an inaccessible paleolithic occurrence of krypto-oranges which appear as pseudo-lemons. Presumably, the very trees from which the ancients picked these citrus fruits were orange trees which resembled lemon trees in every observable way. What discrepancy would then remain to put an alert time-traveling, scientific troubleshooter on the trail of the alleged anomaly? Would his high-powered microscope or his electrical or chemical test equipment warn him of it? Or would he not be taken in, instead, by a prehistoric miracle of botanical transubstantiation?

In another case, Putnam postulates space travelers who remember *none* of the defining characteristics either of aluminum or of molybdenum—not even that both of them are metals or, at ordinary temperatures, matter in the solid state. Yet these voyagers miraculously succeed somehow in fixing on just those combinations of individual items scattered around inside the spacecraft which happen to have the required sets of unknown characteristics, so that they may successfully confuse just those sets in the required way.

Examples like these suggest that the core-facts theory embodies an *ad hoc* attempt to get us to identify scientifically systematized natural kinds with common-sense natural kinds in those cases in which there is a very high, though not necessarily a complete, overlap in their extensional membership. It would seem less laborious to recognize that a lay native speaker, in contrast to his scientist neighbor, might typically betray in his speech behavior a commitment to an implicit system of natural kinds which is of relatively low efficiency for cognitive pursuits—involving what Carnap would call extensive "zones of vagueness," and also, from time to time, even some logical inconsistency.

Could it not be, then, that the optimum application of Putnam's core-facts mechanism is to extensionally overlapping hybrids of everyday natural kinds with scientific ones? For I do not see that he has discredited the use of abstract or dispositional property lists for the discrimination of those natural kinds which are systematized in one or another of the natural sciences. And if not, then the traditional theory is vindicated in the only area in which its more sophisticated proponents ever intended to apply it, and furthermore, retains its ascendancy over other semantic devices, largely because it deals with whole systems of properties which can be specified with precision and whose instances can be predicted or willfully caused.

To the extent that Putnam urges us to consult the scientific experts as to what we might *better* mean than what we now mean by general names for commonplace kinds, I feel that he is deserting the behavioral study of language use in favor of a normative or prescriptive account of what the user *ought* to mean, since the user, it is said, ought to seek the *best* theory of what a lemon, for example, really is. This theory would tell us, presumably, whether lemons are more truly fruit of a certain kind, or more accurately trees of a certain description which produce such fruit (my unabridged dictionary lists both!), or, perhaps, something quite different from either which we must accept as the best meaning on the authority of the experts.

In all of this, it seems to me, Putnam is giving us a nonmentalist analogue of John Locke's distinction between substances and modes. For Putnam's natural kinds (classes whose normal characteristics are "held together" by deep-lying mechanisms that mysteriously resist clear description) contrast with his property lists, which he tells us Carnap and Katz would misguidedly have us use, in much the same way that Locke's substances, whose essential nature mysteriously eludes us, contrast with his modes—complexes which we concoct in an arbitrary way from simple ideational elements. The analogy is even more compelling since Locke contrasts *real* definitions, which would pinpoint his elusive substances, with the merely *nominal* definitions which more successfully specify the arbitrary modes.

How could Putnam have been led to do this? I suspect that two cardinal factors are involved. First of all, I detect in his paper an allegiance to a physicalist parallel to the mentalist gallery myth identified recently by Quine.[1] For Putnam seems to assume that for every so-called natural-kind word there is one, and only one, normal use—a use which traditional semanticists like Carnap miss, and which other devotees of semantic theory may eventually count on finding, although it may escape them for long stretches of time. Thus Putnam speaks in several places of *the* meaning, or of the normal use, of the word 'lemon' where others would speak of the meanings or of the normal uses of that word, or perhaps, simply of the meanings or uses of the word 'lemon'.

The second factor in Putnam's move from empirical methods for determining natural-language usage to the search for the best or the normal usage seems to stem, paradoxically, from his admiration for the intellectual achievement of the natural scientist, a feeling which I believe is shared by most philosophers of science. But while the scientific botanist's technical use of the word 'lemon' to stand for trees of the species *Citrus limon* in some cases, and for other species of trees in other cases, is part of the English usage for the word 'lemon', it is not, from the standpoint of his colleagues in the science of linguistics, the sole important use of that word. If we are concerned here with the semantics of whole natural languages, and not, as were Carnap, Philipp Frank, Reichenbach, and others a number of years ago, primarily with usage in theoretical scientific sublanguages—then surely Putnam is legislating, rather than reporting, when he appeals to the notion of the "best theory" of what a lemon is, or to the unique competence of the botanical scientist in the unmasking of prehistoric quasi-lemons as veritable crypto-oranges—all in the name of discovering the one real meaning or *the* normal usage for the word 'lemon'.

For, to sum up, even where the same word is applied in everyday and in scientific contexts to largely overlapping extensions, the common-sense quest for rules governing its scientific meaning will be quite different from the scientific quest for rules governing its common-sense meaning. A linguistic analysis of scientific usage will rarely coincide with a scientific analysis of linguistic usage.

NOTES

1. See Quine, W. V., "Philosophical Progress in Language Theory," in this volume.

THE ASYMMETRY OF SUBJECTS
AND PREDICATES

P. F. Strawson

I

In *Analysis* for December 1965 Miss Anscombe says:

What signally distinguishes names from expressions for predicates is that
expressions for predicates can be negated, names not. I mean that negation,
attached to a predicate, yields a new predicate, but when attached to a
name it does not yield any name.[1]

In the *Philosophical Review* for the same year Geach says:

What distinguishes predicates from subjects, I suggest, is . . . that by
negating a predicate we can get the negation of the proposition in which
it was originally predicated (plainly there is nothing analogous for subject terms);[2]

and in *Reference and Generality* he has a somewhat longer passage to
the same or a similar effect:

When a proposition is negated, the negation may be taken as going with
the predicate in a way in which it cannot be taken as going with the subject. For predicables always occur in contradictory pairs; and by attaching
such a pair to a common subject, we get a contradictory pair of propositions.
But we never have a pair of names so related that by attaching the same
predicates to both we always get a pair of contradictory propositions.[3]

These remarks do not perhaps all come to quite the same thing.
But they come nearly enough to the same thing to give the thing a
name. I shall call it the *thesis of the asymmetry of subjects and predicates regarding negation,* or, for short, the asymmetry thesis.

I shall not dispute the truth of the asymmetry thesis, but shall, instead, try to explain why it is true. Of course, in undertaking such an attempt at explanation, I am disputing—if anyone upholds it—a different
contention, viz. the contention that the asymmetry thesis of itself ex-

pounds or makes clear the nature of the distinction between subject and predicate, so that there is simply no room for the question *why* the thesis is true. But this would not be a very plausible contention. In any case, the best rebuttal of the view that there is no room for a certain question is to produce a satisfactory answer to that question. So I will not linger further on this view now.

II

Instead, I shall begin a little obliquely by considering a possible objection to the asymmetry thesis, an objection which would rightly be held by upholders of the thesis to miss its point altogether. But it may clarify the nature of the thesis a little to see just this. Consider the following three remarks about Tom, his camera, and the relations between them:

If anyone has sold his camera, it is not Tom.

If Tom has disposed of (or otherwise modified his relation to) his camera, it is not by selling it.

If Tom has sold anything, it is not his camera.

As regards their truth-conditions, these remarks appear to be equivalent to each other and to the negation of

Tom has sold his camera,

i.e. to

Tom has not sold his camera.

Indeed by varying the distribution of stress in our pronouncing of the last sentence, we could confer upon it the force of each of the three previous remarks in turn (first stress "Tom," then "sold," then "camera"). We could then perfectly properly characterize the difference in force between the three remarks, as made in the second way, i.e. with shifting stress, by saying that negation was to be taken in each case with a different part of the proposition which is negated alike in them all. Introducing now the terminology of subject and predicate, and making one presumably acceptable application of it, we could add that in none of the instanced cases was negation to be taken with the predicate as a whole; in one case it was to be taken with one part of the predicate, viz. ". . . sold . . . ," in another with another part, viz. ". . . his camera," and in the remaining case with the subject, viz. "Tom." In general, the argument concludes, negation has no natural affinity for one part rather than another of a negated subject-predicate proposition. Its attachments may vary from part to part, depending on the force with which the proposition is propounded; or it may simply attach to the proposition as a whole.

The upholder of the asymmetry thesis will reply that the facts adduced in this objection are quite beside the point. The sense, invoked in the objection, in which negation may be taken now with one part, now with another part, of a proposition belongs to a different level of theory altogether from that to which the asymmetry thesis belongs. The thesis is not at all concerned with differences in the force with which a proposition or its negation may be propounded, but with the common propounded thing, the proposition or its negation. The point is that negation can never be taken together with the subject of the negated proposition *as yielding a new expression of the same kind, or having the same role*, as the subject of the original proposition; whereas negation can always be taken together with the predicate of the negated proposition *as yielding a new expression of the same kind, or having the same role*, as the predicate of the original proposition. But this reply, though it may be perfectly correct, merely sharpens our sense of the need for an explanation.

III

Before embarking on the explanation of the asymmetry of subjects and predicates regarding negation, we should note that this is not the only asymmetry we shall have to explain. Asymmetry regarding negation (negatability) carries with it as a consequence a certain asymmetry regarding composition (compoundability). To see that this is so, let us regard the original asymmetry thesis as supplying a *test* for subjects and predicates, and a test which we sufficiently well understand to be satisfied that when applied to a proposition such as "Tom is tall," it yields "Tom" as subject and "is tall" as predicate: i.e. we are to be supposed to understand the requirement about sameness of kind of expression sufficiently well to appreciate that when we introduce "not" into the original proposition so as to yield its negation, we can take "not" together with "is tall" to yield a new expression of the same kind as "is tall," whereas, even if it is allowable in some sense to take "not" with "Tom," we should not thereby obtain an expression of the same kind as "Tom."

Consider now the following four propositions:

(1) Tom is either tall or bald
(2) Tom is both tall and bald
(3) Both Tom and William are tall
(4) Either Tom or William is tall

Each of (1) to (4) is, evidently, equivalent to some disjunction or conjunction of two of the three (atomic) propositions "Tom is tall," "Tom is bald," "William is tall." If we apply our test to the first two of the four numbered propositions, we seem to come out with the satisfactory result that "Tom" is the subject in each case and "is either tall or bald" and "is both tall and bald" are compound predicates. This result is satisfactory because we see at once the possibility of a smooth and coherent formal theory of the logic of propositions with simple and compound predicates, a theory in which the relations of "Tom is tall and bald," "Tom is tall" and "Tom is either tall or bald" can be clearly exhibited.

But now what of propositions (3) and (4), i.e. "Both Tom and William are tall" and "Either Tom or William is tall." We might be inclined unreflectively to say that what we have here is a pair of propositions with compound subjects just as what we have in the other case is a pair of propositions with compound predicates. The logical relations these propositions have to each other and to "Tom is tall" are just as intuitively clear as the logical relations which the propositions with compound predicates have to each other and to "Tom is tall." There should be no impediment to constructing as satisfactory a formal theory for propositions with compound subjects as can be constructed for propositions with compound predicates.

This optimism, however, receives a decisive check as soon as we bring the asymmetry thesis regarding negation to bear on the propositions with putative compound subjects. For the negation of "Both Tom and William are tall" is not "Both Tom and William are not tall" but "Not both Tom and William are tall" and the negation of "Either Tom or William is tall" is not "Either Tom or William is not tall" but "Neither Tom nor William is tall." That is to say there is a clear and unexceptionable sense in which negation *must* be taken with the putative subjects, rather than the putative predicates, of the original propositions in order to yield the negations of these propositions. Thus "is tall" and "are tall" fail the test for being predicates of these putative subjects and their failure carries with it the failure of the putative subjects to qualify as subjects of their putative predicates.

What, then, does the asymmetry thesis license our saying about these propositions? Should we say that "Both Tom and William" and "Either Tom or William" pass the tests for predicates, and hence that "is tall" and "are tall" should be allowed as subjects of these predicates? There are fatal objections to this: (i) it is highly counter-intuitive; (ii) so far from advancing the prospects for a smooth logical theory capable of exhibiting the logical relationships of all the propositions concerned, it would put an obstacle in the way of those prospects; and (iii) it is not sanctioned by the asymmetry test itself. What kind of understanding of the notion of "same kind of expression" would we have to possess in order confidently to disallow "not Tom" as an expression of the same kind as "Tom" while confidently allowing "not both Tom and William" as an expression of the same kind as "Tom and William"?

Of course the adherent of the asymmetry thesis has not come to the end of his resources. There is something else he can say. He can say that the appearance of symmetry between propositions (1) and (2) on the one hand and propositions (3) and (4) on the other is misleading. The expressions "is either tall or bald" and "is both tall and bald" are indeed compound predicates, disjunctive and conjunctive respectively, whereas the expressions "Both Tom and William" and "Either Tom or William" are not predicates at all and hence not compound predicates: but they are not compound subjects either; for there are no such things as compound (conjunctive or disjunctive) subjects. Alongside the asymmetry of subjects and predicates regarding negation, we must install another asymmetry regarding conjunctive or disjunctive composition. Compound predicates have a place in logical theory, compound subjects have not. This does not mean that we are at a loss for anything at all to say about propositions (3) and (4). One thing we could say, for example, is that "Both Tom and William are tall" is simply a linguistically legitimate abbreviation of the compound (conjunctive) *proposition,* "Tom is tall and William is tall" and that "Not both Tom and William are tall" is the corresponding abbreviation of the negation of the compound proposition. In the case of propositions (1) and (2), on the other hand, there is no need for any such resource. For while propositions (1) and (2) are also equivalent to compound propositions, the terms "is both tall and bald" and "is either tall or bald" have a place in logical theory as they stand, as compound predicate-terms; whereas no such place is available for the expressions "Both Tom and William" and "Either Tom or William." These last are not logical-subject-terms, but only pseudo-logical-subject-terms.

So, then, if the asymmetry thesis regarding negation is true, we must accept a further asymmetry between subjects and predicates as regards composition. There are compound predicates but no compound subjects. Evidently it would be satisfactory if we could see this restriction not merely as an imposed consequence of the acceptance of the asymmetry thesis but as something intrinsically acceptable. It would be more satisfactory still if the reasons why the asymmetry thesis regarding negation is true proved to have a certain harmony with, to be reasons of the same general kind as, the reasons why there are compound predicates but no compound subjects.

IV

I shall argue that we can find such harmonizing reasons for these asymmetries if and only if we attend to certain other asymmetries; and that these other and underlying asymmetries require for their description a more extended terminology than that of *formal* logic alone. To find these underlying asymmetries we must attend in the first place to propositions of a certain class, which I shall describe somewhat artificially as follows. In any proposition of this class there are presented as assigned to each other a specified empirical particular (or spatio-temporal individual) and a specified general character or kind of empirical particulars. I speak, in symmetrical style, of the particular individual and the general character or kind being presented as *assigned to each other* because asymmetries of direction of fit do not here concern us. I speak of their being *presented as* assigned to each other because the question whether such a proposition is *asserted* or introduced into discourse in some other way is equally irrelevant.

Of course different empirical particulars may be presented as assigned to the same general character, and different general characters may be presented as assigned to the same empirical particular. So far there is still symmetry; but there are also asymmetries. Every general character is such that, whatever individual particular it may be presented as assigned to, there is some other general character, or range of characters, the possession of which, or of any member of which, by the individual in question would be *incompatible* with its possession of the specified character. It is not the case, however, that every (or indeed any) individual particular is such that, whatever general character it may be presented as assigned to, there is some other individual or range of individuals the possession by which, or by any member of which, of the character in question would be incompatible with its being possessed by the specified individual. In brief: Every general character competes for location, in any and every particular individual it might belong to, with some other general character. But it is not the case that every particular individual competes for possession of any and every general character it might possess with some other particular individual. Indeed no particular individual does so. We might speak of this asymmetry as *asymmetry between particulars and general characters of particulars in respect of the possession of incompatibility-ranges.*

Now for another asymmetry. This is of the same family as the first though it cannot be stated quite so simply. We may express it roughly by saying that it is typical of general characters of particulars to stand to other general characters of particulars in certain relations which can be expressed in the terminology of necessary and sufficient conditions; whereas no symmetrical sense can be found in which particulars can be said to stand to other particulars in such relations. These relations between general characters are of different degrees of complexity. It will be sufficient for the immediate purpose to mention the simplest kind of case. This is the case exemplified by any general character—and there are many—which is such that, whatever individual particular it is presented as assigned to, either there is some other general character (or characters) the possession of which by the specified individual would be *sufficient* for that individual's possession of the assigned character or there is some other general character (or characters) the possession of which by the specified individual would be *necessary* for that individual's possession of the assigned character. Neither for this simplest case nor for the more complex cases is it possible to find any symmetrically explicable relationships between particular individuals. It is not the case that *any* particular individual at all is such that, whatever general character is presented as assigned to it, either there is some other individual (or individuals) the possession by which of the specified character would be *sufficient* for the assigned individual's possession of that character or there is some other individual (or individuals) the possession by which of the specified character would be *necessary* for the assigned individual's possession of that character. We might speak of this asymmetry as *asymmetry between particulars and general characters of particulars in respect of the possession of sufficient and/or necessary conditions.*

To express these asymmetries differently: We are considering the class of propositions in each of which a specified particular individual *i* and a specified general character *g* are presented as assigned to each other. Then for all *g*, for all *i*, by keeping *i* constant and varying *g*, we can obtain a proposition (or propositions) incompatible with the proposition we started with, and, for some *g*, for all *i*, by keeping *i* constant and varying *g*, we can obtain a proposition (or propositions) related to the original proposition in one direction or the other by the relation of one-way entailment. But it is not even the case that for *some i*, for all *g*, by keeping *g* constant and varying *i* we can obtain a proposition (or propositions) incompatible with the original proposition; and it is not the case that for some *i*, for all *g*, by keeping *g* constant and varying *i*, we can obtain a proposition (or propositions) related to the original proposition in one direction or the other by the relation of one-way entailment. General characters, we may say, come in groups the members of which are related by relations of mutual exclusiveness or (sometimes) of one-way involvement vis-à-vis any and every particular they may be assigned to. But particular individuals do not come in groups the members of which are related by relations of mutual exclusiveness or of one-way involvement vis-à-vis any and every general character they may be assigned to.

These asymmetries seem to be as obvious and (nearly) as fundamental as anything can be in philosophy.

V

Let us now simply *appropriate* the expressions "subject" and "predicate" as follows. In any proposition in which a specified individual particular and a specified general character are presented as assigned to each other, the expression which has the function of specifying the assigned particular (say, a proper name of that particular) is the subject; and, in any such proposition, the expression which, whatever other function it may also have, has the function of specifying the assigned general character, is the predicate. We now ask whether, given this appropriation of the expressions "subject" and "predicate," the asymmetries just remarked on explain and vindicate, for this class of propositions, the asymmetries of subjects and predicates in respect of negation and composition. I think they do.

Let us begin with the case of asymmetry as regards negation. Consider any proposition in which a specified particular individual i and a specified general character g_1 are presented as assigned to each other. Call this proposition P_1:

$$P_1 \quad \text{ass } (i \; g_1)$$

Because of one of the features of general characters just remarked on, we know that by replacing the predicate of P_1 by an expression specifying some other suitably chosen character, say g_2, and leaving its subject unchanged, we can obtain a proposition incompatible with P_1, say P_2. (The incompatibility of P_1 and P_2 is represented below by the symbol

'X'.):

$$\begin{array}{l} P_1 \quad \text{ass } (i \; g_1) \\ \text{X} \\ P_2 \quad \text{ass } (i \; g_2) \end{array}$$

We can describe the incompatibility of P_1 and P_2 by saying that they have the same subject and incompatible predicates; and we can represent this relation between the predicates as under:

$$\begin{array}{l} P_1 \quad \text{ass } (i \;\; | \;\; g_1 \;\; |) \\ \text{X} \qquad\qquad \text{X} \\ P_2 \quad \text{ass } (i \;\; | \;\; g_2 \;\; |) \end{array}$$

Now consider the negations of P_1 and P_2. They are the propositions, we may say, in which the individual in question and the relevant character are presented, not as assigned to, but as withheld from (or negatively assigned to), each other. Call them P_1' and P_2'. Negative assignment we may represent by putting a negation sign above "ass" thus:

$$\begin{array}{l} P_1' \quad \overline{\text{ass}} \; (i \; g_1) \\ P_2' \quad \overline{\text{ass}} \; (i \; g_2) \end{array}$$

Since P_1 and P_2 are incompatible with each other, P_1 entails P_2' and P_2 entails P_1'. Thus we have, using "→" for "entails":

$$P_1 \text{ ass } (i \mid g_1 \mid) \rightarrow \overline{\text{ass}} \ (i \ g_2) \quad P_2'$$

Fig. I ✗ ✗

$$P_2 \text{ ass } (i \mid g_2 \mid) \rightarrow \overline{\text{ass}} \ (i \ g_1) \quad P_1'$$

The fact that P_1 and P_2 are incompatible with each other is, as we have seen, really identical with (or dependent upon) the fact that they have the same subjects and incompatible predicates. And the fact that P_1 entails P_2' and P_2 entails P_1' is really identical with (or dependent upon) the fact that P_1 is incompatible with P_2. These identities (or dependences) are clearly registered if, in the case of each negating or withholding proposition, we take negation, together with the predicate of the proposition of which it is the negation, as forming a new, a negative, predicate; i.e. if, in Figure I, we transfer the negation sign in P_2' and P_1' from "ass" to "g_2" and "g_1" respectively:

$$P_1 \text{ ass } (i \mid g_1 \mid) \rightarrow \text{ass } (i \mid \overline{g}_2 \mid) \quad P_2'$$

Fig. II ✗ ✗

$$P_2 \text{ ass } (i \mid g_2 \mid) \rightarrow \text{ass } (i \mid \overline{g}_1 \mid) \quad P_1'$$

Incompatibility of predicates in the case of P_1 and P_2 then appears as the same thing as the *entailment (involvement) of the negative predicate* of P_1' by the predicate of P_2 and the *entailment (involvement) of the negative predicate* of P_2' by the predicate of P_1. In this way we do justice to the logical (but not formally logical) relations of incompatibility and entailment in which the members of any such pair of propositions as P_1 and P_1' (i.e. a proposition of our chosen class and its negation) stand to other propositions (e.g. P_2 and P_2') in virtue of the logical relatedness (incompatibility) of general characters. Here we have an argument for taking negation with the predicate; but we can construct no parallel argument for taking negation with the *subject* of the original proposition in each case as forming a new, a negative, subject. We could construct such an argument only if there were such things as incompatible subjects in a sense symmetrical with the sense in which there are incompatible predicates; only, that is to say, if by keeping g_1 constant, *whatever it was*, we could always form another proposition incompatible with P_1 by replacing the designation of i, whatever i was, with an expression specifying a different particular individual. But the fact that we can always perform the operation with changing characters and not with changing particular individuals is precisely the asymmetry we started with.

The relations I have been speaking of can be presented in a simplified figure. Thus we have:

$$\text{Fig. III} \quad i \left\{ \begin{array}{cc} g_1 \times g_2 \\ \downarrow \quad \downarrow \\ \overline{g_2} \quad \overline{g_1} \end{array} \right.$$

where g_1 and g_2 are incompatible general characters and i represents any particular to which either might be assigned. Taking the character-specifying part of any proposition in which either of them is so assigned as the predicate of that proposition, we then have the entailment (involvement) of the relevant negative predicate in each case represented by the downward arrows.

There is no counterpart diagram we can draw in which "g" replaces "i" and "i_1," "i_2" replace "g_1," "g_2."

The argument can be clinched by considering the limiting case, and bearing in mind that it is only the limiting case, of the kind of relationships just described. This is the case which we have when there are a pair of characters g_1 and g_2 which are not only incompatible but complementary. That is to say, it is the case in which, given a proposition P_1 in which g_1 and some specified particular i are presented as assigned to each other, and a proposition P_2 obtained from P_1 by replacing the expression specifying g_1 by an expression specifying g_2, there is no logical room for a third proposition incompatible with both and obtained from either by replacing the expression specifying g_1 or g_2, as the case may be, with an expression specifying a third character g_3. Perhaps the expressions "is stationary" and "is moving" may be regarded as specifying complementary characters in this sense. And there are many pairs of expressions which might be tentatively offered, involving such prefixes or suffixes as "non-" "un-" "-less": e.g. harmful, harmless; happy, unhappy; toxic, non-toxic; obtrusive, unobtrusive and so on. It may well be that our need for nuances makes this class rather less extensive than we might at first be inclined to think. Certainly there are enormous and varied ranges of character-specifying expressions for which ordinary language offers no plausible candidates as their complementaries: e.g. asparagus, elephant, red, two inches long and so on.

Given, then that g_1 and g_2 are complementary characters and allowing, as before, that P_1' and P_2' are the negations of P_1 and P_2, then we not only have the relations we had before, viz. that, since P_1 is incompatible with P_2, P_1 entails P_2' and P_2 entails P_1', we also have the converses of these last relations. (We can add, in these cases, upward arrows to our last diagram.) And here the case for taking negation, in P_1' or P_2', together with the original predicate of P_1 or P_2, as forming a new, a negative, predicate—a term of the same kind—is too clear for it to be worthwhile setting it out in form. It reflected, of course, in ordinary language in the use of the negative prefixes and suffixes just mentioned, where a formal sign of negation is absorbed into a character-specifying expression. But it must be pointed out that the case *is* a limiting case and that the *general* justification of taking negation as part of the predicate in propositions of our chosen class rests on the prior identification of predicates with the character-specifying expressions which figure in such propositions. Because every general character is incompatible, in the required sense, with some other, there is at least the possibility of complementary characters. Because there is no symmetrical sense in which any particular individual is incompatible with any other, there is no sense in the notion of complementary particular individuals.

VI

Now we pass to asymmetry as regards composition. I expressed the underlying asymmetry in this case by saying that while characters may typically stand in the relations of being sufficient or necessary conditions of other characters, there is no symmetrical sense in which particular individuals may be said to stand in such relations. Note that in denying that there are any such relations in the case of particular individuals, I am not claiming that there are no particular individuals such that there are no ways of specifying those individuals such that there are no general characters at all such that a proposition assigning a general character to one of those individuals entails or is entailed by a proposition assigning that general character to the other. Thus suppose there is a chair C, made of pure gold. Then the proposition that C is of pure gold entails the proposition that the seat of C is of pure gold. But of course the proposition that C weighs twenty pounds does not entail the proposition that the seat of C weighs twenty pounds. So it would be a great misunderstanding of the general principle to suppose that any such case constitutes a counter-example to it; but I will not linger tediously on the point.

Because we can sensibly speak of characters standing in these necessary-or-sufficient-condition relations to other characters, we can sensibly define certain more complex relations in which characters might stand to other characters. Thus I define two triadic relations as follows: (1) g_3 is the conjunctive character of g_1 and g_2 when g_1 and g_2 are jointly sufficient and singly necessary for g_3 and neither is sufficient or necessary for the other; (2) g_3 is the disjunctive character of g_1 and g_2 when each is singly sufficient for g_3 and each is necessary in the absence of the other. We can not only define such relations, we can find examples of them. Thus the character expressed by "is a deaf-mute" is the conjunctive character of the characters expressed by "is deaf" and "is dumb." The character expressed by "has a sibling" is the disjunctive character of the characters expressed by "has a brother" and "has a sister."

Ordinary language perhaps provides relatively few examples of expressions, not formally compound, which signify conjunctive or disjunctive characters of other characters; but it would be possible to vastly extend the class of such expressions. Consider any two characters, e.g. tall, bald, such that there is a class of particular individuals such that each character could, independently of the other, be consistently assigned to one and the same specified particular individual of that class. Then the definitions just given of disjunctive or conjunctive characters in general seem to provide us with the means of defining the disjunctive or conjunctive character of those two characters; (though we must stipulate also, in the case of conjunctive characters, that the two characters are not incompatible with each other). But then again, we can dispense with any such definitions by utilising some standard formal means of representing the relationships which would be invoked in such definitions. This we do by linking the character-specifying expressions concerned by the same signs as are used in the formation of conjunctive or disjunctive propositions. Given our decision about the appropriation of the terms "subject" and "predicate" in the case of propositions in which a specified particular individual and a specified general character are presented as assigned to each other, we obviously need no further argument for counting a formally compound expression specifying a disjunctive or conjunctive character as the predicate of a proposition in which that character and a specified individual are presented as assigned to each other.

The case for compound predicates is complete. For compound subjects, on the other hand, there can be nothing but the illusion of a case. We can indeed take the *first* step towards framing the idea of a compound (i.e. conjunctive or disjunctive) particular individual. That is to say, we can consider two particulars, say Tom and William, such that there is a class of characters such that each of the two particular individuals could, independently of the other, be consistently assigned to any character of that class. But no basis exists for taking the *second* step, i.e. the step which would correspond to defining the conjunctive or disjunctive character of two characters. For this step could be taken only if we could speak of one particular individual being a necessary or sufficient condition of another in a sense which symmetrically corresponds to that in which we can speak of one general character being a necessary or sufficient condition of another. And, as we have seen, there is no such sense.

How does the illusion of a case for compound subjects arise? It arises, evidently, from the fact that we can legitimately frame sentences with the following characteristics: (1) their *grammatical* subjects are compounds of expressions specifying particular individuals and their grammatical predicates are expressions specifying general characters of particulars; (2) they express propositions equivalent to conjunctions or disjunctions of propositions of which the several individual subjects are those which appear as compounded in the sentences with apparent compound subjects, and of which the predicates specify the same general characters as those specified by the grammatical predicates of those sentences. And here we have a deceptive analogy with the case of compound predicates. That it is no more than a deceptive analogy we see as soon as we set up the conditions, symmetrically analogous to those for compound characters, which would have to be satisfied by conjunctive or disjunctive individuals, and see the senselessness of supposing that they could be satisfied. Hence we are obliged to rule, with regard to such sentences, that their grammatical subjects are not logically compound subjects and their grammatical predicates are no true logical predicates to such subjects. Instead we read them as permitted and linguistically natural abbreviations of compound propositions of which the constituents have different subjects and share the same predicate. But this conclusion we arrive at now, not as a consequence of accepting the asymmetry thesis regarding negation, but by an independent argument based upon the provisional decision about the identification of subject and predicate in a proposition in which a specified particular individual and a specified general character are presented as assigned to each other. Given that decision, it follows by independently statable, though consilient, arguments *both* that in the negation of such a proposition negation is properly taken with the predicate of the original proposition as forming a new predicate *and* that compound predicates are admissible whereas compound subjects, like negative subjects, are inadmissible.

There may remain a lingering doubt about compound subjects. Could we not, after all, it might be said, find direct analogues among individuals for disjunctive or conjunctive characters—by recognizing slightly unusual types of individual? Why not, to take the more promising-looking case, a conjunctive individual? Might not *a couple* be, in precisely the required sense, a conjunctive individual? Jane is handsome and Thomas is handsome. They are a handsome couple. The possession of this character by Jane (i_1) and its possession by Thomas (i_2) are jointly sufficient and singly necessary to its possession by the third individual (i_3), the couple. So far, if a little shakily, so good. But suppose Jane has seven children and Thomas has seven children. Does it follow that the couple has seven children? In one sense (as a couple) they may have none; in another the couple may have (between them) fourteen— or any smaller number down to seven. Or suppose that they are a very diverse couple. Does it follow that Jane is very diverse? or that Thomas is? So much for the couple as a conjunctive individual of two individuals. I am tempted to pass over in silence the disjunctive individual as unlikely to appeal to anyone. But lest it should seem that I am avoiding a possible difficulty, let it suffice to point out that in order for it to be true that either Tom or William is always on duty it is not necessary, if Tom is not always on duty, that William should be, or if William is not, that Tom should be.[4]

VII

I have been arguing that, given *our* choice of a certain class of propositions and given *our* appropriations of the expression "subject" and "predicate" in relation to propositions of that class, then we have an adequate explanation and vindication of the asymmetry thesis regarding subjects and predicates, both in respect of negation and in respect of composition, *so far as propositions of that class are concerned.* But to say that the explanation and vindication are *so far* adequate is not to say that they are adequate in *general.* For, in the first place, even if we restrict our attention to propositions of the *fa* form—singular subject-predicate propositions—not all such propositions are propositions in which an individual spatio-temporal particular and a general character of particulars are presented as assigned to each other. In the second place, even if we succeed in generalizing our explanation for propositions of the *fa* form, there arises the question of whether our logical conception of subject and predicate should not be extended beyond propositions of the *fa* form. This second question has many ramifications and I shall not discuss it in this paper. But I should, in conclusion, like to say something about the problem of generalizing our explanation for propositions of the *fa* form.

Let us look back to the underlying asymmetries invoked in our explanation for the chosen class of propositions. One way in which I stated them was as follows:

general characters come in groups the members of which are related by relations of mutual exclusiveness or (sometimes) of one-way involvement vis-à-vis any and every *individual particular* they may be presented as assigned to;

but *individual particulars* do not come in groups related by relations of mutual exclusiveness or one-way involvement vis-à-vis any and every *general character* they may be presented as assigned to. Let us write this, for short:

general characters come in exclusiveness/involvement groups vis-à-vis *general characters.*

individual particulars do not come in exclusiveness/involvement groups vis-a-vis *general characters.*

But here we have a generalizable form of contrast. Let us substitute "*y*" for "*general character*" and "*x*" for "*individual particular,*" thus obtaining a general form of statement of a certain condition which we will call the "*x/y* condition." Suppose we have any proposition which can be viewed as a proposition in which an *x* and a *y* are presented as assigned to each other, where it is understood that *x*s and *y*s fall, relatively to each other, under the *x/y* condition. Then we *already* have a vindication of the thesis that the *x*-specifying part and the *y*-specifying part of that proposition are asymmetrical in respect of negation and compoundability in just the ways we have been concerned with. For generalizing the condition automatically generalizes the argument based upon the condition. So one way—I do not say the only, or even the best way, but certainly the quickest way—of obtaining a generalization of our explanation is this. Simply take "Expressions *e* and *e'* are respectively subject and predicate of proposition P" to be equivalent to: "Proposition P can be viewed as a proposition in which an *x* and a *y* are presented as assigned to each other (where it is understood that *x*s and *y*s fall, relatively to each other, under the *x/y* condition) and expression *e* is the *x*-specifying part and expression *e'* the *y*-specifying part of proposition P."

To illustrate the application of the generalized definition to one type of proposition not belonging to our originally chosen class. I take as an example the proposition, "Happiness is found in all stations in life." The expression "is found in all stations in life" specifies a character of characters which has its own incompatibility and involvement ranges in relation to any and every character such that that character and it may be presented as assigned to each other. Thus *being found in all stations in life* is this way incompatible with *being found in few stations in life* and entails (involves) *being found in most stations in life.* But it is not the case that the character-specifying expression "happiness" specifies a character which has its own incompatibility and involvement ranges in relation to any and every character of characters such that it and that character of characters can be presented as assigned to each other. If we consider, say, *happiness, misery,* and *bliss* (or being in a state of bliss) in relation to individual particulars to which they may be presented as assigned, then we may indeed say that happiness is incompatible with misery and is involved or entailed by bliss. But if we consider them in relation to characters of characters to which they may be presented as assigned, then we can say no such thing. "Happiness is found in all stations in life" is not incompatible with "Misery is found in all stations in life" and "Happiness is of short duration" is not entailed by "Bliss is of short duration." [5] Our definition, then, yields "Happiness" as the subject and "is found in all stations in life" as the predicate of our proposition.

VIII

Suppose it granted that the general criterion, or definition, of subject and predicate contains the underlying ground of the originally alleged asymmetries regarding negation and composition. Then why, it might finally be asked, should we present that definition *as* a generalization from a particular kind of case, viz. the case of the proposition in which a specified empirical particular and a specified general character of particulars are presented as assigned to each other? One might answer simply that the underlying asymmetries stand out with peculiar clarity in this kind of case. But this answer is too weak. It is not simply that these cases present very good *examples* or *illustrations* of the general thesis. These cases—or rather these cases together with *relational* propositions about specified particulars, which I neglected for the sake of expository simplicity—really are the fundamental cases of predication. They really are the model for the rest. For every other kind of subject-predicate proposition presupposes them and they presuppose no other kind of subject-predicate proposition. I will not try to argue this case now, though the evidence for it seems to me overwhelming. (I suspect, in any case, that few would wish to dispute it.) I will simply point out —to put it loosely—that the appearance of any type of item other than a particular in the role of subject is dependent upon, or presupposes, its capacity to appear in another propositional role.[6] We could not predicate anything of happiness unless we could predicate happiness of people. We could not predicate anything of a number unless we could predicate having a certain number of a set. We could not predicate anything of propositions unless we framed propositions in which nothing was predicated of propositions. The propositional role of the particular, on the other hand, is—with one dubious exception—always that of subject. The dubious exception is the case which I have elsewhere described [7] as that of a proposition in which a dependent and an independent particular are presented as "attributively tied" to each other, e.g. "That shout was John's." In such a case, it might be held, the dependent particular (the shout) and the independent particular (John) respectively satisfy, as far as incompatibility-ranges are concerned, the x-part and the y-part of the x/y condition; so the independent particular has a predicative role. Few would dispute, however, that this type of formation is derivative from the type exemplified by "John shouted." So even if we allow the dubious exception, we must add that the particular's capacity to appear in this type of case as a predicate is dependent upon, or presupposes, its capacity to appear elsewhere as a subject. Hence we still have the result that the appearance of any type of item other than a particular in the subject-role is dependent upon, or presupposes, its capacity to appear in another propositional role, while the appearance of a particular in the predicate-role, if admitted at all, is dependent upon its capacity to appear in the subject-role. So particular-specifying expressions really are the basic logical subjects, and the class which I selected as the base class of subject-predicate propositions really is the base class of such propositions.

NOTES

1. p. 33.
2. p. 461.
3. p. 32.
4. I have, surprisingly, found that the hankering for disjunctive or conjunctive particulars is not always dispelled by these arguments. Surely—I have heard it said—we can just *define* an individual particular as the disjunctive particular of the two others (say, Tom and William); or as their conjunctive particular. So let me just illustrate some consequences of such attempts.

(1) Take Tom and William and their supposed disjunctive particular, Tilliam. Suppose the following proposition is true:

Tom is taller than William.

Since from the fact that Tom has a certain property it follows that Tilliam has it, and from the fact that William has a certain property it also follows that Tilliam has it, it follows that Tilliam is taller than himself.

(2) Take Tom and William and their supposed conjunctive particular, Tolliam.

Suppose Tom and William are both in the drawing room. Then since Tolliam has all and only the properties that both Tom and William have, Tolliam is in the drawing room too. Suppose, however, that Tom (and every part of him) is in the eastern half of the drawing room and that William (and every part of him) is in the western half of the drawing room. Then where in the drawing room is Tolliam? He is not in the eastern half, for William is not there. And he is not in the western half, for Tom is not there. Nor does he straddle both halves, for neither Tom nor William does. So he is not in the drawing room at all. So he both is and is not in the drawing room.

The idea of the complementary particular of a given particular has not seemed so attractive, perhaps because the general difficulties are more obvious in this case: e.g. if the given particular possesses a certain determinate member of a range of incompatible characters (as a certain shape, or size, or age), it also possesses the complementary character of each of the other members of the range. Hence the supposed complementary of the given particular would have to possess the complementaries of all those complementary characters, i.e. it would have to possess all but one of the incompatible characters of the range.

5. It might be suggested that the involvement relation holds in the other direction, on the ground that "Happiness is of short duration" entails "Bliss is of short duration." But no such relation holds in their direction either. For "Happiness is found in all stations in life" does not entail "Bliss is found in all stations in life." And "Bliss is more rarely enjoyed by the old than by the young" neither entails nor is entailed by "Happiness is more rarely enjoyed by the old than by the young."

6. This is to put it very loosely. Strictly: the introduction or presentation of any type of item other than a particular by means of an expression having the role of subject is dependent upon, or presupposes, the possibility of introducing or presenting an item of that type by means of an expression having another propositional role.

7. *Individuals*, Ch. 5, pp. 167 ff (Methuen), pp. 168 ff (Doubleday).

COMMENTS ON
MR. STRAWSON'S PAPER

Roderick M. Chisholm

I believe Mr. Strawson's paper to be a philosophical contribution of first importance and I am in substantial agreement with much of what he has to say. But I shall raise the following **four** controversial points with respect to his asymmetry principles, as I interpret them: (1) that the case for the first and second of his principles is problematic; (2) that the third and fourth are consequences of more general principles; (3) that, as a result of this fact, the third and fourth principles do not yield any truths peculiar to *individuals,* as contrasted with what Mr. Strawson calls "general characters"; and (4) that they are a selection from a larger number of such principles, some of which are more simple than those that Mr. Strawson cites.

(1) When Mr. Strawson discusses his third and fourth principles, he uses the metaphysical terms "individuals" and "general characters," but when he discusses the first and second, he uses the grammatical terms "subject" and "predicate." But I believe he means to say, in connection with the first and second principles, as he formulates them, that there are two corresponding metaphysical principles about individuals and general characters. The latter two principles, I suggest, are problematic—not because of what they say about individuals, but because of what they say about general characters.

I shall begin with the second of these principles, the one pertaining to composition. Perhaps we should remind ourselves that some philosophers and logicians have held that there *are* conjunctive individuals. Thus Brentano held that, for any individual things A and B, there is a *conjunctivum* which is another individual thing composed of just A and B; so, too, for McTaggart, and for those logicians in the tradition of Lesniewski who hold that, for every nonempty class, there is exactly one "sum" which is an individual having the members of that class as its parts. But Boethius said: a man and a fish are not a thing. And I take Mr. Strawson to be denying such "conjunctivism" with respect to individual things, but to be affirming it with respect to general characters. He is saying, as I interpret him, that for any general characters A and B, there is a conjunctive general character made up of just A and B. But I wonder whether the considerations that lead him to reject the first form of conjunctivism ought not also to lead him to reject the second.

We might summarize the case against individual conjunctivism as follows: "To assume that, for any two individual things, there is a third thing composed of just those two things is to multiply entities beyond necessity. To reject such conjunctivism is not to deny, of course, that there are genuine wholes: some individual things are composed of other individual things. Nor is it to deny that we may consider any two individual things and talk as though they were one. We may give them a name (say 'continental United States') and form true sentences in which that name is used. But such sentences are only ostensibly about *conjunctiva*. For they may be translated or paraphrased into other sentences with terms denoting only genuine individuals, the individuals that are thought to make up the so-called *conjunctiva*. *Conjunctiva*, therefore, are only pseudo-objects. And analogously for *disjunctiva*."

I would think that a similar case may be made against what I take to be Mr. Strawson's version of conjunctivism—conjunctivism with respect to characters. "To assume that, for any two characters, there is a third character which is the conjunction of just those two characters is to multiply entities beyond necessity. To reject such conjunctivism is not to deny, of course, that there are complex characters (e.g., that of being found in many stations in life) or that there are many sets of characters that are always exemplified together. Nor is it to deny that we may consider any two characters and talk as though they were one. We may give them a name and form true sentences in which that name is used. But such sentences are only ostensibly about conjunctive characters. They may be translated or paraphrased into other sentences with terms denoting only genuine characters, the ones that are thought to make up the so-called conjunctive characters. Conjunctive characters, therefore, are only pseudo-objects."

And a similar case may be made against the assumption of those so-called negative characters to which Mr. Strawson's first asymmetry principle, as I interpret it, refers. No one, I believe holds that there are *negativa* among individuals. But Mr. Strawson, I believe, holds that there are *negativa* among characters. I think he would say, for example, that in addition to the character of being green, there is also the negative character of being nongreen. And so one might reason as before:

"To assume that, for any character, there is another character which is the negation of the first character is to multiply entities beyond necessity. This is not to deny, of course, that there are many characters and many things such that those things do not have those characters. Nor is it to deny that many general characters are incompatible with other characters (we know that nothing can be both red and green). Nor again is it to deny that we may consider any character and talk as though there were another character which is its negation, just as we talk as though there were a certain entity named by 'the class of things not having that character.' We may give these supposed negative characters names (e.g., 'being nongreen') and form true sentences in which such names are used ('Ripe apples exemplify the character of being nongreen'). But such sentences may be translated or paraphrased into other sentences in which the only characters denoted are those of which the so-called negative characters are thought to be the negation ('Ripe apples do not exemplify the character of being green'). Negative characters, therefore, are only pseudo-objects."

(2) I take Mr. Strawson's third and fourth asymmetry principles to be consequences of certain more general principles about the relation of exemplification. Mr. Strawson does not use the term "exemplification," I believe, and I introduce it only for simplicity. Let us say that if a character is "assigned to" a thing, in Mr. Strawson's sense of that expression, then the thing "exemplifies" the character and the character "is exemplified by" the thing.

Mr. Strawson puts his third principle this way: "Every general character is such that, whatever individual particular it may be presented as assigned to, there is some other general character, or range of characters, the possession of which, or of any member of which, by the individual in question would be *incompatible* with its possession of the specified character. But it is not the case that every (or indeed any) individual particular is such that, whatever general character it may be presented as assigned to, there is some individual or range of individuals the possession by which, or by any member of which, of the character in question would be incompatible with its being possessed by the specified individual." I suggest that this is a consequence of the following more general principle about the relation of exemplification:

The formula "$(x)(y)[xRy \rightarrow (\exists z) \approx (xRz)]$" is true if "R" is taken as "exemplifies" and false if "R" is taken as "is exemplified by."

Thus if x exemplifies y, then y will be a general character, and there will be another general character such that it is not the case that x exemplifies that other general character. But if x is exemplified by y, then x will be a general character; and it is not true of every general character x that, for everything y such that x is exemplified by y, there is a z such that x is not exemplified by z. For some general characters—e.g. being self-identical—are exemplified by everything.

Mr. Strawson's formulation of his fourth principle is somewhat longer. In introducing the principle, he writes: "We may express it roughly by saying that it is typical of general characters of particulars to stand to other general characters of particulars in certain relations which can be expressed in the terminology of necessary and sufficient conditions; whereas no symmetrical sense can be found in which particulars can be said to stand to other particulars in such relations." I suggest that this fourth principle is a consequence of the following:

The formula "(x)(y){xRy → (∃z)[≈(z = y) & ((xRz → xRy)
v (xRy → xRz))]}" is true if "R" is taken as "exemplifies" and
false if "R" is taken as "is exemplified by."

Thus if x exemplifies y, then y will be a character, and there will be, therefore, some other character z such that "x exemplifies z" either entails or is entailed by "x exemplifies y." But it is not the case that, for every character x, if x is exemplified by some thing y, then there will be a z other than y such that "x is exemplified by z" either entails or is entailed by "x is exemplified by y." (If there are no conjunctive characters, then will there be anything for the "y" in our formula to refer to when "R" is taken as "exemplifies"? I think there would be. Being red, for example, is sufficient for being colored, and being colored is necessary for being red. But being red, I believe, is not a conjunction of being colored with some other character. For what would that other character be?)

(3) We may say that, for any entity x, if there is anything that exemplifies x, then x is a character (for we may assume that individuals do not exemplify themselves). But we may not say "if and only if"; for x may be a character even though there is nothing that exemplifies x. We may also say that, for any entity x, if x is an individual thing (particular, *concretum*, primary substance, or *ens reale*), then there is something that x exemplifies. But again we may not say "if and only if"; for x may exemplify something even if x is not an individual. Thus characters themselves possess characters. Redness, after all, has the characteristic of being a color; it also has the characteristic of being incompatible with greenness, of having been favored by Giorgione, of being exemplified by apples, and so on *ad indefinitum*.

Now Mr. Strawson formulated his third and fourth principles as principles pertaining to the relations between *individuals* and the characters that individuals exemplify. The principles I have formulated are more general in that they pertain to the relations holding between entities of *any* category, whether they be individuals or nonindividuals (e.g., characters), and the characters that those entities exemplify. Hence, if I am right in saying that the principles Mr. Strawson has formulated are consequences of the more general principles I have formulated, it follows that his third and fourth principles do not tell us of anything that is peculiar to individuals. For what they tell us about individuals also holds of *anything*, individual or nonindividual, that may be said to exemplify anything. What they tell us of individuals and their relations to their characters also holds of characters and their relations to *their* characters.

(4) Finally, I have said that Mr. Strawson's third and fourth principles may be thought of as a selection from a larger number of such principles. At any rate, this is true of the two principles I have formulated, and I have suggested that Mr. Strawson's principles are consequences of these.

The principles I have formulated are such that (i) they involve a formula which contains, in addition to logical expressions, only the relational expression "R", and (ii) the truth value that the formula has when "R" is read as "exemplifies" is different from the truth value it has when "R" is read as "is exemplified by." And there are indefinitely many principles of *that* sort. I shall cite only two.

The formula "$(x)(y)[xRy \rightarrow (\exists z)(yRz)]$" is true if "R" is taken as "exemplifies" and false is "R" is taken as "is exemplified by."

Thus whatever exemplifies anything exemplifies something that itself exemplifies something. But the characters that are exemplified by individuals and by unexemplified characters are exemplified by things that aren't exemplified by anything. (This principle may recall Aristotle's definition of primary substance: "Substance, in the truest and primary and most definite sense of the word, is that which is neither predicable of a subject nor present in a subject; for example, the individual man or horse." *Categories*, 5, 2a, 11.) Following Mr. Strawson's procedure, we might give this principle a name—say, "the principle of the asymmetry of exemplifying and being exemplified with respect to posterity." For if one thing exemplifies a second thing, then the second exemplifies a third; but not so for "is exemplified by."

The following principle is more simple:

The formula "$(x)(\exists y)(xRy)$" is true if "R" is taken as "exemplifies" and false if "R" is taken as "is exemplified by."

For everything is such that there is something that it exemplifies. But there are some things—for example, individuals and unexemplified characters—which are not exemplified by anything. Perhaps we could call this "the principle of the asymmetry of exemplifying and being exemplified with respect to universality." [1]

NOTES

1. The formula "For every x, it is false that there is one and only one y such that xRy" is true when "R" is taken as "exemplifies" and false when "R" is taken as "is exemplified by." For there is nothing that exemplifies only one character, but there are many characters (e.g., being satellite of the earth, being an even number between two and five) that are exemplified by only one thing. Analogously, if we replace "one and only one" by "two and only two," and by "three and only three," and so on *ad indefinitum*. Perhaps one could also say that the formula "$(\exists y)(x)N(xRy)$", when "N" is read as "it is necessary that," is true if "R" is taken as "exemplifies" and false if "R" is taken as "is exemplified by." For one might hold that the character of being self-identical is one that everything necessarily has. But there is no individual or character y which is such that, for every character x, x is necessarily exemplified by y; for there is nothing that possesses every character.

THE NATURE OF BELIEF

DECIDING TO BELIEVE

Bernard Williams

When the subject of belief is proposed for philosophical discussion, one may tend to think first of such things as religious and moral beliefs, belief in the sense of conviction of an ideological or practical character. Indeed, many of the most interesting questions in the Philosophy of Belief are concerned with beliefs of this type. However, this is not in fact what I shall be talking about, though what I say will, I hope, have some relevance to issues that arise in those areas. I wish to start with the question of what it is to believe something, and then go on from that to discuss (rather briefly) how far, if at all, believing something can be related to decision and will. In order to discuss this, I am not going to take religious and moral beliefs, but cases of more straightforward factual belief; cases of the sort of belief one has when one just believes that it is raining, or believes that somebody over there is one's father, or believes that the substance in front of one is salt. It is this kind of belief that I shall be concerned with.

When I talk about belief in these remarks, I shall be talking about belief as a psychological state. The word "belief," of course, can stand equally for the state of somebody who believes something, and for what he believes. And we can talk about beliefs in an impersonal way, when we talk about certain propositions which people believe or might believe. But my principal concern will be with belief as a psychological state: I shall be talking about people believing things.

The ultimate focus of my remarks is going to be on the relations between belief and decision and certain puzzles that arise about the relation between these two ideas. But before we can get into a position to discuss the questions that concern the relations between belief and decision, we must first ask one or two things about what belief is. I shall begin by stating five characteristics—as I take them—of belief. This will not be very accurate; and each of the five things that I am going to mention as a characteristic of belief, can itself give rise to a good bit of dispute and philosophical consideration. In the course of mentioning the five features, it will be necessary to mention things which may seem problematic or completely platitudinous.

The first of these features is something which can be roughly summarized as this: beliefs aim at truth. When I say that beliefs aim at truth, I have particularly in mind three things. First: that truth and falsehood are a dimension of an assessment of beliefs as opposed to many other psychological states or dispositions. Thus if somebody just has a habit of a certain kind, or merely has some disposition to action of some kind, it is not appropriate to ask whether this habit of his is true or false, nor does that habit or disposition relate to something which can be called true or false. However, when somebody believes something, then he believes something which can be assessed as true or false, and his belief, in terms of the content of what he believes, is true or false. If a man recognizes that what he has been believing is false, he thereby abandons the belief he had. And this leads us to the second feature under this heading: to believe that p is to believe that p is true. To believe that so and so is one and the same as to believe that that thing is true. This is the second point under the heading of "beliefs aim at truth."

The third point, closely connected with these, is: to say "I believe that p" itself carries, in general, a claim that p is true. To say "I believe that p" conveys the message that p is the case. It is a way, though perhaps a somewhat qualified way, of asserting that p is true. This is connected with the fact that to say "I believe that p, but p is not true," "I believe that it is raining but it is not raining" constitutes a paradox, which was famously pointed out by G. E. Moore. This is a paradox but it is not a formal self-contradiction. If it were, then in general "x believes that p but p is false," would also be a self-contradiction. But this is obviously not so. Thus I can, without any paradox at all, say "Jones believes that p but p is false"; it is only in the first person, when I say "I believe that p but p is false," that the paradox arises. The paradox is connected with the fact that I assert these two things; it is connected with this, that "I believe that p" carries an implied claim to the truth of p.

This trio of points constitutes the first of the features of belief I want to mention, that which I vaguely summed up by saying "beliefs aim at truth."

The second feature of belief is that the most straightforward, basic, simple, elementary expression of a belief is an assertion. That is, the most straightforward way of expressing my belief that *p*, is to make a certain assertion. And I think the following is an important point: the assertion that I make, which is the most straightforward or elementary expression of my belief that *p*, is the assertion *that p*, not the assertion "I believe that *p*." The most elementary and straightforward expression of the belief that it is raining is to say "it is raining", not to say "I believe that it's raining". "I believe that it's raining" does a rather special job. As a matter of fact, it does a variety of special jobs.[1] In some cases, it makes what is very like an autobiographical remark; but very often in our discourse it does a special job of expressing the belief that *p*, or asserting that *p*, in a rather qualified way. On the whole, if somebody says to me, "Where is the railroad station?" and I say "I *believe* that it's three blocks down there and to the right", he will have slightly less confidence in my utterances than if I just say "It's three blocks down there and to the right".

We have a near parallel to this in the field of action, in the contrast between saying "I will do so and so" and saying "I intend to do so and so". The direct or primitive expression of an intention to do so and so, is not saying "I intend to do so and so"; it is saying "I *will* do so and so". This is not to deny that beliefs can be ascribed to non-language-using animals. There are reasons, however, for saying that these are beliefs in a somewhat impoverished sense. There are many interesting questions in this field; I shall refer briefly to one of them. There is a certain conventionality about the ascription of something like a belief to an animal. Suppose that we present to a rabbit or some similar animal, something that looks like the mask of a fox; and that when the animal notices this object it displays characteristic fear behavior. It may run away or take evasive action, or freeze where it is, whatever. We might say in this case that the rabbit had *taken* what it was presented with for a fox. We probably would not use the rather pompous phrase of saying that the rabbit *believed* that it was a fox, though even this might not be in every case entirely unnatural. In the case of animals whose behavior is, in our terms, more obviously sophisticated, and especially in the case of animals such as dogs which perform a very special role for humanity as being things on which we project an enormous amount of anthropomorphic apparatus—in those cases the word "belief" may come more happily to hand. In any case, we do say about animals that they take things for things, and that they recognize things as things; and in at least certain cases even that they *believe* that something is something. The puzzle about this is: where does this *concept* come from, which, as it were, we pretend the animal is using? We can scarcely have a picture, or if we do have this picture it is a false picture, that the animal extends a kind of thought-balloon which says "fox." We don't think that in an effective sense the animal has the *concept* "fox." We have some idea what it is for a human being to have a concept "fox"; we have a different idea of what it is for him to have the more general concept, for instance, "predator." If we were faced with the question: did the rabbit think that it was a fox, or did the rabbit merely think it was a predator that was in front of it? we have some difficulty in deciding this question, indeed, in knowing how to set about deciding this question.

There is an interesting sideline to this. For instance, let us take the case of a human being, who sees a certain figure in the distance and takes that figure for the President of the United States. This man might not know that the President of the United States was Lyndon B. Johnson. It would certainly not follow from the fact that this man had taken the figure in the distance for the President of the United States, that he had taken him for Lyndon B. Johnson. These would come to the same thing only if that man himself had the operative piece of knowledge that the President of the United States was Lyndon B. Johnson, as was the case at the time in question. The odd thing is that in a kind of way we can apply this feature of intentionality to a dog. Suppose there is a dog whose master is the President of the United States; a certain figure comes to the door, and this dog, as dogs often do, wakes up and pricks up his ears when he hears the person crossing the step—we say "this dog took the person who was coming up the drive for his master." If this dog's master was the President of the United States, we would hardly say that the dog had taken this figure for the President of the United States. Is this because it is a better shot to say that the dog has got the concept "master" than it is to say that the dog has got the concept "President of the United States"? Why? The concept "master" is as much a concept that embodies elaborate knowledge about human conventions, society, and so forth as does the concept "President of the United States". There seems to be as much conventionality or artificiality in ascribing to a dog the concept "master" as there is in ascribing to a dog the concept "President of the United States". So why are we happier to say that a dog takes a certain figure for his master than we are to say that the dog takes a certain figure for the President of the United States? I think the answer to this has something to do with the fact, not that the dog really has got an effective concept "master," which would be an absurd notion, but that so much of the dog's behavior is in fact conditioned by situations which involve somebody's being his master, whereas very little of the dog's behavior is conditioned by situations which essentially involve somebody's being President of the United States. That is, the concept "master" gets into our description of the dog's recognition or quasi-thought or belief because this is a concept we want to use in the course of explaining a great deal of the dog's behavior. It is something on those lines, I think, which is going to justify the introduction of certain concepts into an animal's quasi-thoughts or beliefs, and the refusal to introduce other concepts into an animal's quasi-thoughts or beliefs. In the case of human beings, however, the situation is not just like this, because we have other tests for what concepts the human being in fact has.

This, then, was the second feature of belief: that the most straightforward expression of a belief is an assertion, but this does not prevent our using concepts of belief or something rather like belief with regard to animals which are incapable of making assertions and do not possess a language—although we will have to warn ourselves that such beliefs, recognitions and so on, are going to be ascribed to animals in an impoverished and (I think I have said enough to suggest), a somewhat conventionalized sense.[2]

The third feature of belief is that although the most straightforward, simple, and elementary expression of a belief by a language-using creature is an assertion, the assertion of p is neither a necessary nor, and this is the point I want to emphasize, a sufficient condition of having the belief that p. It is not a necessary condition, because I can have beliefs which I do not express, which I shall not utter. In fact it is very plausible to say that most people most of the time have a very large number of beliefs which they are not expressing, never have expressed, and never will express. The point, however, that I want to emphasize is the converse, namely that it is possible for someone to assert that p and try to bring it about that others think that p and think that he believes that p, although he does not; that is to say, assertion can be insincere. The fact that assertion can be insincere, which is an extremely important fact about assertion, shows, what in any case is obvious, that belief cannot be defined as acceptance, at least if "acceptance" is taken as the name of an action which we can overtly perform. If you take "accepting" to be something like accepting an invitation— that is, somebody comes up to me and says "Will you come to my party tomorrow?" and I accept it if I say something like "Yes, I will"; then in that sense of "accepting," "acceptance" is the name of something like a speech-act, and belief cannot be equated with acceptance in such a sense. Suppose somebody comes up to me and says, "Do you accept that p?"; "Do you accept that such and such is true?" If I just say "Yes," then in a speech-act sense of accepting that proposition, in that sense I will have accepted; just like the speech-act of accepting an invitation. But, of course, that is not a sufficient condition of my believing that p; because this acceptance may have been insincere. Belief lies at the level of what makes my acceptance sincere or insincere; it does not lie at the level of those acceptances themselves. So we have a picture of belief as of the internal state which my overt assertions may represent or misrepresent, and this is a very important feature about the concept of belief. Similarly, statements of intention or promises can be sincere or insincere because they do or do not represent an internal state of intention. "Intention," and "belief," are not the names of speech-acts; they are the names of things which speech-acts can represent correctly or misrepresent. Where the expression of a belief is the typical one of an assertion, that assertion itself can be called insincere just in that case in which the man does not really believe what he is asserting. This then is the third point; that assertion is not a necessary condition of belief, nor is it a sufficient condition, since assertion can be insincere.

The fourth point is that factual beliefs can be based on evidence. This can mean at least three things. The weakest sense of this is that the content of a given belief can be probabilified or supported by certain evidential propositions. If I just say that the belief that ancient Crete was occupied by Greek-speaking persons at a certain date is based on, or supported by, the evidence of such and such excavations, the existence of pots in certain places, I am not, in saying this, talking about any particular person's beliefs. I am just talking about a certain proposition which concerns the history of Crete and saying that that proposition is in fact supported by certain evidence which exists. Let us turn from this to a case in which we are referring to a particular person's belief; in saying that his belief was based on particular evidence, we might just mean that he could defend the proposition he believes, or support it in argument by certain evidential propositions which he could cite. However, there is a stronger sense in which his beliefs can be based on the evidence, which is not just that he has the belief and can defend it with the evidence, but that he has the belief just because he has the evidence. This says that if he ceased to believe the evidence, then, other things being equal, he would cease to have that belief. In this case, something that is true of him, namely, that he believes that p, depends upon something else being true of him, namely, that he believes these evidential propositions. In this strongest sense of somebody's actual belief being based upon his belief in certain evidential propositions, we have a statement the form "A believes that p because he believes that q"; and such statements are very often true of most of us.

Where the connection between p and q is a rational connection, that is to say, q really is some sort of evidence for p, then, of course, we can also say "p because q"; if a man says to me "Why p, why do you believe that p?" I can say "because q". We have a genuine connection of a rational character between the two propositions. Of course there are other cases in which A believes that p because he believes that q, which are not cases of rational connection, or even supposed rational connection, at all. It is just a fact about him that he believes the one thing because he believes the other, by some kind of irrational association. In this case he cannot rightly say "p because q", that is, claim a rational connection between the two propositions. Here we have a case where he believes one thing because he believes another, and that is a pure causal connection. The point I want to make is that where the connection is rational—that is, not only does he believe that p because he believes that q, but we, and he, can also say "p because q,"—that does not stop the "because" in "A believes that p because he believes that q" from being causal. The fact that there is a rational connection between p and q does not mean that there is not a causal connection between A's believing p and his believing q. We tend to bring out the mere causal connection between his beliefs in the irrational cases because in those cases there is nothing but a causal connection between them. But that does not mean that in the case in which the man has one belief rationally grounded on another that it is not the case that there is a causal connection between his believing the one thing and his believing the other; and in fact I think it is, in general, true that when A believes that p because he believes that q, this "because" is a causal "because". It is a "because" of causal explanation, the explanation of how one of his states is causally connected with another.

We do have a genuine and systematic difficulty in the philosophy of mind in filling in the content of that causal "because", and this is mainly because we have a very shadowy model of the kind of internal state belief is. However, this can be no particular objection to causal connections between beliefs in the case of evidential connection; because there are many other cases in which we must invoke a causal connection between such internal states while we still have only a shadowy notion of what that causal connection consists in. The most obvious case of this is the case of remembering things that one has experienced in the past. Suppose we say concerning a certain man that he remembers being lost in the park when he was five. What are the necessary conditions for its being the case that he remembers being lost in the park when he was five? The first is that he should, in fact, have been lost in the park when he was five and have experienced that at that time. The second is that he should now know that he was lost in the park when he was five and be able to make some more true remarks about his experience. That is not enough. Suppose it were the case that he was lost in the park when he

was five but everything he now knows about it he was told by his
mother a few years ago. Then it would not be the case that he remembered being lost in the park when he was five. The further condition
which makes it the case that he does remember being lost in the park is
that he now knows about it because he experienced it. That is, that the
knowledge he now has of this is the causal product of a record left by
the experience of his having been lost in the park. This necessary condition of event-memory appeals to exactly that kind of indeterminate
causal "because", the stuffing of which we are not clear about, which I
think we need in the case of one belief being based upon another, of a
man's believing that p because he believes that q.

People sometimes argue against the idea that we can have a causal
connection here, on the following ground. It cannot be the case that in
rational thought I arrive at one belief causally because I have another
belief, since then it would be a perpetual miracle that the laws of nature
worked in such a way that we were caused to have beliefs by rational
considerations. Granted the different sort of fact that q actually supported
p, that q was evidence for p, does it not seem a happy accident or even miraculous that when I believe that q it comes about that I believe that p?
The answer to this objection is extremely simple, and falls into two
parts. It is not a miracle, but a necessary truth, that if men are creatures
with beliefs, they are creatures with rational beliefs; and that they are
creatures with beliefs is no more miraculous than any other phenomenon
of natural evolution. If the causal connections did not hold, then there
would not be anybody with any rational beliefs. If there were not anybody with any rational beliefs, there would not be anybody with beliefs
either, because it is only because beliefs are to some extent that they are
beliefs. The fact which is being referred to, namely, that having a belief
of a certain kind can quite a lot of the time bring it about that one has
a belief which is rationally connected with that first belief, this fact is
a necessary condition of there being rationally thinking creatures at all.
You may say that it is a miracle that there are any such creatures. But
if it is, it is not *another* miracle that, when they exist, they satisfy this
condition; they have to satisfy this condition if they are to exist as
rational creatures.

Not every belief that I have which is *based*, is based on *evidence*.
There are some beliefs that I have which are not (relative to the probability of their being true) random or arbitrary, and which are very
proper beliefs to have, but which are not based on further evidence;
that is, are not based on other beliefs that I have. Indeed, there is a very
good reason why it cannot be the case that every belief which one has is
based on another belief that one has—namely, one could never stop (or

start). Quite evidently there are nonrandom beliefs which are not based on further evidence. The most notable examples of these, of course, are perceptual beliefs, beliefs that I gain by using my senses around the environment. I certainly do not want to go or try to go into questions of the philosophy of perception at this time. I want to say only the following: that one element, an essential element, in perception is having beliefs caused in one by the environment via the senses. There is more to it than that, and I do not think we can say (as some philosophers do) that perceiving just *is* acquiring beliefs in this way—but it is an essential element.

In the case of human perception, we have something which we found lacking in the earlier discussion of animals' "beliefs". We can understand what it is for somebody to acquire a belief from his environment, and we have a kind of guarantee that the terms in which we describe the cause, that is, the environment which gave rise to his belief, can match the concepts that he uses in describing the environment and therefore, by the same token, in expressing his beliefs. The very condition of having a shared experience, having a shared language and having a common perceived environment which we can know to be such, is this: we share concepts which simultaneously enable us to express our beliefs about our environment, to describe that environment, and to describe other people's perception of the environment. Therefore we get a match between our descriptions of the environment which causes another person's belief, and the concepts which he himself uses in expressing the belief and in describing the environment. This avoids the essentially conventional element which we met in the case of animals, the kind of arbitrariness about which concepts one uses in describing its recognitions or beliefs. In the case of a human being we have his own assertions, his own conceptual apparatus, which will make clear how he sees the world. The cause and the effect are described alike from the resources of a common language.

So much for the causality of beliefs; this was the fourth feature of beliefs. Beliefs can be based upon evidence. It is sometimes true that a man believes that *p* because he believes that *q*. I take that to be a causal "because," and have tried to dispose of at least one objection to thinking that it is so. The fifth, and last point about the nature of belief (and this is something which I shall mention without elaborating at all), is that belief is in many ways an *explanatory* notion; we can, in particular, explain what a man does by saying what he believes. But it is very important that one cannot explain a man's actions in terms of his beliefs without making an assumption about what his projects are, just as one cannot infer from his actions what his projects are without making assumptions about his beliefs. The trio: project, belief and action, go together. Granted that I know his projects and beliefs, I may be able to predict his actions. Granted that I know his actions and his projects, I may be able to infer his beliefs. And granted that I know his actions and his beliefs I may be able to infer his projects. But I do need basically to know, or to be able to assume, two out of the three in order to be able to get the third. A standard example of this is: I see a man walking with a determined and heavy step onto a certain bridge. We say that it shows he believes that the bridge is safe. But this, of course, is only relative to a project which it is very reasonable to assume that he has, namely to avoid getting drowned. Suppose that there were doubt about this, suppose it was a man who rather surprisingly had the project of falling in the river, then of course his walking with firm step onto this bridge would not manifest the belief that the bridge was safe but perhaps precisely the opposite, namely, the belief that the bridge was unsafe. This is a fairly obvious point. It is in terms of the trio of project, belief, and action that we offer our explanations.

These, then, are the five characteristics or features of belief that I have wanted to emphasize.

Now I want you to consider a certain machine which satisfies, more or less, three of the conditions which I have mentioned: the first, second, and the fourth conditions. In a weak sense, it produces assertions. That is to say, it produces prints-out, or, if you like, it has a speech synthesizer in it—though this would be really a rather unnecessary luxury. In any case, it produces messages which express propositions. And it has a device which distinguishes between propositions which it asserts, as opposed, for instance, to propositions which it is prepared to hypothesize in the course of an argument. It comes out with something which roughly, it "claims to be true." These things that it comes out with can be assessed for truth or falsehood; and so derivatively can be the states of the machine, which issue in these assertions. Further, the states which go with some of these assertions are based in an appropriate way on other states, and the machine arrives at some of these states from others. It goes through a causal process which is at least something like inference. We can add the fact that it gathers information from the environment; it has various sensory bits and pieces which acquire information about the environment and these get represented in the inner states of the machine, which may eventually issue in appropriate assertions.

Now this machine, I claim, would not manifest the concept of belief; its states would not be beliefs. They would be instances of a much impoverished notion which I shall call a "B state". This machine would be in B states; they are the states which issue in these various assertions and these B states can be called, I have already suggested, true or false. Why would a B state fall short of the state of a belief? I claim the essential reason for this is that this machine would not offer any satisfaction of the third condition in the list I earlier gave, namely, that it be possible to make insincere assertions, to assert something other than what you believe. In the case of this machine there is a direct route from the state that it is in to what it prints out; or if something goes wrong on this route, it goes mechanically wrong, that is, if something interrupts the connection between the normal inner state for asserting that p and its asserting that p, and it comes out with something else, this is merely a case of breakdown. It is not a case of insincere assertion, of its trying to get you to believe that p when really all the time it itself believes that not-p: we have not yet given it any way of doing that. The fact that we have not yet given it any way of doing that has, I think, deeply impoverished the concept of belief, as applied to this machine. It also, of course, means that when I said this machine made assertions, I should have actually put that in heavy scare quotes; "assertion" itself has got to be understood in an impoverished sense here, because our very concept of assertion is tied to the notion of deciding to say something which does or does not mirror what you believe. "Assertion" in the case of this machine just means, bringing out something in an assertoric mode, without putting qualifications around it. This is an impoverished sense of "assert."

It is, however, a notable feature of this machine that it could have true B-states which were nonaccidentally arrived at, that is, which were not randomly turned out but were the product of the environment, the programming and so on; and these might be called "knowledge." We could say of this machine that it knows whether so and so is the case, that it knows when the aircraft leaves, that it knows where somebody left something, that it knows where it is itself, that it knows where certain buildings are in the town, it knows all sorts of things. I would claim in fact that the use of the word "know" about this machine is not terribly far away from a lot of uses we make of the word "know" about human beings, whereas a use of "believe" to refer to the B-states that this machine is in, is quite a long way away from the way in which we use the word "believe." There might be *some* machine to which we could properly ascribe beliefs; the point is that a machine to which we properly ascribed knowledge could be a lot more primitive than one to which we properly ascribed beliefs.

This goes against what is a rather deep prejudice in philosophy, that knowledge must be at least as grand as belief, that what knowledge is, is belief plus quite a lot; in particular, belief together with truth and good reasons. This approach seems to me largely mistaken. It is encouraged by concentrating on a very particular situation which academic writings about knowledge are rather notably fond of, that which might be called the *examiner* situation: the situation in which I know that *p* is true, this other man has asserted that *p* is true, and I ask the question whether this other man really knows it, or merely believes it. I am always represented as checking on someone else's credentials for something about which I know already. That of course encourages the idea that knowledge is belief plus reasons and so forth. But this is far from our standard situation with regard to knowledge; our standard situation with regard to knowledge (in relation to other persons) is rather that of trying to find somebody who knows what we don't know; that is, to find somebody who is a source of reliable information about something. In this sense the machine could certainly know something. Our standard question is not "Does Jones know that *p?*" Our standard question is rather "Who knows whether *p?*"

As a matter of fact, even with "Jones knows that *p,*" we do not have to have all this elaborate exercise of reasons. Consider the following situation. They are engaged in this illicit love affair; she comes running in, and says "He knows". Her lover says: "You mean he believes it? Well we know it's true. Now has he got good reasons for what he thinks?" She says, "I think he just picked it up from the gossip next door." Would her lover then be right in saying "In that case, he doesn't know"? This would be absurd; absurd, basically, because "he knows" here means "he's found out", and not that he has very well grounded true beliefs. "He's found out", however, does express more than "he's guessed". What "he's found out" means is, very roughly, that he has acquired a true belief by an information-chain which starts somewhere near the facts themselves.

In his case, of course, we can speak of a belief. The point is that reflection on this and other common uses of 'know' suggests that much of the point of the concept of knowledge could be preserved if it was applied to things such as our machine which had, not beliefs, but something less.

With regard to the B-states, there could be false B-states that the machine was in; accidentally or randomly true B-states; and nonaccidentally true B-states, that is B-states which were true and which came about in ways which were connected with the fact that they were true, and these last we could call knowledge. But for belief, full-blown belief, we need the possibility of deliberate reticence, not saying what I believe, and of insincerity, saying something other than what I believe. So in a sense we need the will; for it is only with the ability to decide to assert either what I believe or what I do not believe, the ability to decide to speak rather than to remain silent about something, that we get that dimension which is essential to belief, as opposed to the more primitive state, the B-state, which we can ascribe to the machine which satisfies the elementary conditions.

From the notion of what belief is, then, we arrive at one connection between belief and decision, namely, the connection between full-blown belief and the decision to say or not to say what I believe, the decision to use words to express or not to express what I believe. This is, however, a decision with regard to what we say and do; it is not the decision to believe something. Thus far, belief is connected with decision because belief is connected with that decision to say. It is not the case that belief is connected with any decision to believe. We have not got anything like that yet. Indeed, from what has already been said it seems that we have some rather good reasons for saying that there is not much room for deciding to believe. We might well think that beliefs were things which we, as it were, found we had (to put it very crudely), although we could decide whether to express these or not. In general one feels that this must be on the right track.

It fits in with the picture offered by Hume of belief as a passive phenomenon, something that happens to us. But there is something very peculiar about Hume's account; he seems to think that it is just a contingent fact about belief that it is something that happens to us. He says, in effect: There are some things you can decide and some things you cannot, and that just means that some things happen to respond to the will while others do not. It will be a blank contingent fact if belief does not respond to the will. Now we must agree that there are cases of what we may call contingent limitations on the will. For instance, suppose somebody says that he cannot blush at will. What would it be to blush at will? Well think of the following: something which quite a lot of people could do—you could put yourself in a situation which you would guess would make you blush. That is getting yourself to blush— by a route—but it could not possibly count as blushing at will. Consider next the man who brings it about that he blushes by thinking of an embarrassing scene. That is getting a bit nearer to blushing at will, but is perhaps best described as making oneself blush at will. The best candidate of all would be somebody who could just blush in much the way that one can hold one's breath. I do not know whether people can do that, but if they cannot, it will be a contingent fact that they cannot.

Belief cannot be like that; it is not a contingent fact that I cannot bring it about, just like that, that I believe something, as it is a contingent fact that I cannot bring it about, just like that, that I'm blushing. Why is this? One reason is connected with the characteristic of beliefs that they aim at truth. If I could acquire a belief at will, I could acquire it whether it was true or not; moreover, I would know that I could acquire it whether it was true or not. If in full consciousness I could will to acquire a "belief" irrespective of its truth, it is unclear that before the event I could seriously think of it as a belief, i.e. as something purporting to represent reality. At the very least, there must be a restriction on what is the case after the event; since I could not then, in full consciousness, regard this as a belief of mine, i.e. something I take to be true, and also know that I acquired it at will. With regard to no belief could I know—or, if all this is to be done in full consciousness, even suspect—that I had acquired it at will. But if I can acquire beliefs at will, I must know that I am able to do this; and could I know that I was capable of this feat, if with regard to every feat of this kind which I had performed I necessarily had to believe that it had not taken place?

Another reason stems from our considerations about perceptual belief: a very central idea with regard to empirical belief is that of coming to believe that p because it is so, that is, the relation between a man's perceptual environment, his perceptions, and the beliefs that result. Unless a concept satisfies the demands of that notion, namely that we can understand the idea that he comes to believe that p because it is so and because his perceptual organs are working, it will not be the concept of empirical belief; it will hardly even be that more impoverished notion which I have mentioned, the B-state. But a state that could be produced at will would not satisfy these demands because there would be no regular connection between the environment, the perceptions and what the man came out with, which is a necessary condition of a belief or even of a B-state.

However, even if it is granted that there is something necessarily bizarre about the idea of believing at will, just like that, it may be said that there is room for the application of decision to believe by more roundabout routes. For we all know that there are causal factors, unconnected with truth, which can produce belief: hypnotism, drugs, all sorts of things could bring it about that I believe that p. Suppose a man wanted to believe that p and knew that if he went to a hypnotist or a man who gave him certain drugs he would end up believing that p. Why could he not use this more roundabout method, granted that he cannot get himself into a state of believing just by lifting himself up by his own shoe straps; why could he not bring it about that he believes that p by adopting the policy of going to the hypnotist, the drug man or whatever? Well, in some cases he could and in some cases he could not; I am going to say something about the two sorts of cases. I am not going to discuss the issue of self-deception. The issue of self-deception is a very important and very complex issue in the philosophy of mind which gives rise to a very large number of problems; of course it is true that people can deceive themselves into believing things that they know are false. But I am not going to discuss self-deception; what I am going to raise is rather this question: Why, if we're going to bring it about that we believe something in this kind of way, do we have to use self-deception; that is, what, if anything, is wrong with the idea of a conscious project to make myself believe what I want to believe?

The first thing we have to do is to distinguish between two senses or two applications of the notion of "wanting to believe" something. I am going to distinguish these under the terms "truth-centered motives" and "non-truth-centered motives." Suppose a man's son has apparently been killed in an accident. It is not absolutely certain he has, but there is very strong evidence that his son was drowned at sea. This man very much wants to believe that his son is alive. Somebody might say: If he wants to believe that his son is alive and this hypnotist can bring it about that he believes that his son is alive, then why should he not adopt the conscious project of going to the hypnotist and getting the hypnotist to make him believe this; then he will have got what he wants —after all, what he wants is to believe that his son is alive, and this is the state the hypnotist will have produced in him. But there is one sense—I think the most plausible one—of "he wants to believe that his son is alive" in which this means *he wants his son to be alive*—what he essentially wants is the *truth* of his belief. This is what I call a truth-centered motive. The man with this sort of motive cannot conceivably consciously adopt this project, and we can immediately see why the project for him, is incoherent. For what he wants is something about the world, something about his son, namely, that he would be alive, and he knows perfectly well that no amount of drugs, machinery and so on applied to himself is going to bring that about. So in the case of the "truth-centered motives," where *wanting to believe* means *wanting it to be the case,* we can see perfectly clearly why this sort of project is impossible and incoherent.

However, he might have a different sort of motive, a non-truth-centered motive. This would be the case if he said, "Well, of course what I would like best of all is for my son to be alive; but I cannot change the world in this respect. The point is, though that even if my son isn't alive, I want, I need to believe that he is, because I am so intolerably miserable knowing that he isn't." Or again a man may want to believe something not caring a damn about the truth of it but because it is fashionable or comfortable or in accordance with the demands of social conformity to believe that thing. Might not such a man, wanting to believe this thing, set out to use the machinery of drugs, hypnotism, or whatever to bring it about that he does? In this case the project does not seem evidently incoherent in the way in which the project was incoherent for the man with the truth-centered motive. What it is, is very deeply irrational, and I think that most of us would have a very strong impulse against engaging in a project of this kind however uncomfortable these truths were which we were having to live with. The question I have to leave you with, is Why? What is the source of our very strong internalized objection to this kind of project?

I will raise two questions which may assist in the discussion of this. The first is this: is the project of trying to get yourself to believe something because it is more comfortable fundamentally different or not from the project (more familiar, and, it might seem, more acceptable) of trying to forget something because it is uncomfortable? That is, if I just wanted to forget what was disagreeable, would this be very different in principle from the project of actually trying to believe something which is untrue? Is the project of trying to forget the true morally or psychologically different from the project of trying to get oneself to believe the false? If so, why? Is one of them easier than the other? If so why? That is the first question I would like to leave you with; together with the suggestion that there is almost certainly a genuine asymmetry here, tied in to the asymmetry that while every belief I have ought ideally to be true, it is not the case that every truth ought ideally to be something I believe: belief aims at truth, knowledge does not similarly aim at completeness.

The second consists of a couple of considerations. Perhaps one objection to the projects of believing what is false is that there is no end to the amount you have to pull down. It is like a revolutionary movement trying to extirpate the last remains of the *ancien régime*. The man gets rid of this belief about his son, and then there is some belief which strongly implies that his son is dead, and that has to be got rid of. Then there is another belief which could lead his thoughts in the undesired direction, and that has to be got rid of. It might be that a project of this kind tended in the end to involve total destruction of the world of reality, to lead to paranoia. Perhaps this is one reason why we have a strongly internalized objection to it. If we are not going to destroy all the evidence—all consciousness of the evidence—we have to have a project for steering ourselves through the world so as to avoid the embarrassing evidence. That sort of project is the project of the man who is deceiving himself, and he must really know what is true; for if he did not really know what was true, he would not be able to steer around the contrary and conflicting evidence. Whether we should or should not say that he also believes what he really knows to be true, is one of the problems that surround self-deception. But at least the project that leads to that condition, the project of self-deception, is something different from the blank projects of belief-inducement which we were considering.

NOTES

1. It is important to notice this point. It is even more important not to suppose that discussions of "I believe that *p*" provide the main highway to an understanding of belief. That they do not, follows from this point itself.

2. I do not think that to say that a psychological concept is applied to other animals in an "impoverished" sense either merely follows from the fact that they lack a language, or is in itself in the least explanatory. Some psychological concepts, like some concepts of action, apply *straightforwardly* to animals. The claim of "impoverishment" or "conventionality" has to be made good by special considerations, such as those concerning the choice of concepts figuring in that application.

SOME LOGICAL INCONGRUITIES BETWEEN THE CONCEPT OF KNOWLEDGE AND THE CONCEPT OF BELIEF

Justus Hartnack

I

During almost the whole history of epistemology the logical difference between the concepts of knowledge and belief has been emphasized. It is one thing, however, to understand that these two concepts are different; it is quite another thing to understand the nature of the difference and to be able to explain some of its details and reasons. In this paper I shall try first of all to describe some of the essential differences; next, to show some problems connected with these differences; and finally, to attempt a solution to some of these problems.

II

Since Plato it has been an epistemological commonplace that knowledge cannot be wrong but that belief may be. In other words, it would be a conceptual misunderstanding to speak of false knowledge, and redundant to speak of true knowledge, but it would be neither a misunderstanding nor a redundancy to speak of true or false beliefs. If I say that I know that p, then, if p is false, I have said something false. A necessary, although not a sufficient condition for saying that one knows that p, is that p is true. However, if I believe that p and it is discovered that p is false I shall cease to believe that p, but it is nevertheless the case that I did believe that p. If, however, I say that I know that p and it is discovered that p is false I cannot say that I do no longer know that p; nor can I say that I nevertheless did know it. One way of expressing this difference has been to say that to believe is a psychological verb, used to characterize a person's state of mind, while to know is a nonpsychological verb; it is not used to characterize or describe a person's state of mind. There is something called belief behavior, but there is nothing called knowledge behavior.

If I assert that I believe that p I can be challenged on two accounts. It may be argued that p is false. What is false then is that which I believe but not the fact that I believe. Or it may be argued that I ought not to believe that p. That is, I am accused of believing without sufficient evidence. I may believe too lightly; I may be naive. This accusation may be justified even if it turns out that p is in fact true.

If I say that I know that p I can likewise be challenged on two accounts. If it is argued that p is false, what is false, then, is both that which I claim to know (again we notice a difference between knowledge and belief: I cannot say that what is false is that which I knew—as I can say that what is false is that which I believed), and my statement that I know that p (while my statement that I believe that p is not falsified just because p is proven to be false). It may also be argued that independently of whether p is true or not I ought not to say that I know that p; there simply is not enough evidence. (Again: If in such cases I claim to know, it is not due to naiveté—it is due to a lack of epistemological education; furthermore, it cannot be said that I ought not to know that p, as it can be said that I ought not to believe that p).

Both knowledge and belief are related to evidence. The evidence for belief is evidence for the truth of a belief but, since one can have belief without evidence, it is not evidence for the existence of the belief. The evidence for knowledge, however, is evidence for the existence of the knowledge; if there is no evidence I cannot claim that I know. If I claim that I know that p, I may be asked how I know. My answer to that question is to reveal my evidence for the truth of p. But the point of my answer is not to prove p but to prove that I did have the right to say that I know, that in other words it is not an ill-grounded assumption but an instance of knowledge.

Furthermore, if there is evidence for a proposition p it is logically impossible to assert that p cannot be believed. I can ("can" in a psychological sense) believe something without having any evidence (although, perhaps, I ought not so to believe), but I cannot ("cannot," in a logical sense) disbelieve a proposition p if there is evidence for it and no counterevidence: it is a logical "cannot" since evidence obviously is evidence for the truth of a proposition, and it is contradictory to say that one does not believe in the truth of a proposition for the truth of which there are good reasons to believe. But even if there is evidence for a proposition p, it is logically in order to say that one does not know that p.

Let me try to sum up these differences:

(1) To say that a proposition p is an object of knowledge entails that p is true; but to say that p is an object of belief does not entail that it is true.

(2) The verb 'to know' is not a psychological verb in the sense in which the verb 'to believe' is.

(3) If a proposition p is false then the claim I may have made to know that p is unjustified. I may have believed that I know p but then my belief was false. If, however, p is false, my belief, though a false belief, would still have been a belief.

(4) The evidence for a proposition p entails belief in p, but belief in p does not entail evidence for p. Evidence for p, however, does not entail knowledge of p, while knowledge of p does entail evidence for it.

III

Can knowledge be defined in terms of belief? If it is asserted, as it sometimes is, that knowledge is true belief, this proposition is obviously false. I may believe that p on very slight evidence, yet p may be true: but I could not therefore claim that I knew p. I may know that Smith is fifty years of age, and my evidence may be that he looks to be of the same age as Jones, whose age I happen to know to be fifty. On such evidence I could not claim to know that Smith is fifty years old. I could only say that I believe it. This belief cannot be said to be knowledge just because it so happens that Smith is in fact fifty years of age. I may even believe that Smith is fifty on false evidence; I may believe it because somebody who knows Smith well has informed me—however, due to some misunderstanding the other person was talking not about Smith but about Jones, who happens also to be fifty. It would be absurd to assert that for this reason I knew that Smith was fifty years of age.

In order to correct the above inadequacies it may be added that one must have the right to believe. It is equally obvious that such an addition does not help us. How much evidence is sufficient to have the right to say that one believes? It is either sufficient to have the right to say that one believes but does not know—in which case one does not know; or sufficient to say that one knows: that is, it is more than is required for having the right to say that one believes; it is to go beyond what is required. It would be one of these situations in which one could say that one does not believe, because one knows; but there is something drastically wrong in talking of having or not having the right to believe. It is to confuse the logic of knowledge with the logic of belief. I may not have the right to a knowledge claim, namely if the evidence for my claim is not good enough, and consequently I do not know. But I do not need any right to have a belief. If my evidence is slight my belief may be naive, foolish, or superstitious, but I believe all the same. I can believe naively, foolishly, or superstitiously, but I cannot know naively, foolishly, or superstitiously. My claim to knowledge can be justified or not; but I do not make any claim to a belief. I either have it or I do not have it.

The concepts of belief and knowledge play different parts in our language. They belong to different language games. This constitutes another and, so it seems, decisive reason against the possibility of defining knowledge in terms of true belief. The truth-conditions for the statement 'A knows that p' is the evidence for p which A is able to give. The truth-conditions for the statement 'A believes that p' is A's behavior, or, if one prefers, A's mental state. The truth-conditions, however, are independent of the evidence for the truth of p. But two concepts whose applications in statements require quite different types of truth-conditions cannot be defined in terms of each other or be reduced one to the other.

Knowledge and belief exclude each other. If I know that something is the case I cannot say that I believe it, and if I believe it I cannot say that I know it. I cannot at one and the same time do both.

This seems to create a problem. If I say that I know that p then I cannot say that I believe that p; but if I cannot say that I believe that p, it seems to imply that I do not believe that p. That this is a pseudo-problem is easy to see: What is implied by the fact that I cannot say that I believe that p is, that when I make a knowledge claim, the concept of belief cannot be applied—that is, if I say I know that p, I have ruled out statements to the effect that I believe or that I do not believe.

It has been argued that knowledge and belief do not exclude each other. Thus Anthony Quinton argues: "I should mislead people if I described my wife as the woman I live with, and I might say, No, she is my wife, if I were asked whether she is the woman I live with. Nevertheless, my wife is the woman I live with. What is true is that I do not *merely* live with her. Likewise, if I know that p, I do not merely believe it, but I do believe it all the same." [1]

The above argument rests, I think, on a confusion between two different things. It would indeed be paradoxical if I said that I know that p but that I am utterly convinced that p is false. That is, I must be convinced of the truth of p. But from this it does not follow that I can say that I both know and believe that p, because part of what I mean by saying that I believe that p is that I have not made sure. If I say that I believe there is an interesting play on T.V. tonight I may be asked to look at the T.V. program in order to find out for sure; but if I say that I know it, I imply that I already have found out. It is one of the purposes of the use of the verb 'to know' to function as a block for further proposals about finding out for sure. The verb 'to believe' has more than one function. It is partly a psychological verb; it is psychological in the sense that it informs about the speaker's attitude toward the truth of a proposition. But it is also an epistemic verb; it is epistemic in the sense that it informs the hearer that the speaker does not have enough evidence to make a knowledge claim. The use of the verb 'to believe' does not block, but on the contrary invites proposals about finding out for sure. If I say that I know, I can be asked to reveal my evidence but not to find it. If I say that I believe I can be asked to do both. In other words, while it is necessary that doubt is excluded if I know that p, it does not follow that I can say that I both know that p and believe it. Or, rather, it follows that I cannot say both. For I cannot at one and the same time say both that I have enough evidence to make a knowledge claim and that I do not have it.

Although I cannot know without also being absolutely certain that the proposition I claim to know is true, I cannot say: "I know that p and I am absolutely certain that p is true." The reason I cannot say so is not that it would be contradictory; rather, it would be like saying: "After some deliberation I have finally decided to send in my application for the job, and, furthermore, I intend to do as I have decided to do." This is an instance of the not uncommon phenomenon that we cannot express in language that which is in fact the case. Later on in this paper I shall take up other instances of the same phenomenon. At the present, the following remarks suffice. We have to solve the apparent conflict between the following two statements: (1) "A claims to know that p, and one can therefore infer that A feels absolutely certain that p is true," and (2) "If A states that he knows that p, he cannot in that statement also state that he is absolutely certain that p is true." The solution to the problem is, I think, as follows: To say that one knows that p, is, among other things, to say that one has all the evidence one can wish for in order to establish the truth of p. And, as I have argued earlier in this paper, it is a contradiction to say that there is evidence, and no counterevidence, for the proposition p but that one does still not believe that p is true. In saying that one knows p, therefore, it is implied that one is absolutely certain that p is true. Consequently, if I state that I know that p I have *presupposed* that I have enough evidence to guarantee the truth of p; and as evidence entails belief (or, according to the strength of the evidence, other psychological concepts, e.g., being convinced of) I therefore also presuppose belief (or being convinced of). A presupposition of a statement, however, cannot be stated in that very statement; and since a presupposition for stating that I know that p is that I am utterly convinced of the truth of p, this presupposition cannot be stated in that statement for which it is a presupposition. There is therefore no conflict between (1) and (2).

Knowledge entails truth. We cannot say that p is an object of knowledge but that nevertheless p may not be true. This fact has created familiar puzzles such as that of the logical positivists who have been eager to emphasize that no empirical proposition can be an object of knowledge. An empirical proposition implies an infinite number of propositions, and as it is logically impossible to verify an infinite number of propositions we can never know whether there might not be a false proposition—and if just one is false the implicans is false. This is unacceptable. It surely is unacceptable that we *never* have the right to say that we know that p if p is an empirical proposition. So we feel we have to say with Austin: "surely . . . we are often right to say we *know* even in cases where we turn out subsequently to have been mistaken— and indeed we seem always, or practically always, liable, to be mistaken. . . . It is naturally *always* possible ('humanly' possible) that I may be mistaken—but that by itself is no bar against using the expression 'I know.' " [2] To accept this Austinian line, however, also creates puzzles. To say that one has the right to claim that this book is my book must mean that the book is in fact my book. To have the right to say that I have passed the examination must mean that I have in fact passed it. To say that I have a right to assert that the proposition p is true must mean that the proposition p is in fact true: so to say that I have the right to claim that I know that p must mean that I do in fact know p. Now suppose that I have the right to say that I know that p; suppose furthermore that p turns out to be false. If we grant Austin his point I shall be permitted to say that although p is false I nevertheless had the right to say that I knew that p. But surely I cannot say that I did know that p; because I cannot say that when I asserted that I knew p I did know it although my knowledge proved to be false. If Austin is right, therefore, there are situations in which I can say that I know that p despite the fact that I do not know that p. I cannot know that p if p is false. If p is false it is correct to say that I do not know that p. To say that I have the right to say that there are cases when I know that p even if p is false is to say therefore, that there are cases where I have the right to say that I know that p despite the fact that it is incorrect to say that I know that p.

This is, of course, unsatisfactory, to say the least. It is unsatisfactory that we can also have the right to say that we know in cases in which it is incorrect to say that we know—that is, in cases where in fact we do not know. We seem to have been caught in the following dilemma: Either we say that we can claim to know that p if and only if we cannot be wrong; and as there are infinitely many sentences that can falsify p we can never make sure that we cannot be wrong, and, consequently, can never have knowledge. Or, we may say that there are situations in which we have the right to say that we have knowledge even if it may turn out that we are wrong—which leads to the paradox that we can say that we know even when we do not know. The only way out seems to be to say with the Austinians that we do sometimes, even often, have the right to say that we know, but against the Austinians to deny that there are cases where we can say that we know where we in fact do not know. It means that we shall also have to deny the logical positivists' point that there always are infinitely many sentences that can falsify the proposition we claim to know.

Suppose I answer the question, what day of the week is it today, by saying that it is Friday. I am asked whether I am sure, and I say that I know it. How do I know? Well, I have looked at today's newspaper; I know it is on Fridays that I have my seminar on The Philosophy of Science—a seminar I have just had; I know that yesterday was Thursday—which I know on account of many other reasons; I know that my cleaningwoman came this morning, and she comes on Fridays only. I can state these and many other facts, not as ways of *discovering* but as ways of showing that I know it is Friday. In fact I do not really have to prove, in a sense of *discovering*, that it is Friday; I have to do that as little as I have to *discover* my own age or *discover* my own home address. What could possibly falsify my statement that today is Friday? Let us suppose that historical research has discovered that centuries ago a mistake was made in the calculation of the calendar. If the mistake had not been made we really should have had Saturday today. Would this constitute a falsification? All we could do would be to issue a contrary-to-fact conditional: If they had not made the mistake, we would now have had Saturday. But this is the same as to say that, now that they did make the mistake, we do have Friday.

Furthermore, there are situations in which the truth of a proposition p is so well established that no further experience can falsify it—that is, the truth of p is so well established that the alleged falsifications by the other proposition cannot be accepted. The claim to the truth of these other propositions is weaker than the claim to the truth of p. They cannot count, therefore, as a falsification of p.

Of course, there are situations in which we have all the available evidence for a proposition, and therefore it is justifiable, at least so we think, to claim the truth of it. Nevertheless, later on, new evidence is discovered which definitely falsifies the proposition. It is evidence which it was impossible for us even to think of when we proclaimed that we knew the proposition. Could we say that we had the right so to proclaim? According to what I have argued above, we could not. What we may say, or, rather, will have to say, is that in this particular situation it was *excusable* to claim that we knew. But a presupposition of using the word 'excuse' is precisely that something wrong has been done, or that an error or a mistake has been made. We cannot talk about excusing acts which were right. That is, Austin's statement that "we are often right to say we know even in cases where we turn out subsequently to have been mistaken" is correct if by the word "right" we mean the same as 'excusable'—but this is an interpretation which hardly is the one Austin had in mind. Some other difference between the concepts of knowledge and the concept of belief should be noticed. Compare the following statements: (1) "I believe there is an interesting play on T.V. tonight"; (2) "There is an interesting play on T.V. tonight"; (3) "I know that there is an interesting play on T.V. tonight." One difference between (1) and (2) on the one hand and (3) on the other hand is this: Both (1) and (2) can be uttered without any special occasion for doing so. They can both be my first remark. I can enter a room and start my conversation by asserting either (1) or (2). But it would be an oddity if my first remark were (3). If it was, I would invite questions like: "Who says that there isn't?" In other words, we only use the expression: 'I know that *p*' if we have been challenged. If we have not been challenged we express that which we believe we know by asserting (2). If I say: "There is an interesting play on T.V. tonight" I can be challenged; and if I cannot show sufficient evidence to justify a knowledge-claim, I have said something more than I should have. I shall have to admit that I really should have said that I only believed or assumed it.

The fact that it is only when we are challenged that we use the expression 'I know that *p*,' somehow explains and gives plausibility to the Austinian claim that there is a performative force in the use of that expression. It is when we are challenged and want to emphasize that we do have sufficient evidence and want to emphasize that what we assert cannot be wrong that we use the verb 'to know.' By using the expression 'I know that *p*,' we, so to speak, guarantee that we have sufficient evidence to assert that we cannot be wrong. If, however, we are unchallenged, or do not expect to be challenged, we state that which we know without the use of the verb 'to know.' The fact that we possess knowledge does not call for the use of the expression 'I know that *p*' but only of '*p*'—*that is, knowledge is, at least ordinarily, stated without the use of the concept of knowledge.* If I know that the cat is on the mat and consequently assert "The cat is on the mat," I use the concept 'cat' and the concept 'mat' but not the concept 'knowledge'—and this, incidently, is parallel to the use of the concept of truth. We state that which is true without the use of that concept, and it is only if, in one way or another, we are challenged, provoked, or interrogated, that we use that concept.

If I know, do I then know that I know? This is a question which has been asked more than once in recent philosophic literature. If I state the proposition p without such qualifying expression as 'I believe,' 'I think,' or 'I assume,' I must be able, if challenged, to say I know that p; it is to be committed, therefore, to show that the evidence I have for p is sufficient. I cannot state p without being able to show my evidence. I must have it ready at hand. If I assert that there is an interesting play on T.V. tonight, and I cannot answer the question how I know, I surely should not have asserted it. To say that I know that I know that p, according to what I said above, must be to say that I am able and ready to show and state my evidence that I have evidence for the proposition p. But to understand what we mean by evidence is to understand that we cannot ask the question whether we have evidence for evidence. Or rather, to need evidence for evidence is the same as to say that it really is not evidence. In order for something to count as evidence it must be something which *in itself* is either a proof or an argument for a proposition. I can no more talk of evidence for evidence (but may talk of explaining or analyzing evidence) than I can talk of proof for proof (but may talk of explaining or analyzing a proof). The expression 'evidence for evidence' is a spurious expression. The expression 'knowing that one knows' is consequently also a spurious expression.

Against this view the following two objections may be raised. The first objection is this. I can say that I know that p; but I cannot say that I know that p but I do not know that I know that p, which seems to imply that I must know that I know that p.[3] The answer to the objection is that as the expression 'knowing that one knows' is a spurious expression, it follows that also the expression 'I know that p but I do not know that I know that p' is also a spurious expression. I can say neither that I know that I know that p nor that I do not know that I know that p.

The second objection is based on the fact that if I say that I know that p and p turns out to be false, I may say, and say correctly, that I believed that I knew, but, apparently, my belief was false. Now, if I can believe that I know it seems that I must be able also to know that I know; but to say that I believed that I knew does not entail that at the time I stated p I could have said: "I believe that I know that p," because it would be to say that I assume but cannot guarantee that I have sufficient evidence for a knowledge-claim—which of course is the same as to say that I cannot make a knowledge claim, and consequently cannot say that I know. We never say that we knew that we knew. Suppose that, despite the fact that my evidence is doubted by others, I make a knowledge-claim. If my claim is justified I may say something like: "Well, I did say that I knew it, didn't I?" Or "Well, this was what I said, wasn't it?" Which is something different from saying that I knew that I knew.

It should be too obvious to need saying that the concept of knowledge I have been concerned with in this paper is the concept 'knowing that.' To say this is neither to affirm nor to deny that this concept can be analyzed in terms of the concept 'knowing how,' because independently of which analysis we accept of the concept of 'knowing that,' it cannot eliminate the different uses of these two concepts—the concepts of 'knowing that' and 'knowing how.' We still acknowledge the difference between knowing how to swim and knowing that there is an interesting play on T.V. tonight. I can know *that* I know *how* to swim; but I cannot know how *that* there is an interesting play on T.V. tonight.

Even if I have limited myself to an analysis of 'knowing that' and its differences from belief, there are, needless to say, many more things about this concept that are in need of further investigation.

NOTES

1. *The Encyclopedia of Philosophy* (The Macmillan Company and The Free Press, New York, 1967), vol. 4, p. 346.
2. J. L. Austin, *Philosophical Papers* (Oxford, 1961), p. 66.
3. See Arthur Danto, "On knowing that one knows," in *Epistemology, New Essays in the Theory of Knowledge*, edited by Avrum Stroll (Harper and Row, New York, 1967), p. 32 f.

BELIEFS AS SENTENTIAL STATES OF PERSONS

Arthur C. Danto

One widely underwritten difference between "*m* knows that *s*" (hereafter, when convenient, *mKs*) and "*m* believes that *s*" (hereafter, when convenient, *mBs*) is that only the former entails, since only the former presupposes, that *s* is true. It is a commonplace of philosophical usage that one cannot know that *s* if *s* is false, but that belief is indifferent as to the truth-value of the sentence which expresses its content. This suggests then a radical difference in the analysis and ascription of knowledge and of belief respectively. The truth-conditions for *s* figure in some fashion amongst the truth-conditions for *mKs*, though not for *mBs*, and accordingly it is implausible to suppose that in ascribing knowledge that *s* to *m*, we are ascribing some absolute condition to *m* himself. Rather, *mKs* says something about *m* and something about whatever it may be, call it *o*, which makes *s* true. It is natural, therefore, to regard *mKs* as asserting, or as presupposing, a relation between *m* and *o*, in that the failure of *o* to exist means that *s* is false and hence that *mKs* is false. "*K*," therefore, may be regarded as a two-place predicate taking (for example) *m* and *o* as its terms.

Some writers (e.g., Malcolm) have taken the difference between *mKs and mBs* to be solely a difference in the truth-value of *s*. This is suggestive, since if it is correct it is compatible with the thesis that nothing about *m* taken alone will tell whether he knows that *s* or not, a thesis which is trivially entailed by the relational status of K. But it is a poor analysis because it leaves no room for a relation between *m* and *o* except the indirect relation that *m* is related to *s* and *s* is related to *o*. The relation to *s* stands, then, whether the relationship between *s* and *o* is satisfied, and the former relation holds whether *m* believes or *m* knows that s, the difference between the latter turning only on whether the relation between s and o holds. Moreover, the analysis destroys the semantical neutrality of mBs relative to s; for it now *has* to follow from mBs that s is false.[1]

Doubtless there is an innuendo of falsity implied in certain uses of ". . . (merely) believes that . . . ," but then there are other cases in which we should wish to say that *we* know what m only believes. So we ought to leave room for true as well as false beliefs. There can be little argument that the difference between true and false belief is altogether an external matter of the truth or falsity of the sentence which expresses the belief, but then this latter difference is irrelevant to the ascription of belief as such, i.e., semantically unmodified. And inasmuch as ascriptions of belief are semantically neutral, we *can* plausibly be taken as ascribing some absolute condition to m when, of m, we say that he believes that s; for we are saying nothing about whatever makes the difference between the truth or falsity of s, and so the truth or falsity of mBs *can* depend upon facts concerning m alone, that is, that we should be able to determine whether it is true that a man believes something by examination only of him.

It is natural, then, to take "believes that s" as a one-place predicate, true absolutely of m when "m believes that s" is true.[2] To be sure, it is not a run-of-the-mill one-place predicate, containing, as it does, a *sentential shape*. I shall acknowledge this abnormality by characterizing the *class* of predicates of which "believes that s" is paradigmatic, as composed of *sentential predicates*. The identification of sentential predicates is, unfortunately, not a mechanical matter of applying syntactical or grammatical criteria. For ". . . knows that s" is not a sentential predicate despite its syntactical and grammatical indiscernibility from ". . . believes that s." On the other hand, neither is it plain that the semantical neutrality of s with regard to the truth-conditions for sentences of the form "mFs" entails that Fs is a sentential predicate, true or false absolutely of m in case "mFs" is true; for though "m wrote that s" is semantically neutral with regard to s, the sentential shape (supposing *oratio recta*) had in fact to be written, and the truth of the sentence thus does not conspicuously depend upon facts which pertain to m alone: it depends also upon successful modification of an external graphic medium.

II

There are some manifest advantages in treating ". . . believes that s" as a (sentential) predicate, which connects with another widely acknowledged feature of ascribing beliefs to people. This concerns the so-called referential opacity of terms which occur in *s* in such a way that were *s* to be a free-standing sentence, i.e., not occur embedded in a predicate, those terms would have conspicuously referential status. In the free-standing state, it is generally held that if *t* is a referential term in *s*, then any term *t'* coreferential with *t* may replace it, leaving unaffected the truth-value of *s*—the latter depending upon satisfaction of reference without regard to differences in meaning. The principles implicit here license uninhibited interchange of coreferential terms in given sentential contexts, a license indispensable for algorithmic work. But it is notorious that this privilege does not extend to sentences when these occur in sentences ascribing beliefs: If it is true that *m* believes . . . *t* . . . , it is not necessarily false, but certainly not automatically true, that *m* believes that . . . *t'* . . . , the coreferentiality of *t* and *t'* not withstanding.

It is not altogether clear why this should be so, and I can see the temptation for ruthlessly overriding it. One might argue that if a man believes that . . . *t* . . . , well, he just believes that . . . *t'* . . . , and our reluctance to suppose otherwise must be due to some tacitly held, perhaps metaphysically suspect, theory of belief. Thus there is no requirement that we must report upon a man's beliefs in terms he would have used to report them, and often we must use terms he *could* not have understood. Mo Tzu believed that ghosts exist, and that he did so is a historical truth of Chinese philosophy; but he could not—since the language had not yet been invented—have understood this straightforward English description of what he believed. This ruthlessness is appealing, but will not survive some implausible consequences. It would require Mrs. Newton's neighbors to have believed—since they believed that Issac Newton would not survive the first six months of his life—that the author of *Principia Mathematica* would not survive the first six months of his life. At such junctures, the most uncompromising extensionalist might allow an exception, rather than allow our intuitions regarding beliefs to go so completely under. It is, therefore, something of a relief not to have to do *either*. For the principle of coreferential interchange will apply to terms only when they occur in nonpredicative positions anyway, and in counting ". . . believes that . . . *t* . . ." as a (sentential) predicate, we have removed it from exposure to the principle to begin with. So in effect the principle encounters here no exception whatever, and our intuitions regarding beliefs remain intact.

As we shall see, this happy resolution is only a temporary respite, but the coherency we are allowed to preserve by means of the sentential-predicate analysis of sentences which ascribe beliefs, is some presumptive evidence in favor of the correctness of that analysis.

III

These advantages may be thought trifling in contrast with certain others of a more strikingly metaphysical order. If . . . believes that . . . is taken as a relational predicate, the question becomes pressing regarding *what* m must be related to when $m\mathrm{B}s$ is true. Notice that, whatever this relatum may turn out to be, it must be neutral relatively to the truth or falsity of s, since $m\mathrm{B}s$ is by common consent true even when s is false. So the problem is not so simple as in the case of . . . knows that . . . In the latter case, when it is true that $m\mathrm{K}s$, then m may be related to whatever makes s true. Let this be o. Then if o does not exist, the relation collapses and $m\mathrm{K}s$ is just false. Trivially, there is no false knowledge, but part of our problem is to account for false belief, so the relatum for m when m believes that s cannot be the same, or even of the same type, as that which serves for knowledge.

The demand that belief be relational, together with the collateral demand that belief-sentences be semantically neutral, forces us to furnish semantically neutral *objects* of belief, e.g., intensions, essences, propositions, abstract actualities (which remain whether there are concrete actualities which correspond to them or not) and comparable ontological monstrosities, the nature of which are determined in advance by the problem they are manufactured to solve. They are always, by a nice convenience, outside of space and time and corruption, and *there*, whatever the semantical vagaries of the beliefs that take them as objects. The temptation to postulate such entities is aborted, however, when "believes that" is not taken as relational, but as predicable absolutely of single individuals, one at a time.

To be sure, a mere shift in philosophical grammar leaves the universe as it is, and there may indeed *be* just those entities, those objects of belief, in some crooked corner of a universe ontologically more generous than our mingy imagination would credit. The loss, then, will be ours. Since, however, the only reason we have for supposing there are such entities is an antecedent view that belief is relational, we can hardly use the possibility that they may exist as support for the relational interpretation. It is not as though we were talking about nefrits or hammer-toed clams!

The stock arguments in favor of relationalism descend from *Theatetus* 189b,[3] where Socrates proposes that to believe is to believe something, since to believe nothing is not to believe, and implies that there must therefore be an x, which m believes, when it is true that m believes ". . . x . . . ." Minor quantificational prophylaxis might preserve what is intuitive while eliminating what is dubious in this account, but there are subtler arguments and less compromising ontologies than those traditionally proposed in response to the Socratic demand. Israel Scheffler [4] thus generates a relational theory of belief from three philosophical theories, each of which, though contestable, possesses an undeniable philosophical power. (1) The Nomological-Deductive Theory of Explanation, which requires of every valid explanation at least one general law in its premises. (2) The Want-Belief Model of Explanation for human actions, according to which we explain a man doing a with reference to his wanting b and believing that a is a means to b. But then by (1) there must be a general law (roughly) to the effect that, whenever men want x and believe that y is a means to x, then they do y. But (3) by a Principle of Ontological Commitment, we are committed to the existence of objects of belief if we must quantify over objects of belief, since the existence of whatever is a value of a variable that we are constrained to bind is something *we* must then countenance. Obviously there *is* no constraint if (1)–(3) can be gotten round, but Scheffler has arguments which are not to be dismissed lightly, and he has, moreover, some genial candidates for objects of belief, namely *inscriptions*. Inscriptions are homely objects to be found the time-space world over—easy, furthermore, to furnish samples of, so all we need now is to analyze belief as a relationship between a person and an inscription.

Scheffler's theory is vulnerable chiefly through its extreme artificiality, and though naturalness is not an overriding criterion for accepting or rejecting philosophical theories, if we can find a natural theory of belief which is not conspicuously incompatible with (1)–(3), then we may regard ourselves as having outflanked Scheffler's position and hence the obligation to deal with it directly. Moreover, the relational conclusion is, setting aside the problems of inscriptions, inconsistent with aspects of the psychology of the concept of belief.

There are various psychological accounts of belief, ranging from the view that belief is something (purely) internal—a modification of a *res cogitans*, an imprint upon a *tabula rasa*, a certain (unanalyzable) feeling accompanying certain impressions—to the view that beliefs are dispositions to behave, habitual patterns of behavior, and the like. In large measure, we are going to have a different analysis of belief as we move to a different view of the mind-body problem, with various shades and compromises exactly reflecting the shades and compromises on the latter question. Yet it is common epistemological ground throughout this range of positions that, in order to ascribe a belief to m, it is sufficient to make observations upon m alone, and that, if there should be an uncertainty attaching to any such ascription, this will at least *not* be due to the fact that there is something *other* than *m* upon which we ought to be making observations. Thus, if a belief is a mental trait, observable solely to *m*'s infallible reflective introspection, then *m* and *m* alone can say with certainty what he believes and that he believes it. Or if belief is a habitual pattern of behavior (and dispositions are not hidden springs which cause tendencies, but tendencies as such), so that *m* is in no specially privileged, and perhaps even in a disadvantaged position, and must, as you and I, read his beliefs off the surface of his behavior, there remains *m* alone upon whom observation must be made in order to certify ascriptions. Of course it will be in response to various items of the *environment* that *m*'s beliefs will be activated, but none of these can be regarded in general as *objects* of belief in the sense required by the relational theory, for we still would have to account for false and semantically vagrant beliefs, and the objects of belief would have to exist invariantly as to the truth or falsity of the belief. In order that there should be things, external to *m*, which activate beliefs, his relation to the object of belief would *not* be his relation(s) to *these* objects, and in the relevant respect, there remains *m* alone upon whom observations are to be made. If there *are* objects of belief, however, then we must observe something other than *m*: we must observe the objects and determine whether the relation is satisfied in any given instance. And this is incompatible with (perhaps) the (one) common ground under the various psychological theories of belief. These theories *as a class* reinforce the view that it is solely facts regarding *m* which are relevant in ascribing beliefs to individuals. Compatability, then, with the entire class of psychological theories regarding beliefs represents some evidence in favor of a nonrelational theory, inasmuch as relational theories are incompatible with them as a class; so we have here a notion which captures another intuitive sector of our antecedent beliefs about beliefs.

IV

The fact that we can use terms which the believer would be prohibited through linguistic ignorance from using, while at the same time we are severely restricted in descriptions he might have had the linguistic equipment for understanding but lacked the requisite knowledge to apply, suggests that we have liberty of interchange for synonymous terms (expressions) in sentential predicates though not for nonsynonymous but coreferential ones. This, however, is hasty. As we shall see, there are restrictions upon intra- and inter-linguistic interchanges of synonyms which are quite instructive.

Let us now recall our *Sinn-Bedeutung* distinctions, and turn from referential matters (*Bedeutungsfrage*) to matters of meaning (*Sinns-*

frage). Surely, one wishes to say, a term does not suffer modification of *meaning* when shifted into predicative position, even though it is referentially emasculated. And surely, again, reference to one side, interchange of synonymous expressions, must leave unaffected the truth-value of the context. But it is not by any means clear that we have license even of synonymy interchange in sentential predicates. Let us suppose that "is a widow" means "has survived a legal husband" and let *m* believe, in consequence of a series of jolly adventures with women ostensively identified as widows, that widows are merry women. It plainly is not automatically true that *m* believes that women having survived their legal husbands are merry, and indeed he may not believe this at all, having had a series of dismal encounters with women ostensively identified as having survived their legal husbands. This *could* be taken as evidence that the expressions are not synonymous. But why then not have said on similar grounds that the pair of terms in our earlier example are not coreferential after all? Such strategies are, at any rate, dangerous. It is always possible to find contexts in which interchange of synonymous expressions will alter truth-values without our wishing to say, because of this, that they are after all not synonyms. Consider, thus, quotations. If *m* says ". . . *t* . . ." then it is false that *m* says ". . . *t'* . . . ." Yet one would hardly wish to argue that *t* and *t'* must therefore *not* be synonyms. An incapacity to sustain truth-values by interchanging terms in quotational contexts leaves undetermined the synonym-status of these terms, and we don't want to let the existence of quotational contexts serve to subvert the possibility of establishing synonymy. We must therefore, at least decide whether contexts formed by sentential predicates are like quotational contexts or not; and, if not, then why interchange of synonymy breaks down. Whatever the case, sentential predicates appear not only referentially opaque, but meaning-opaque as well; yet it is difficult to suppose that we can explain this latter opacity as we explained the former. The former, it seemed plausible to think, would be due to the fact that being relocated in a predicate would render a term a-referential; a term would not become a-meaningful in consequence of such transportation, and the plausible assumption would be that it would retain its meaning, and so its synonymy kinships, in and out of sentential predicates.

Of course there are some prophylactic strategies available. One is that terms embedded in sentences which are, in turn, embedded in sentential predicates, do not occur there in a sufficiently loose state to make interchange possible. Suppose *m* believes that widows are merry. Then we will be predicating ". . . believes-that-widows-are-merry" of *m*. Here the hyphens are punctuational reminders that the terms have been melted down, so to speak, to form simple, seamless lexical units, which must be taken as wholes; and the erstwhile words are reconstituted virtually as syllables; but we have no license for the interchange of syllables, much less for speaking of synonyms for syllables, and the only substitution licit would be with the sentential predicate *as a whole*. If we are at liberty to make predicates out of names, we need hardly balk at transforming words into syllables.

This strategy is nevertheless intuitively artificial, and I shall endeavor now to explain the source of what I feel as philosophical queasiness in connection with it. Typically and in principle, the meaning of a term is independent of its reference much (or just) in the same way in which the meaning of a sentence is independent of its truth-value. We may, in principle, understand a term, just as we may understand a sentence, independently of any consideration of *knowledge*, i.e., independently of the establishment of any epistemic relation between ourselves and the referendum of a term, or between ourselves and whatever conditions, external to a sentence, confer upon it a truth-value. I shall not argue this claim here but merely advance it,[5] acknowledging that there are problems, at one end, with terms the meaning of which it is sometimes said we cannot get unless we have experienced instances to which they apply and, at the other end, with sentences, the meaning of which is said to determine which truth-value they are to bear. In the general case, I should argue, *Sinn* is logically independent of *Bedeutung*, or, in other terms, *Bedeutung* varies in independence of *Sinn*. But it is implausible to suppose that *Sinn* may vary in this way. A term retains its meaning in and out of quotational contexts, and so, one would believe, does it retain its meaning in and out of predicative contexts. We *understand* it invariantly as to contexts of these sorts and, in view of this, altering its status from a term *simpliciter* to an ersatz syllable in a hyphenated neologism, appears to leave meaning and understanding unaltered.

In addition to this, the strategy raises serious linguistic problems. For we must now be accorded the same generative powers for *terms* as we possess for sentences, and a definitive dictionary becomes impossible in principle: it would be like asking for a finite *phrasikon* of all the sentences in a language. Doubtless we *do* have the ability to generate infinite terms, viz., by means of subscripts and the like; but these will not be spontaneously intelligible to speakers of the language, as are the infinite sentences we may generate. Furthermore, *these* terms are not somehow invented: they seem accessible to exactly those mechanisms of understanding which enable hearers to take in and comprehend sentences never before encountered. Well, we could continue to regard the terms

as terms and merely rule that interchange between them and their synonyms will not be allowed. But this is philosophically unsatisfactory. Is
it merely a *rule* that we will not allow interchange of synonyms in quotational contexts? We want some sort of an *explanation*.

V

When a man says or writes something, he produces what I shall un-
ingratiatingly call a *wordthing*. Sentences, for example, are wordthings,
made of ink or of soundwaves. A quotation of a wordthing is, as it were,
a picture of it, standing to it in a replicative rather than a descriptive relationship; so a quotation says nothing about the wordthing it replicates,
though the fact that a given wordthing should be quoted at all says
something obliquely about it: not just everyone gets his portrait
painted. The reason, then, that we have no liberty of substitution in
quotational contexts is that, if we replace a portion of it with a synonymous portion, it may retain its meaning, but it collapses as a replication.
It is a misquotation at best, and at worst a bit of editorializing on the
part of the quoter, whose business it is to show what a man said without
comment. The license we have with wordthings, then, extends only to
replacement of portions with other portions which may, by conventions
of portraiture, stand in the same replicative relation to the original as
the replaced part, *viz.*, if we replace cursive with uncial.

The ethics of quotation have a certain direct interest. The wordthings produced by a man are *his* property and *his* responsibility. When
I quote, I take responsibility only for replicative accuracy: so I am not
to be attacked for quoting *m*'s words to *n*: "*n* is a swine"—for it is not
me who says it. Neither am I to be praised for some especially striking
sentence which I quote, and if I do not make it plain that I am quoting
and not saying, I have stolen another man's words, pretending they are
my own. This is in general a self-confession of internal inadequacy: I
should *like* to have produced the wordthing, but was not capable of it,
so in pretending the words are *mine*, I in effect masquerade as a different person than I am.

Of course it is difficult sometimes to tell whether a given wordthing
is original or replication, inasmuch as the replication of a wordthing is
often an exact copy of its original, and the two are, just as wordthings,
indiscernable. Similarly it is difficult (or can be) to tell whether a given
paint-thing is a copy of a paint-thing—a copy of a Poussin, say—or is an
original artistic statement by Poussin himself: a difficulty compounded
when Poussin is his own copyist (and, like Socrates we all quote ourselves on occasion). A paint-thing will belong in a quite different history, and require to be judged by vastly different criteria, depending

upon whether it is an original artistic statement or the exact copy of one; and quite distinct talents are called for in either case (imagine Jackson Pollack having to *copy* one of his things). Some men may be able to paint anything already painted, but have no capacity for original artistic statement. The same holds true with words: a man might have phenomenal ability to recover the words of others, and have nothing to say himself.

Consider now the wordthing *s*—a sentence originated by *m*. As a wordthing, *s* is a part of the world, as much so as a stone, and like the replication of a stone, the quotation of *s* will picture one of the world's minor components. Let now S as it occurs in "S" replicate *s*, i.e., share parity of structure with *s* conformably with the conventions of word-portraiture. Merely taken as a wordthing, *s*, no more than a stone, is true or false. Neither, of course, is S in "S" true or false, quotations never being true or false, only accurate or inaccurate. They cannot be true or false primarily because nothing is *said* with them. Let us now suppose that *s* is true—that is, that it satisfies a truth-relation with another part of the world, say o. There is no reason why o should not be another wordthing, e.g., an English sentence. Since *s* is true, we shall suppose that *s* says "o is an English sentence." But this will be replicated by S in "S" which has the shape "o is an English sentence." But while *s* is made true by o, "S" is not: "S" is semantically neutral, saying nothing but only showing *s*.

Typically, of course, o will *not* be a wordthing, for we do not commonly speak about the components of the world which are made of words. My concern has only been to stress the different sorts of relationships which hold between *s* and o, and between "S" and *s*. It is a difference which has some collateral interest for the philosophy of language. There are famous episodes in the history of that subject wherein an ideal language was considered ideal through the manner of its relationship to the world. It was to *show the world forth*, standing to it in the relation in which "S" stands to *s*. In order for it to succeed, there had to be supposed an isomorphism between language and the world, a parity of structure which virtually demanded that the world not merely contain but that it consist of wordthings; for wordthings replicate but wordthings and so are indiscernible from one another as the accuracy of the one approaches optimality. The world, therefore, which is made of facts, could as readily be taken as a picture of its language. The ideal language truly *says* nothing: it only *shows:* so in satisfying the one relation—the relation of "S" to *s*—it is precluded from satisfying the other—that of *s* to o—just because it *does* not say. The ideal language is curiously mute, a mere reflection for the accuracy of which we check against the world.

And presumably the world itself is mute: for there is nothing other than it about which it could talk, and there are deep Tarskian reasons why it cannot talk about itself.

The same wordthing can be used to say or to show; but in showing it does not say, and in saying it does not (except incidentally and irrelevantly) show. A Correspondence Theory of Truth does not require (if anything it requires that there not be) a replicative relationship between language and the world. In some special circumstance, perhaps, a sentence can show what it wants to say something about, but showing accurately and saying truly would be different relations only freakishly satisfied by the same sentence. And in general a sentence may be true quite independently of whether it shows whatever makes it true. Our concern, however, lies with the topic of belief from which we may appear to have wandered. So let us return.

VI

It is beyond controversy that the world contains wordthings—bits of itself in sentential shape, for example. Why should it be implausible to suppose that, as bits of the world ourself, we should not be constituted, in part, of wordthings? Let me recklessly speak now of men as being in certain *sentential states*. We shall obviously wish to distinguish being in sentential states from such extrinsic happenstances as bearing tattoos or startling birthmarks: I shall think of sentential states as *internal* to men: but the time for precision here is not yet. I shall now suppose that in predicating "believes-that-s" of m, we are asserting that m is in a sentential state. The sentence s, embedded in the predicate, serves to individuate the sentential state ascribed to m by being, literally, a picture or quotation of that state. We now may say that "m believes that s" is true only if, m is in a sentential state o, and s replicates o. Since s functions quotationally, *showing* the sentential state in question, this would explain the opacity of belief-contexts not only with regard to reference but with regard to meaning as well. For quotations may do neither more nor less than to replicate the wordthings they mean to quote. Thus ". . . said 's'" is true of m if, and only if "s" replicates what m said. There are certain problems with *oratio obliqua*, perhaps, but the sole liberties which may be taken with this form of quotation are grammatical—matters affecting the inflections of nouns (so far as the language permits a distinction between nominal and accusative cases) and moods of verbs, and the like.

It may at this point be asked whether it is any more felicitous to postulate sentential states than merely to rule out substitutions of coreferential and synonymous expressions in belief-contexts. My reply is that these opacities are genuine discoveries, and that sentential states would at least provide an explanation of the facts which they reveal. Let me now marshall some further support for the theory in which sentential states function as quondam theoretical entities.

(A) Let o be a sentential state of m, and let s replicate o. Let t be a term in s and t' a synonym for t. By replacing t in s with t' we get the sentence s', which we may henceforward regard as a sentence synonymous with s. Still, it would be false that m said that s' when he said that s, for s' fails to replicate his words; but so would it be false that s' replicates the sentential state o in case s replicates *that* state. Still, the question remains as to whether the falsehood of m believes that s' is entailed by this fact, and the answer to this is No: neither the truth nor the falsehood of this is entailed by the truth or falsehood of m *believes* that s. The reason for this is plain. It simply does not follow from the fact that, if a man is in one sentential state, he must be in another, any more than it follows from the fact that a man says one sentence that he must say another. This is so even if the states (and sentences) in question are replicated by synonymous sentences. A man believes that s, so he may or he may not believe that s'. In our previous example, m will believe that wives with one dead husband are merry, given that he believes that widows are merry, providing that (at least) he (a) knows that the terms are synonymous and (b) has applied this knowledge in the present instance. There is, however, no need that he should ever have connected the two. It is, then, physically possible that he should at once believe that s and disbelieve that s', even where there is a rule of language in which s and not s' is inconsistent, and even when the man in question knows the rule of language. Granted, he ought, knowing that rule, to believe that s' if he believes that s; but the theory of sentential states gives a natural explanation of why he need not: for the sentential states which s and s' replicate would be distinct sentential states of m.

(B) Similar considerations apply when we replace a term t in a replica of some sentential state with another term, coreferential but nonsynonymous with it. It is usually just a matter of fact that a pair of terms should be coreferential, e.g., that Lady Murasaki should be the author of *Genji Monogatori*. It is possible to know that person without knowing *who* she is, and it is a fact that many who knew Lady Murasaki did not believe that she was the author of *Genji*. It is natural, because of certain natural facts about knowledge, that we should have opacity in replicae of sentential states, it being a natural fact regarding knowledge, that even though one knows something under one description, one need not and perhaps *cannot* know it under another description, viz., one could not be in a certain sentential state, given the causal conditions under which one is another.

(C) In our casual remarks on the ethics of quotation, the suggestion emerged that there is an intimate connection between a man and his words. We can quote his words, but in so doing, our relation to those words is thoroughly external. They no more are *our* words than they would be the words of a recording tape which plays them back. Yet we can steal the words in the sense of pretending them to be ours, and, insofar as there is the intimate connection between a person and *his* words, we are, as I suggested, in effect pretending to be a different person than we are.

In addition to stating a fact, i.e., in addition to being true, words may *express* a fact about the person who says them, and indeed, they may express *this fact* whether they are true or false. Suppose I know that Lady Murasaki wrote *Genji,* and say as much. Then I give *you* a fact about Oriental literature, and you have a right henceforward to assert it as something which you know—another exotic fact. The fact itself does not express a trait of either of our personalities, but that I should have this knowledge *might* express a trait of mine. Thus my having this knowledge could be due to a passionate interest in Oriental literature. *This* I do not transfer to you along with the knowledge which I do transfer; for it may be a dominating internal trait of mine that I am involved with this literature, whereas with you the knowledge is only an external ornament. You could, of course, pretend that the knowledge here expresses an internal trait of yours, but all that is expressed here is the internal trait of wanting to be like me.

Knowledge itself is transitive. I cannot speak of *my* knowledge in the way in which I speak of *my* beliefs. Can I now transfer my beliefs the way I transfer my knowledge? I transfer knowledge easily, since *s* is detachable from *m* knows that *s;* but *s* is *not* detachable from *m* believes that *s.* When I know that *m* knows that *s,* then *I* know that *s;* but if I know that *m* believes that *s,* I only might believe that *s.* When I transfer my knowledge, I teach; but when I transfer my beliefs, I indoctrinate. To transfer my beliefs is to transform the persons to whom I transfer them, into my own image: for when they acquire a new belief, they acquire a new sentential state, and when thenafter they *state* that *s,* they are expressing an internal trait of themselves, whether what they state is true or false.

(D) That a man's statements of belief, when sincere, express traits of himself which it is natural to regard as sentential states, may be underscored by the slight degree of control we often have regarding what we are to believe. Under inquisitorial pressure, I can pretend that certain beliefs are mine, but the beliefs I avow notoriously can remain hopelessly external. I may *want very badly* to believe them. I may pray in the hope that the sentences I want to believe should become part of me, and so internal. Should this happen, and it is commonly regarded an exercise of grace when it does, then in a very profound sense the person to whom it happens is changed and, in his own eyes, reborn. It is not clear that by a mere act of will, we can make a certain belief *ours*. When, as Al Ghazali marvelously put it, "the glass of [one's] naive beliefs is broken," then:

This is a breakage which cannot be mended, a breakage not to be repaired by patching or by assembling of fragments. The glass must be melted once again in the furnace for a new start, and out of it another fresh vessel formed.[6]

We may find more domestic examples of this. Consider any sentential predicate ". . . believes-that-*s*" which is not true of you, e.g., ". . . believes-that-babies-are-brought-by-storks." I think I understand how someone may believe this, and I think I understand well enough to believe false the sentence embedded in the predicate. What I cannot do is achieve an *internal* understanding of what it is to instantiate the predicate myself, what it *would be like to hold* this belief.[7] I cannot imagine, even, what it is like, for in imagining myself to hold this belief, I at the same time know that the belief is not mine, and there is always a distance intervening, as it were, between the belief and me. This distance is never a part of the person who holds the belief. The only way to know what it is like to hold this belief is in fact to hold this belief naively, and the conditions which are presupposed for successful imagining rule out imaginative success. No: a new vessel would have to be formed: I should have to be a different person from what I am in order for this belief to be mine.

(E) It may be an interesting fact regarding *m* that *m* believes eccentrically that storks bring babies: but *m* does not take this to be an eccentric autobiographical fact but rather an uneccentric fact about the *world*. He does not refer his beliefs to himself but to the world, and in effect, to change one's beliefs is to change ones *world*. The world will have to be different for one who believes that storks bring babies than for one who holds the ordinary generative-obstetrical beliefs: A belief is not an isolated thing, but functions in a system, and to change a belief is to change a system, and one's system of beliefs defines one's *world*.

This would have a natural explanation if beliefs were sentential states; for sentential states are, since replaceable with sentences, to be regarded as sentences themselves, and sentences are *representations*. Obviously, "representation of *x*" is an absolute property of a sentence, it is the meaning of a sentence, not a relation *between* a sentence and *x*. A sentential state is thus not merely (say) a grammatical ornamentation on the ghostly flanks of a *res cogitans*. Sentences mean to be about the world, and *my* world is defined by my representations of the world, whether these be true or false. It is for this reason that to change a belief is to change one's world. And it may be for this reason that one cannot by, a mere act of will, change one's beliefs: for since they are referred to the world, it is presumptuous of me to suppose that by an act of will I can modify the world. If a belief is held, it is because he who holds it believes it to be true. This may perdure, even when he knows it to be false, a fact which may be explained in terms of the difficulty of erasure once one's soul has been scored with what later proves to have been a semantically vagrant sentential state.

VII

Israel Scheffler regards the relata of individuals who stand in the belief-relation as believers, to be inscriptions. Inscriptions are interesting entities, perhaps, but philosophically unexceptionable ones, being in space and time, and easily generated as *graffiti*. It is this metaphysical responsibility which is especially appealing about Scheffler's position, and one might say that, after all, sentential states are *exactly* inscriptions. The same inscriptions, therefore, which Scheffler ingeniously suggests, will serve their role in virtue of being replicae of sentential states—portraits, as it were, of the relata of believers, *showing* what *saying* that they believe *describes*. Thus far, then, postulating sentential states removes a measure of artificiality from Scheffler's account by means of a proto-scientific strategy which Scheffler must consider congenial. This being so, it may be wondered why we ought any longer to insist upon the absolute predicative status of ". . . believes-that-*s*?" Why not now regard the decision as between a relational and a nonrelational analysis of belief to be a matter of no special philosophical moment?—For if the sentential state is the relatum of believers, who are so called because the relation is satisfied, then this relation holds independently of the semantical value borne by the sentential state (read: inscription). There can thus be none of the sorts of objections there were before to "objects of belief."

This objection cuts deeper, I think, than it intends, for it touches the quick of *categorial grammar*. Consider any sentenial value of F, viz., "*a* is yellow." Here we could be talking about a relationship between a particular - *a* - and the color yellow, considered as an entity, the universe containing *a* and *yellow*, at perhaps different levels, with the copulative "is" standing for a complicated participatory relationship between them.

We then would have a general license for recasting anything which now stands as an absolute predication as a relational one, the decision turning only upon extra-grammatical and perhaps extra-logical considerations of what sorts of entities we were prepared to budget for in our ontologies. This is not a matter I can go deeply into here, except to remark that since the entities involved would be of different "levels," so the relations between them would then be intertypical, and so themselves relations of a different sort than the intratypical relations which hold amongst entities of one level. And so bit by bit we should find reinstated all the old distinctions, and the gain in making entities out of properties would have to be paid for elsewhere, as though there were some principle of the Conservation of Distinctions operative over philosophical revisions. But again I press past this fascinating suggestion to what is immediately of relevance here.

The yellowness of *a* is, in some not easily formulated sense, sufficiently an internal character of *a* that we would want to say that *a* were different, that *a* itself were changed, should *a* lose its yellowness (it being interesting to reflect that yellowness would not change were it to lose *a*). But relations are external. If *a* is next to *b*, there is no internal change in *a*, if *c* is inserted between it and *b*. The *world* will have changed, for a relation will have collapsed, but the terms of the relation are what they are in and out of the relation. I have proposed that a man's beliefs are in something like this sense internal to him, in that when he changes his beliefs, *he* changes; so, unless the relationship in which it is proposed that believing is to consist may be counted an internal relationship, penetrating its terms or at least one of its terms, I should want to persist in regarding believes-that-*s* as an absolute trait of *m* when "*m* believes that *s*" is true. It is a trait which depends upon no other thing than *m* himself, who provides, as it were, all the truth-conditions required by the sentence; for as was momentously recognized in the first great pages of modern philosophy, our beliefs might be just as they are, representing the world just as they do, whether or not there *exists* a world for them to represent truly or falsely. I might, therefore, be just the person I am, with just the beliefs I have, though nothing besides me existed.

I am not concerned with the epistemological agonies felt to be engendered by this latter consideration, using it only as a mechanism here to underscore: if those agonies are possible, beliefs have to be internal properties of individuals, considered one at a time. To say that is, perhaps, not to say much, and for the reason that I am convinced of a fundamental difference between persons and things, I am convinced that I possess (or am possessed by) my sentential states in a different way than that in which a thing possesses (or is possessed by) its properties. After all, one might say that a piece of paper or of recording gear, or a tattooed skin or—to use a more traditional example—a wax tablet may bear inscriptions and so be regarded as in sentential states. But they are so in a manner too external to capture the intimacy I wish to suggest. Perhaps, however, bearing inscriptions or imprintments in these cases *is* an external relationship between media and inscriptions. A tape is restored to itself, retaining its integrity minus an irrelevant measure of wear and tear when its messages are erased; so perhaps what I wish to say is that *I am my sentential states,* that (perhaps) I contain them not as a book contains sentences but as a *story* does: the story is made of its sentences, whereas the book is only inscribed with the sentences of the story which it houses.

I am made of sentential states, but not wholly made of them; for then I should be but a set of inscriptions. Rather, I think, believing involves *assenting* to a representation of the world, and assenting to *s* involves something more than a linear juxtaposition of *s* and Yes. The connection, rather, is like the Fregean notion which serves to assert the sentence it operates upon. The assertion of *s* consists, then, not in *s* alone, but rather in an *action with s;* and so, I suggest, a belief is a kind of action with *s.* The connection between an action and what the action is done *with* is at once philosophically crucial and philosophically complicated, and while I have ideas regarding its analysis, I shall make no effort in this paper to further them. A sentence is part of me as my arm is part of me, namely, when I am able to perform an action with them. There is no lifting of an arm without an arm, as there is no assenting to a sentence without a sentence. And it is the latter, perhaps, which is all that is required to capture and domesticate the Socratic claim that when I believe, I must believe something. There are no *pure* beliefs, no sententially unqualified beliefs.

VIII

I have introduced sentential states in order to offer a natural explanation of those perturbations in the orderly processes of Leibnizian substitution which the discovery of opaque contexts has brought to our attention. A *natural* explanation is in order since the perturbations are due to certain natural facts regarding beliefs as such: and we verge here thus upon science. I have no special view as to what, scientifically, sentential states may be, viz., informational charges on protein molecules, or neural loops, or whatever. But I would like to suggest a few of the philosophical implications of what is essentially a scientific theory.

First, the intentionalities which philosophers have taken as definatory of "the mental" are in fact due not to something intractably psychic, but to the pictorial semantics of quotation: we *show* what a man's belief is. Thus *s* individuates what a man's belief is when ". . . believes that *s*." is true of him. This uniquely individuating device is crucial for at least the following reason: we have no license for saying that *m* believes that *s'*, given that he believes that *s* and *s'* is a logical consequence of *s*. We only have license for saying that he *ought*, under these conditions, to believe that *s'*. Inasmuch as there is room for this doxastic discrepancy, unique individuation of beliefs taken one at a time is all we are entitled to give.

Second, *what* we show with a sentence is a sentence; and this yields a classical theory of the mind-as-representation. Thus we owe to our masters the theory that the mind is characterized by *ideas*, which are what they are, and mean what they mean, whether true or false—and if ideas may be true or false, as well as *"modes ou façons de ma pensée"*, as Descartes puts it, then ideas will be but forerunners to the theory of sentential states. Indeed, Descartes himself at times used language as a model for characterizing ideas, as well as their relation to the world when true: [8] a true idea, he often says, need no more resemble what *makes* it true than a true *sentence* need resemble that which satisfies its truth-conditions. What is less like the white snow than "The snow is white?"

Finally, if our essence is language, as I believe it to be—word made flesh—then the celebrated Identity Theory may receive a curious, disappointing confirmation. There is little doubt that the sentences we speak and write are made of matter, and if they are, why should not the sentence we are made of be themselves made of matter—of protein, say? This would be a fact about such sentences, but conspicuously it would not be the most important fact about them. But this diverts us to questions beyond my immediate horizons, and I leave the issues until a later time.

NOTES

1. "As philosophers, we may be surprised to observe that it *can* be that the knowledge that *p* is true differs from the belief that *p* is true *only* in the respect that in the one case *p* is true and in the other false. But that is the fact." Norman Malcolm, "Knowledge and Belief," *Mind*, LXI, 242 (1952). Reprinted in his *Knowledge and Certainty* (Englewood Cliffs, New Jersey, Prentice-Hall, 1963). See p. 60. Malcolm speaks of knowledge "in the weak sense," but that is the only sense that matters anyway.

2. The suggestion comes directly from Quine: "This means viewing 'Tom believes [Cicero denounced Catiline]' no longer as of the form 'FaG' with $a =$ Tom and $G =$ [Cicero denounced Catiline], but rather as of the form 'Fa' with $a =$ Tom and complex F. The verb 'believes' here ceases to be a term and becomes part of an operator 'believes that,' or 'believes [   ],' which, applied to a sentence, produces a composite absolute general term whereof the sentence is counted an immediate constituent." Willard V. O. Quine, *Word and Object* (The Technology Press of M.I.T. and John Wiley, 1960), p. 216.

3. See also the discussion in *The Republic*, 477–478.

4. Israel Scheffler, *The Anatomy of Inquiry* (New York, Knopf, 1963), 88–110.

5. I argue it, however, in *Analytical Philosophy of Knowledge* (Cambridge; Cambridge University Press, 1968).

6. Al Ghazali, "Deliverance from Error and Attachment to the Lord of Might and Majesty," from W. M. Watts (trans.), *The Faith and Practice of Al-Ghazali* (London: Allen & Unwyn, 1953), p. 27.

7. This is elaborated in my "Historical Understanding: the Problem of Other Periods," *Journal of Philosophy*, LXIII, 19 (1966), 566–577.

8. See Robert C. Taliaferro, *The Concept of Matter in Descartes and Leibniz* (Notre Dame, Indiana; University of Notre Dame Press, 1964), p. 1. Descartes says, of *"les signes et les paroles"* that they *"ne ressemblent en aucune façon aux choses qu'elles signifient."*, in *Dioptrique*, IV. A comparable point is in Leibniz's *Nouveaux essais sur l'entendement humaine*, Bk. II, ch. 30.

ON DANTO'S "BELIEF AS A SENTENTIAL STATE OF PERSONS"

(A RESPONSE)

Gertrude Ezorsky

Danto argues against the view that "*m* believes *s*" expresses a relation of any sort. As he sees the matter, "believes *s*" is a sentential state of *m*, a one place predicate, absolutely true of *m*, when *m* believes *s* is true. This sentential state is "exactly an inscription," a philosophically unexceptionable entity, in space and time, "made of ink and sound waves." I am not convinced by his arguments against the relational view of belief. Moreover, I find his own view difficult to grasp.

Danto's Criticism of Malcolm

Danto reports: "Some writers (e.g. Malcolm) have taken the difference between '*m* knows *s*' (*m*K*s*) and '*m* believes *s*' (*m*B*s*) to be solely a difference in the truth value of s. Since '*m* knows *s*' entails that *s* is true, on Malcolm's analysis, *it now has to follow '*m* believes *s*' that s is false.*" (Italics added) Against this Danto argues that "We ought to leave room for true as well as false beliefs." Malcolm thinks, according to Danto, that if *m* believes *s*, *s* must be false. Did Malcolm or anyone else, ever make such a wild claim? Consider for a moment just what the claim implies. If someone in the 14th century, believed the earth is round, it follows that the earth is *not* round. Did Malcolm ever really express such a view? Danto quotes Malcolm as saying: "It *can* be that the knowledge that P is true differs from the belief that P is true only in the respect that in the one case P is true and in the other P is false." (Italics in original.)

Notice Malcolm emphasized that knowledge that *p*, *can* differ from belief that *p*, in that when *m* believes that *p*, *p* is false. Danto mistakenly reads "*can*" as "*must*." Hence he claims that for Malcolm "it had to follow from *m* believes *s*, that *s* is false." But this is plainly not Malcolm's position. Indeed, in the essay Danto quotes, Malcolm describes a case where *m* believes *p* and *p* is true. "You say 'I believe that it [the gorge] won't be dry although I have no particular reason for thinking so.' If we went to the gorge and found a flowing stream we should not say that you knew that there would be water but that *you thought so and were right*" [1] (Last emphasis added.)

Danto's Criticism of Belief Objects

Danto holds (mildly) that philosophers who take inscriptions to be belief objects are wrong; but those ontologists who accept abstract entities (propositions, etc.), are committed to "ontological monstrosities." He suggests that all of his objections to these ontologists arise because for them the truth of *m* believes *p*, (satisfaction of the belief relation between *m* and a proposition) depends on the truth value of *p*. Thus Danto claims that if an inscription ". . . is the relatum of believers, who are so called because the relation (of belief) is satisfied . . . then this relation . . . holds independently of the semantic value (truth value) borne by the . . . inscription. So there can be none of the sorts of objections there were before to (non-inscriptional) objects of belief." Thus, Danto reports, he objected to philosophers who accept noninscriptional, abstract belief objects, because, according to these philosophers, satisfaction of "*m* believes *p*" depends on the truth value of *p*. But on which truth value of *p* is "*m* believes *p*" supposed to depend, according to these philosophers? On *p*'s being false? In that case true beliefs are logically impossible. (The satisfaction of *m* believes *p* demands that *p* be false.) On *p*'s being true? In that case false beliefs are logically impossible. (The satisfaction of *m* believes *p* demands that *p* be true.) Has any philosopher ever maintained either of these views (when sober)? Danto suggests, but does not show, that they have. On the other hand he also implies they have not. In another passage he describes these abstract belief objects as "semantically neutral." "The demand that belief be relational together with the collateral demand that belief sentences be semantically neutral, forces us to furnish semantically neutral *objects* of belief, e.g., intensions, essences, propositions, abstract actualities . . . and comparable ontological monstrosities . . . They are . . . there whatever the semantical vagaries of the beliefs that take them as objects."

Notice that here Danto finds that according to philosophers committed to abstract belief objects, these objects are semantically neutral. In that case the satisfaction of "*m* believes *p*" must be independent of the truth value of *p*. But as we have just seen, Danto also suggests that for philosophers who accept abstract belief objects, "*m* believes *p*" is *not* independent of truth value of *p*. Indeed he confessed that all his objections to these "ontological monstrosities" arise because their acceptance spells doom to the independence of *m believes p* from the truth value of *p*. Since as he now reports, this necessary independence really does obtain, he should have no objections to abstract objects of belief.

Danto's Quotational Notion of Belief

Danto construes "believes that s" as a nonrelational, one-place predicate true absolutely of *m* when "*m* believes that *s*" is true. He claims that in "believes that *s*" *s* functions quotationally and the sentence *s* embedded in the predicate, serves to individuate the sentential state ascribed to *m* by being literally a picture or a quotation of that (sentential state) state. It is a word thing, "made of ink and sound waves," a bit of the world in sentential shape. Let us ignore for the moment the problem of whether "believes that *s*" is a one or two place predicate, and consider whether *s* in "*m* believes *s*" should be construed quotationally.

The fact is that Danto nowhere considers a familiar argument against the quotational treatment of belief sentences. If belief sentences do function quotationally, how is one supposed to translate a belief sentence into another language? An analogy may make this difficulty clear. Consider (1) "The English sentence 'It is raining' is a grammatical sentence." The constituent sentence of (1) " 'It is raining' " must in any translation of (1) appear in its original English form, since it is the quoted English sentence which is referred to in (1). Consider now the sentence "I believe that John is a scoundrel." First, if belief sentences should be treated quotationally, then "I believe John is a scoundrel," should strictly be rendered as "I believe 'John is a scoundrel' (in English)" (It is possible, after all, that "John is a scoundrel" has a different meaning in some languages.) Secondly, suppose someone were translating my remark "I believe John is a scoundrel." He must not translate the constituent sentence " 'John is a scoundrel' " into another language. The constituent sentence must, if it is treated quotationally, appear in its original, undisturbed English. This means that it should be impossible for a translator to communicate my beliefs to anyone who doesn't know English. But translators perform this "impossible" task all the time.

This argument taken from the practice of translators is by now a familiar objection to the quotational treatment of belief sentences. Danto's failure to consider this objection creates a lacuna in his own argument.

"Believes s" As a One-Place Predicate

Danto thinks that "believe s" is a nonrelational one-place predicate, describing a sentential state of a person. These states "are exactly inscriptions." He finds his one-place inscriptional notion, more natural than a relational view. Why? Here are some of his supporting arguments:

1. *Descartes showed that our beliefs are independent of the external world.*

Danto writes: "For as was momentously recognized in the first great pages of modern philosophy, our beliefs might be just as they are, representing the world just as they do whether or not there exists a world for them to represent truly or falsely. So I might be just the person I am with just the beliefs I have though nothing besides me existed." Thus Danto endorses Descartes position that one's beliefs could be just as they are if nothing else besides oneself and one's beliefs existed. But Descartes, did not, like Danto, think that beliefs are "word things made up of ink and sound waves, . . . and easily generated as grafitti." Indeed, when Descartes claimed that his beliefs could have existed without a world external to them, he meant that his beliefs could have existed independently of just such spatio-temporal objects as ink, sound waves, and grafitti. Hence, if Descartes is right as Danto thinks, then Danto's view that beliefs are such spatio-temporal objects must be wrong. I conclude that what "was momentously recognized in the first great pages of modern philosophy" has been insufficiently examined by Danto.

(2) *Beliefs are usually independent of our control.*

Danto writes "that a man's statement of belief, when sincere, expresses traits of himself which it is natural to regard as sentential states, may be underscored by the slight degree of control we often have regarding what we are to believe." But if, as Danto argues here, one can't usually just create one's beliefs, at will, then a belief isn't the sort of thing he claims it to be—an inscription. After all, one can (if one has a pencil or the like) freely and easily create an inscription. Indeed, as Danto points out, inscriptions are "easily *generated* as grafitti." I should say that this ease of generation underscores the difference between inscription and beliefs.

(3) *The truth of "M believes S" depends on facts about M alone.*

What facts about *m* will show, according to Danto, that *m* has a belief? Remember, Danto construes beliefs as inscriptions, spatio-temporal objects, word things, made up of ink and sound waves as easily generated as grafitti. In that case, one should be able to determine *m*'s beliefs, by a thorough physical examination of his body. Where should one look? At his brain? No. I never knew anyone who had ink on his brain. Where else should one look? Some people do have sentences inscribed on their bodies by tattoo artists. A tattooed inscription, can truly be described as a word thing, a spatio-temporal object, made up, at least, of ink.

But, a belief cannot be a tattooed inscription for a man may not believe what is tattooed on his chest. Two people who share the same belief do not necessarily share the same tattoo and the meaning of "belief" cannot be taught ostensively by pointing to the bared, haired chest of a tattooed sailor.

Since I am unable to imagine anything, except a tattoo, that would fit Danto's notion of belief, I suggest he has not proven his case.

NOTES

1. Malcom, M. "Knowledge and Belief," in *Knowledge and Certainty* (New York, Prentice-Hall, 1963).

BELIEF AND THE EXPRESSION OF BELIEF

Wilfrid Sellars

I

1. The following is as good a characterization of "belief" as any for the purpose of introducing the topics I wish to treat here:

Jones believes that-p = Jones has a settled disposition to think that-p

It would be foolhardy—indeed downright mistaken—to claim that this formula captures "the" meaning of "believes," and even more so to put it by saying that "a belief is a settled disposition to think that something is the case"; for, as with most, if not all, of the words in which philosophers are interested, we are confronted with a cluster of senses which resemble each other in the family way.

2. To say that the senses of cognate expressions bear a family resemblence to one another must not be taken to imply that they present themselves as a family, nor even that they constitute a family. Aristotle seems to have thought that philosophically interesting concepts present themselves to us as families in which, with a little effort, we can discern the fathers, mothers, aunts, uncles, and cousins of various degrees. In some cases something like this may be true. But the matter is rarely so simple, and there is more than a little truth to the idea that the families are "created" by reconstruction (hopefully rational) or regimentation rather than found.[1]

3. If the above account of belief gets us started, it does so by confronting us with the equally problematic concepts of *disposition* and *thinking that*-p. Here are other systems of family resemblances, or of resembling systems of family resemblances. Before stepping into this quicksand, let us take another look at the title of this paper. Since it trips reasonably well off the tongue, the concept of belief and expression must fit reasonably well together, and this fact may limit the degrees of freedom which enable each of them, taken separately, to elude our grasp. It should be good strategy to coordinate our regimentation of the

one with our regimentation of the other. Thus if beliefs are to be construed as dispositions, this strategy would have us seek to relate the sense in which beliefs are "expressed" to the sense in which the disposition of things and persons are manifested by what they do. This suggests the schema

x expresses Jones' belief that-$p = x$ is a manifestation of
Jones' settled disposi-
tion to think that-p

If the right hand side of this formula were clear-cut and unambiguous, substantial progress would have been made. But it isn't; and, in general, to hope that in delineating the relationships of interesting concepts to one another we will come to one which is intrinsically clear and will illuminate all the others, is to look for the philosopher's stone. Our only hope is that some spark may result from rubbing unclarities together.

4. Our first unclarity concerns what it is for a disposition to be "manifested" by something which that which has it does, and how the class of episodes in which a given disposition is manifested is to be determined. If the "disposition" is of the familiar kind to which we refer by such expressions as "an angry disposition" or, perhaps, by such a term as "humility," then it would seem that, depending on circumstances, any of a wide range of episodes could be its manifestation. And, indeed, if we had begun by simply characterizing belief as a disposition, we would be confronted by the fact that depending on circumstances any of a wide range of episodes could count as a manifestation of Jones' belief that-p. But, by saying, more specifically, that belief that-p is a settled disposition to think that-p, we have narrowed things down in an interesting way. For by characterizing our disposition as a disposition to *think* that-p, we have introduced a conceptual tie between the designation of the disposition and the description of the episodes which can be said, at least in a primary sense, to manifest it.

5. If we ask what kind of episodes manifest a disposition to V, the answer must be, in the first instance, episodes of V-ing. We have consequently committed ourselves to the idea that it is episodes of thinking that-p which are, in a primary sense at least, manifestations of Jones' disposition to think that-p, and consequently that it is episodes of thinking that-p which are, in a primary sense, manifestations of Jones' belief that-p. This gives us the schema

x is a primary manifestation of Jones' belief
that-$p \rightarrow x$ is a thinking that-p

6. Now our troubles really begin; for there is a prima facie tension between "being a thinking that-p" and being a "manifestation" of anything. The latter term carries with it the implication of "making some-

thing manifest," i.e. apparent, (roughly) perceptible, observable. But, it would seem, what need be less "manifest" than an episode of thinking that-p?

7. It might be thought that all that is necessary is to replace "manifestation" by a term which lacks this implication. And there are, indeed, such at hand—thus "realization," "actualization." The statements:

> episodes of thinking that-p are *realizations* of the settled
> disposition to think that-p
>
> episodes of thinking that-p are *actualizations* of the settled
> disposition to think that-p

trip easily off the metaphysically trained tongue; but they are ruled out by our strategy, for the concept with which we are concerned is that of the *expression* of a belief, and "expression" clearly belongs in the same box as the "manifestation" to which our initial intuitions were led.

8. The boulder may have slipped, but perhaps it has not rolled to the bottom, so that we can continue with this cycle of the Sisyphean task. To do so is to look for a way of making coherent the idea that episodes of thinking that-p are the primary *expressions* of the belief that-p.

9. To do so within the allotted time however, I must abandon the leisurely dialectic which consults intuition at each stage of the argument, and must draw upon the familiarity of standard philosophical moves. Thus the simplest way of (ostensibly) achieving our goal is to espouse a form of logical behaviorism according to which, in first approximation, "thinking that-p" is, in its most episodic sense, to be equated with "candidly and spontaneously uttering p" [2] where the person, call him Jones, who utters "p" is doing so as one who knows the language to which "p" belongs. I need not remind you of all the troubles which beset this move. Some of them will be taken into account as the argument moves along. But since, in any case, my aim is dialectical, the fact that it suffers from serious inadequacies need not prevent it from playing an essential role in the argument.

10. The phrase "candidly and spontaneously" is intended to sum up an open-ended set of conditions without which the position can't get off the ground. Jones' thinking that-p obviously cannot be a quoting of "p" or saying it on the stage in the course of acting a play. The qualifying phrase also clearly rules out the case where Jones is lying, i.e. using words to deceive. Somewhat less obviously it is intended to imply that Jones is not choosing his words to express his convictions. He is neither lying nor speaking truthfully. In a sense, as we shall see, he is not *using* the words at all.

11. According to the position I wish to sketch, thinking that-p is,

in its *primary episodic* sense, thinking-out-loud that-*p*. The utterance of "*p*" is not directed to an audience. It is not, as such, a social act. Explicit performatives are clearly out of place in utterances which are, in the desired sense, to be thinkings-out-loud. Nor is it appropriate to characterize them in the categories of illocutionary performance—at least those which are other directed,[3] though exactly similar utterances would, in a context of "communication" be appropriately so characterized.

II

12. It is important to realize that the ways in which we classify linguistic expressions are not only bound up with the jobs they do, but with the purposes for which the classification is made. Since these purposes tend, for obvious reasons, to concern the role of language as a means of communication, i.e. as that by which we give information, warn, make statements, predict, describe, etc., we should not be surprised if our ways of classifying expressions which are capable of performing certain basic functions in the *noncommunicative* context of thinking-out-loud are conceptually tied to communication, and, hence, to functions of quite a different order of complexity. One needs only think of the difference between classifying "it is not raining" as the "negation" of "it is raining," and classifying it as the "contradictory" of the latter, and to note the conversational implications of classifying something as a referring expression or as a "characterizing" expression.

13. Thus the ways in which common sense, and not only common sense, classifies linguistic expressions, and the verbs which it uses to describe what people do with them are heavily weighted in the direction of linguistic actions and performances in a context of communication. That it is legitimate to view language in this way is not to be doubted. Indeed, it is philosophically important to be clear about two categories in terms of which the variety of ways in which language functions in inter-personal exchange are to be understood. But there is the danger that exclusive concern with this perspective will obscure those connections between thought and language in which the latter does not function as a means of communication.

14. The point is not that there are failures of communication, e.g. the supposed hearer may be a dummy or a foreigner. It is not even that there are soliloquies, if by this is meant cases of "talking to oneself." It is the more radical point that thinking-out-loud is a form of meaningful speech which doesn't consist in talking *to* anyone at all, even oneself, and hence is not, in any ordinary sense, *talking*.

III

15. But before developing this point let me return to the formula we were considering before this digression on the conversational orientation of the categories in terms of which common sense, linguistics, and many philosophies of language approach linguistic behavior. The formula was

> x is a primary expression of Jones' belief that-p
> $= x$ is a primary manifestation of his settled disposition
>   to think that-p
> $\rightarrow x$ is a thinking that-p

The implications of the term "manifestation" (and, for that matter, of "expression") led us in the direction of a logical behaviorism according to which the relevant sense of "thinking that-p" is "thinking-out-loud that-p." Thus reinterpreted, the formula becomes

> x is a primary expression of Jones' belief that-p
> $= x$ is a primary manifestation of Jones' settled disposition
>   to think-out-loud that-p
> $\rightarrow x$ is a thinking-out-loud that-p.

16. The point of this move was to assimilate the sense in which an episode is a primary *expression* of a belief to the sense in which an episode of, for example, a piece of litmus paper turning red is a *manifestation* of its disposition to turn red.

17. Note, in passing, however, that in the case of the litmus paper we are inclined to expand the characterization of the disposition into

> disposition to turn red, if put in acid

this generates the suspicion that if we are to continue with our strategy, we must similarly expand our analysis of "Jones believes that-p" into

> Jones has a settled disposition to think-out-loud that-p, if . . . . .

If what? There are many pitfalls here, though we can, perhaps, cover them up temporarily with a glib "if the question whether-p arises." Whether or not this is legitimate, however, it immediately confronts us with a more serious difficulty. For it simply isn't the case that if a person believes that-p, he utters "p" let alone thinks-out-loud that-p, whenever the question whether-p arises.

18. When confronted with this fact, we are strongly tempted to abandon our strategy and say that if a person believes that-p then (other things being equal) whenever the question whether-p arises, he tends to think (*not* think-out-loud) that-p; to which we might add that if the circumstances are appropriate he *may* express his thought by uttering (saying?) "p!"

IV

19. On the other hand, if we are to continue with our original strategy, we must resolutely put aside the temptation to draw the kind of distinction between thought and its expression which this formulation implies, and continue with the intriguing idea that an uttering of "*p*" which is a primary expression of a belief that -*p* is not merely an *expression* of a thinking that-*p*, but is itself a *thinking*, i.e. a thinking-out-loud that-*p*.

20. Yet the above difficulty does remind us that we must take into account the fact that there is a sense of "express" in which we can be said to express our thoughts by *using* language for this purpose. Thus, we express our thought that-*p* by *saying* "*p*." Can we sophisticate our logical behaviorism to do justice to this fact?

21. Let us take a closer look at the words "thought" and "express." First the latter. It will be noticed that the reference to observability implied by the term "manifestation" in the context "manifestation of the disposition to think that-*p*" was absorbed into the phrase which describes the disposition. Thus, "*manifestation* of the disposition to *think* that-*p*," became, in effect "*actualization* of the disposition to *think-out-loud* that-*p*."

22. Thus our formula becomes

x is a primary expression of Jones' belief that-*p*

= *x* is a manifestation of Jones' settled disposition to think that-*p*

= *x* is an actualization of Jones' settled disposition to think-out-loud that-*p*

→ *x* is a thinking-out-loud that-*p*

It is only too clear that by pushing our analysis of the context "expression of belief" in this direction we have lost contact with the idea that people express their beliefs by using language. The point can be put simply—indeed bluntly—by saying that the concept of the actualization of a disposition is not, as such, the concept of an *action*, whereas expressing their beliefs is something people *do*.

23. The statement

Jones, by saying "*p*," expressed his belief that-*p*

requires an interpretation of *saying* p as an action which is undertaken by Jones in order to express (to someone) his belief that-*p*. If we suspect that Jones is lying, we could equally describe him as saying "*p*", but our complete sentence would be something like

Jones, by saying "*p*," pretended to believe that-*p*.

24. In neither case could Jones' saying "*p*" be construed as a case

of *thinking* that-*p*. Even where Jones is speaking truthfully, the thinking involved, if any, would be of the sort described by such formulas as

Jones thought that saying ". . ." would express his belief that-*p*

Jones intended to express his belief that-*p* by saying ". . ."

or, in the case of lying,

Jones intended to pretend to believe that-*p* by saying ". . . .".

25. Thus, granted the validity of the concept of thinking-out-loud, the thinking-out-loud which would be relevant to the context

Jones, by uttering ". . . ," expressed his belief that-*p*

would be *not*

Jones thought-out-loud that-*p*

but rather

Jones thought-out-loud that saying ". . ." would express his
belief that-*p*

or, where Jones is lying,

Jones thought-out-loud that he would pretend to believe that-*p*
by saying ". . . ."

Needless to say, the latter thinking-out-loud would be inappropriate in the presence of the audience he intends to deceive.

26. All this seems to amount to the idea that the term "express" in contexts pertaining to thought has two radically different senses. The difference can be brought out by relating these senses to two different contexts, namely,

(1) Jones expressed his thought (belief) that-*p* by saying . . .

(2) Jones' utterance of "*p*" expressed *his* thought that-*p*

27. I shall call the former the "action" sense of express, and the latter, for want of a better term, the "causal" sense. Both, as we shall see, are to be distinguished from a third sense illustrated by the context

Jones' utterance of "*p*" expressed *the* thought that-*p*

where the phrase "*the* thought that-*p*" stands for an abstract entity, a thought in Frege's sense. I shall call this the logical (or semantical) sense of "express."

V

28. Although my ultimate aim is to show how a logical behaviorist might draw these distinctions, my initial move will be to discuss them in more traditional terms. I shall, therefore, construct a regimented (I dare not say idealized) model according to which, in the course of learning to speak a language, a child acquires the capacity to be in mental states which are *counterparts*, in a sense to be analyzed, of the utterances which come to belong to his repertory of linguistic behavior. The idea can be blocked out in two steps:

(a) A mental episode which is a thinking that-p is correlated with a piece of behavior which "stands for the proposition that-p" (however *that* is to be understood).

(b) In the initial stages of the child's mastery of the language, whenever it has a thought that-p, this thought is manifested in a purely involuntary way in the corresponding verbal behavior.

29. As our model for understanding the sense in which the uttering of "p" is the involuntary manifestation of a thinking that-p, let us take the instinctive connection between a pain and a piece of unlearned pain behavior. The fact that a connection between states A and B of a child is, in some sense, learned rather than instinctive, acquired rather than part of its initial equipment, by no means entails that either A or B is under the child's voluntary control. Not all learning to *do* consists in the addition of new behaviors to the stock of things that are under one's voluntary control.

30. Thus the key feature of our model is that the connection between the mental act and the verbal behavior is not to be construed on the action model of "using the behavior to express one's thought." Thus, verbal behavior is not in the child's voluntary control in that, although, once the language is learned, a necessary and sufficient condition of the child saying "p" is that it thinks that-p, the saying is the involuntary manifestation of the thinking.

31. Notice that the model allows the child a rich vocabulary, including the language of intention and resolve as well as that of matter-of-fact. It learns to verbalize about verbal behavior and even about the mental acts of which its behavior is the involuntary manifestation.

32. Actually we can weaken our model and still make our point. We need not suppose that the child remains a chatterbox. We can suppose it to acquire the ability to keep its thoughts to itself in the sense that it can effectively tell itself to keep quiet, without ceasing to think. We can grant that to this limited exent its verbal behavior is under its voluntary control. When it is thinking without speaking, we shall say that it is in a keeping-its-thoughts-to-itself frame of mind. When *not* in this frame of mind, it thinks-out-loud.

33. "Thinking-out-loud" remains the primary conception. The child's keeping its thoughts to itself can be compared to the opening of a general switch which breaks or (to mix metaphors) short circuits the initial acquired connection between thoughts and verbal behavior.

34. At this stage, the child has no conception of locutionary acts as verbal behavior which can be engaged in apart from thinking the corresponding thoughts. It has no concept of *saying "p" without thinking that-*p.

35. On the other hand, it is perfectly capable of having concepts of *actions* involving thinking-out-loud. Thus, wondering-out-loud about the weather: "I shall wonder-out-loud about the likelihood of rain." It is important to see that this by no means entails that there is such a thing as an action of *thinking-out-loud that*-p. Even in our more sophisticated framework there is no such thing as an *action* of thinking that-*p*, though there is the *action* of deliberating what to do. By granting, as we must, that it can conceive of action consisting of thinkings-out-loud, we admit a further sense in which its verbal behavior (*as* thinking-out-loud) would be under its voluntary control.

36. *The child's verbal behavior would express its thoughts, but to put it paradoxically, it could not express them.*

VI

37. Notice, also, that although its linguistic behavior would be meaningful, and we could say of each of its utterances what, specifically it meant, e.g.

Jones' utterance meant "it is raining."

It would, on our assumptions, be incorrect to say, for example

Jones, by uttering ". . ." meant (to convey) . . .

For the latter supposes that Jones has the concept of an action of uttering ". . ." as a piece of linguistic behavior which could exist independently of its being the "spontaneous verbal expression" of the corresponding mental act. There being no such action as bringing about a specific mental act, there could be no such thing as bringing about a thinking-out-loud for the purpose of conveying a thought.

38. In other words just as our regimenting fiction enables us to draw a distinction between a sense in which a mode of verbal behavior can *express* thoughts without being *used* to express them, so it enables us to distinguish between the context

utterance of *E* (in L) means - - -

and the sense of "means," closely related to "intends," which involves the context

person, by uttering *E*, means (to convey) . . .

39. The familiar saw that words have meaning only because people mean things by them is harmless if it tells us that words have no meaning in abstraction from their involvement in the verbal behavior of language users. It is downright mistaken if it tells us that for an expression to have a certain sense or reference is for it to be *used* by people *to convey* the corresponding thought. Rather, we should say, it is because the expression has a certain meaning that it can be effectively used to convey the corresponding thought.

VII

40. I want to return to an earlier stage of the argument and reconsider the account there given of "belief and the expression of belief." The first thing to note is that if we were to approach this topic in terms of the framework we have just been developing, we would get something like the following schema

Jones believes that-*p* = Jones has a settled disposition to think that-*p*, if the question occurs to him whether-*p*, and, indeed, to think-out-loud that-*p*, unless he is in a keeping his thoughts to himself frame of mind.[4]

We also get the following formulae with respect to "expression of belief,"

x is a primary actualization of Jones' belief that-*p* → *x* is a thinking that-*p* (or, if Jones is in a thinking-out-loud frame of mind, a thinking-out-loud that-*p*.)

x is a primary expression of Jones' belief that-*p* → *x* is a thinking-out-loud that-*p*.

Thus, where Jones is in a thinking-out-loud frame of mind, the verbal behavior is both an *actualization of* and, in the "causal" sense, an *expression of* his belief, both a thinking and an expression of thought.

VIII

41. But what will our logical behaviorist say of all this? Clearly he will be unhappy about our uncritical acceptance of mental acts as covert inner episodes. What moves might he make? He may well accept our initial formula

Jones believes that-*p* = Jones has a settled disposition to think that-*p*

But he will emphasize the "settled," which we have not yet done, and will call attention to the fact that it presumably contrasts with something. It is not obvious what the contrasting adjective should be, but it, too, should apply to dispositions. Let us, he suggests, try "proximate," drawing on the contrast between "settled" and "near the surface." Another appropriate contrast would be provided by "short term."

42. Objects, as is well known, can have causal properties which are not so to speak, immediately available. Thus iron attracts filings, *if* it

has been treated in a certain way. A proximate disposition can roughly
be characterized as one which is immediately available.

43. Our logical behaviorist, consequently, suggests that

Jones believes that-p = Jones has the *settled* disposition to
have *short term, proximate* dispositions
to think-out-loud that-p, if the question
whether-p arises, and he is in a thinking-
out-loud frame of mind.

In other words, our logical behaviorist construes the contrast between
fleeting thought episodes and settled beliefs as falling within the broad
category of dispositions, and hence construes the "covertness" of
thoughts as simply a special case of the covertness of dispositions.
Flammability, he reminds us, is not a covert flame.

44. Many features of our previous discussion can be fitted into this
framework, once its distinctive character is understood. Thus, we must
substitute for the previous account of the child's candid and spontaneous verbal behavior as the expression (in the "causal" sense) of classically conceived *episodes* of thought, an account according to which a

thinking-out-loud that-p

is simply an "actualization" of a

disposition to think-out-loud that-p

however, exactly, *this* is to be analyzed.

45. In the previous model we stipulated that the child be unable to
verbalize without thinking the appropriate thought, in other words, that
only if it has the mental act of thinking that-p does it utter "p." In our
present framework, the corresponding stipulation would be that all utterances of "p" be thinkings-out-loud that-p.

46. Both stipulations could be formulated in the same words, thus
"the child utters "p" only in the course of thinking-out-loud that-p."
But the concepts of thinking-out-loud are radically different. In the earlier model, the phrase "thinking-out-loud" referred to thoughts together
with their verbal expression. In the new model it is to be taken as an
unanalyzed expression which means roughly the same as "candid," spontaneous verbal behavior," but serves, by its mode of composition, to emphasize that the basic meaningfulness of candid, spontaneous verbal behavior is not to be construed in terms of its being the reverberation at
the tip of the tongue of covert episodes which are thoughts *properly
speaking,* in accordance with the schema

x is candid, spontaneous verbal behavior = x is an outcropping
of thought.

IX

47. It is important not to confuse logical behaviorism with what might be called logical physicalism. I mean by the latter the view which denies that, to quote Chisholm, "when we analyze the kind of meaning that it involved in natural language we need some concepts we do not need in physics or behavioristics." [5] Chisholm thinks that to deny the need for such an irreducible concept is tantamount to trying to "analyze the semantics . . . of natural language in a physicalistic vocabulary of a behavioristic psychology with no undefined semantical term and no reference to thoughts." [6]

48. In the essay which led to the correspondence from which I am quoting, I had argued that the concept of meaning which belongs in the context

$$E(\text{in } L) \text{ means} \text{-}\text{-}\text{-}$$

is not to be analyzed in terms of a reference to "thoughts." Thus I rejected any analysis along either of the following lines:

E (*in L*) means - - - = candid and spontaneous utterances of E causally express thoughts pertaining to - - -

E (in L) *means* - - - = speakers of L use E to express their thoughts pertaining to - - -

where "thought" is to be taken as referring to classically conceived inner episodes or mental acts.

49. On the other hand, though I denied that "means" in the sense appropriate to the context "E (in L) means————" is to be analyzed in terms of a reference to thoughts, I also argued that it cannot be analyzed in physicalistic terms. From Chisholm's point of view this was a blatant attempt to have my cake and eat it. As he saw it, to admit that "to analyze the kind of meaning that is involved in natural language" we need a distinctively semantical term ("means") which *cannot* be analyzed in physicalistic terms, while denying that the explication of this distinctively semantical term requires a reference to thoughts has all the appearance of paradox.

50. The correspondence went on at some length, and although some progress was made, the issue was never really joined. As I now diagnose the situation some ten years later, the cause of this failure was my inability to clarify adequately two points:

(a) The exact nature of statements of the form "E(in L) means - - -"

(b) The exact relation of the concept of *meaning* to that of *thought*.

I shall not attempt here to do anything more than indicate the moves I should have made.

51. My basic move should have been to clarify along the lines of this paper the distinction between the context

person expresses

and

utterance expresses.

52. My second move should have been to clarify "means" as it occurs in the context "*E* (in *L*) means————," as contrasted with the context "person, by uttering *E*, means————.

As I have since argued, to say what an expression means is to classify it by the use of a sortal predicate the application of which implies that the expression in question does the job in its language which is done in the speaker's language by an expression from which the predicate is formed. Thus, roughly

"und" (in German) means *and*

has the form

"und's (in German) are .and.s

53. But above all I should have made it clear that on my view the fundamental concept pertaining to thinking is thinking-out-loud as conceived by our logical behaviorists. This is not to say that I agree with him in rejecting the classical conception of thoughts as inner episodes in a nondispositional sense. Rather I accept mental acts and something like the classical sense, but argue that the concept of such acts is, in a sense I have attempted to clarify, a derivative concept.

54. Finally, I should have emphasized my total commitment to the thesis that the concept of thought essentially involves that of intentionality in the following sense. To say of a piece of verbal behavior that it is a thinking-out-loud, is to commit oneself to say of it that it means something, while to say of it specifically that it is a thinking-out-loud *that*-p, is to commit oneself to say of it that it is a piece of verbal behavior which means *p*.

55. Thus, at the primary level, instead of analyzing the intentionality or aboutness of verbal behavior in terms of its expressing or being used to express classically conceived thoughts or beliefs, this verbal behavior *is already thinking in its own right,* and its intentionality or aboutness is simply the appropriateness of classifying it in terms which relate to one's own linguistic behavior.

NOTES

1. Equally dangerous are such metaphorical contrasts as those between "paradigm" and "borderline," "shadow" and "penumbra." All suggest a sequential

strategy in which, once we are "hep," we know how to begin and what kinds of difficulty to expect.

2. Similarly "wondering whether-p" would be equated with "uttering" "p?," "wishing that-p" with "uttering" "would (that) p" and "deciding to do A" with uttering "I shall do A."

3. We can grant that a thinking-out-loud that-p might be a constituent of a reasoning-out-loud or a deliberating-out-loud on a certain topic.

4. The "if the question occurs to him whether-p" condition can be taken to cover all cases in which where the alternatives "p" and "not p" are relevant to his course of thought, he thinks that-p, even if the question whether-p is not actually raised.

5. *Minnesota Studies in the Philosophy of Science*, Vol. II, p. 523.

6. *Ibid.*

METAPHYSICS

IDENTITY THROUGH TIME[1]

Roderick M. Chisholm

According to Bishop Butler, when we say of a physical thing existing at one time that it is identical with or the same as a physical thing existing at some other time ("this is the same ship we traveled on before"), we are likely to be using the expression "same" or "identical" in a "loose and popular sense." But when we say of a person existing at one time that he is identical with or the same as a person existing at some other time ("the ship has the same captain it had before"), we are likely to be using "same" or "identical" in a "strict and philosophical sense." [2] I shall attempt to give an interpretation to these two theses; and I shall suggest that there is at least an element of truth in each.

To illustrate the first of the two theses—that it is likely to be only in a loose and popular sense that we may speak of the identity of a physical thing through time—let us recall the traditional problem of the ship of Theseus, in a somewhat updated version. The ship, when it came to be, was made entirely of wood. One day a wooden plank was replaced by an aluminum one (this is the updating) and the wooden plank was cast off. But we still had the same ship, it was said, since the change was only slight. Somewhat later, another wooden plank was cast off and also replaced by an aluminum one. Still the same ship, of course, since, once again, the change was only slight. The changes continue, but they are always sufficiently slight so that the ship on any given day can be said to be the same as the ship on the day before. Finally, of course, the ship is made entirely of aluminum. Some will feel certain that the aluminum ship is the same ship as the one that was once made entirely of wood. After all, it preserved its identity from one change to the next, and identity is transitive. Consider, however, this possibility, suggested by Thomas Hobbes: ". . . if some man had kept the old planks as they were taken out, and by putting them afterwards together in the same order, had again made a ship of them, this, without doubt, had also been the same numerical ship with that which was at the beginning; and so there would have been two ships numerically the same, which is absurd." [3] To compound the problem, let us imagine that the captain of the original ship had taken a vow to the effect that if his ship were ever to go down, then he would go down with it. What now, if the two ships collide at sea and he sees them start to sink together? Where does his duty lie—with the aluminum ship or with the reassembled wooden ship?

Putting the problem schematically, we may suppose that on Monday a simple ship, "The U. S. S. South Dakota," came into being, composed of two principle parts, A and B. On Tuesday, part A is replaced by a new part C. (We may imagine that the replacement was accomplished with a minimum of disturbance: as A was eased off, C was pushed on immediately behind and in such a way that one could not say at any time during the process that there was only half a ship in the harbor.) On Wednesday, there was fission, with B going off to the left and annexing itself to F as it departed from C, and with C going off to the right and annexing itself to J as it departed from B. On Thursday, over at the left, B is replaced by L, while, over at the right, C is replaced by H. And now the captain of the original U. S. S. South Dakota sees FL and JH in equal distress.

Mon		AB	
Tue		BC	
Wed		FB	CJ
Thu	FL		JH

One of his advisers tells him: The ship on the left is the one that took the maiden voyage on Monday, and the ship on the right, therefore, is not. But another of his advisers tells him: No, it's just the other way around. The ship on the right is the one that took the maiden voyage on Monday, and the ship on the left, therefore, is not. Agreeing on the need for philosophical assistance, the two advisers appeal to a metaphysician who instructs them in the following way: First of all, he says, we must make a technical distinction between what I shall call an intactly persisting temporal object and what I shall call a nonintactly persisting temporal object. A thing is an intactly persisting temporal object if it exists during a period of time and is such that, at any moment of its existence, it has the same parts it had at any other moment of its existence. We may suppose that AB, the object that came into being on Monday and passed away on Tuesday, was such an intactly persisting object. So, too, for BC, for FB, for CJ, for FL, and for JH. Thus a nonintactly persisting temporal object will be a temporal object that is composed of one set of parts at one time and of another set of parts at another time. If we can say of a ship, that it is composed of *A* and *B* on Monday and composed of *B* and *C* on Tuesday, then a ship is such a nonintactly persisting temporal object." [4]

Appealing now to our diagram, the metaphysician continues: I assume that the situation you disagree about involves the six intact temporal objects you have labelled. It also involves a number of nonintact temporal objects. Thus (i) there is that total object, having the temporal shape of an upside down Y—*that* object is composed of *AB* on Monday, of *BC* on Tuesday, of *FB* and *CD* on Wednesday, and of *FL* and *JH* on Thursday; (ii) there is that object composed of the stem and the left fork of the Y—that object is composed of *AB* on Monday, of *BC* on Tuesday, of *FB* on Wednesday, and of *FL* on Thursday; and (iii) there is that object composed of the stem and of the right fork of the Y—the object that is composed of *AB* on Monday, of *BC* on Tuesday, of *CJ* on Wednesday, and of *JH* on Thursday. The second and third of these temporal objects thus have certain parts in common, and the first one includes both the second and the third among *its* parts.

Given such distinctions as these, our metaphysician now concludes, you can see that there is really nothing for you to dispute about. Just consider the question: Is the ship on the left the one that made the maiden voyage on Monday? If you are asking whether *FL* is identical with *AB*, then the answer is obviously *no*, for *FL* didn't come into being until Thursday and *AB* ceased to exist on Tuesday. On the other hand, if you are asking whether *FL* and *AB* are both parts of our second temporal object, the one composed of the stem and of the left fork of the Y, the answer is clearly *yes*; and *JH* is not a part of that object. And if you are asking whether *JH* and *AB* are both parts of our third temporal object, the one that is composed of the stem and of the right fork of the Y, then the answer, once again, is clearly *yes*; and *FL* is not a part of *that* object. All you need to do then, is to distinguish these various objects and make sure you know *which* ones you are talking about. Then everything will be clear.

I think we might go along with the metaphysician—up to the very **last point.** Consider the reaction that his sort of instructions might produce: You say that everything will be clear. Things were *far* more clear before you entered the picture. We couldn't agree as to which of these two ships was the one that set sail on Monday. But we were clear, at least, that only two ships were involved. Now, with all your intact and nonintact temporal objects, we have *no* idea how many ships there were. We have learned from Webster that a ship is a structure used for transportation in water. Your intact temporal objects satisfy *that* definition;

so they yield at least six ships. What of the nonintact temporal objects? Is the one having the temporal shape of the Y a ship? That would make seven. The stem would give us eight, the two forks would bring it up to ten; the stem plus the left fork makes eleven, and the stem plus the right one makes it *twelve*. Conceivably we might countenance the presence of twelve ships in this situation if by so doing we could solve our problem. But you haven't solved the problem. Consider the poor captain. He wants to go down with his ship and he *still* doesn't know which way to go.

Our metaphysician, I suggest, did not succeed in locating the source of the dispute.

Consider the problem as it pertained to the relation between *FL* (the object that came to be, on the left, on Thursday) and *AB* (the object that had ceased to be by Tuesday). It was agreed that Webster's definition of "*x* is a ship" would do. It was also agreed that *FL*, *AB*, and the other intact objects satisfied that definition. The question was whether *FL* constituted the same ship as did *AB*. And the question whether *FL* constituted the same ship as did *AB* must be distinguished from the closely related question whether *FL* was identical with *AB*; for, as Locke saw, at least in principle, "*FL* constitutes the same ship as does *AB*" does not imply "*FL* is identical with *AB*." [5]

Railroad trains may provide a more perspicuous example of the distinction between "*x* constitutes the same so-and-so as does *y*" and "*x* is identical with *y*." Suppose we ask: Is this the same train we rode on last year? We are not concerned to know whether the set of objects that makes up today's train is identical with the set of objects that made up the train of a year ago. ("I'm not asking whether we rode on *precisely these same cars* a year ago!") The following three statements tell us three quite different things: (1) This set of cars constitutes a train today and it also constituted a train a year ago; (2) This set of cars constitutes the same train as did that set of cars and that set of cars constituted a train a year ago; (3) This set of cars constitutes the same train that that set of cars constituted a year ago. By going to the dictionary we may find a definition or criterion of "*x* is a train"; but we do not thereby find a definition or criterion of "*x* constitutes the same train as does *y*." A definition of the latter expression would be much more complex and would doubtless say something about roadbeds, schedules, and cities. Possibly, for example, if we can agree that the present aggregate of cars leaves Hoboken at 7:30 P.M. for Chicago via Scranton and the Poconos, we may be willing to concede that this is the same train that we took a year ago, even if all the cars are different. (We may note, in passing, that in this case applicability of "*x* is the same train as *y*" will presuppose applicability of some such expression as "*x* is the same roadbed as was *y*" or "*x* is the same city as was *y*.")

"The same ship" would seem to require a kind of continuity that "the same railroad train" does not. That is to say, if this is to be the same ship that that was, then this ship must be *evolved* in some clear-cut way from that. The requisite sense of "evolves" is illustrated by our diagram. Thus *BC* is continuous with *AB* in that they have a part in common; we may say, therefore, that the latter object *BC* "directly evolved" from the earlier object *AB*. Analogously for the relation of *FB* to *BC*, of *FL* to *FB*, of *CJ* to *BC*, of *JH* to *CJ*, and of *FB* to *AB*. And since *FL* directly evolved from something that directly evolved from *AB*, we may say simply that *FL* evolved from *AB*.[6]

What more is needed if this is to be the same ship that that was? The best we can do, I believe, is to formulate various additional criteria which are such that, if they are satisfied, then this is the same ship that that was. Let us consider only one such criterion—one involving reference to sameness of sailing schedule. Suppose we know, with respect to each object, that it satisfies Webster's definition of a ship: each object is a structure that is used for transportation in water. Suppose we also know that everything that evolved from that and into this was also a structure used for transportation in water (none of these things was ever towed on land and used there as a dwelling-place or as a restaurant). Suppose we know, moreover, that they all followed the same sailing schedule (they were used, say, to ferry passengers between Hoboken and lower Manhattan). And suppose we know, finally, that if at any time one of these objects underwent fission at that time and evolved into more than one structure that was used for transportation in water, then only one of those structures kept to the original schedule. If we know all these things, then, I think, we may say with confidence, that this is the same ship as that—or, more accurately, that this constitutes now the same ship that that constituted then.

Hence one possible criterion (as distinguished from a definition) of "*x* constitutes now the same ship that *y* constituted then" would be this: *x* evolved from *y*; everything that evolved from *y* and into *x* was a structure used for transportation in water and followed the same sailing schedule that *y* does; and if at any time more than one such structure evolved at that time from *y*, then only one of them followed the same sailing schedule that *y* does.

If we should be fortunate enough to find that Wednesday's left hand object followed the same sailing schedule as did those of Monday and Tuesday, and that Wednesday's right hand object took off on a course of its own, then we may conclude that the one on the left, and not the one on the right constitutes the same ship as the one that came to be on Monday.

Reverting to the terminology of our metaphysician, we may say that the situation we have been concerned with involved at least six different intactly persisting objects and at least six different nonintactly persisting objects. Does this mean, then, that the situation involved at least a dozen ships? No, for if we speak in a strict and philosophical sense, we will say that counting ships through a given period of time is not the same as counting structures that are used for transportation in water during that time; it is, rather, to count sets of objects that constitute the same ship during that time. For example, to say that there is *one* ship is to say that there is one set of things all constituting the same ship. To say that there are two ships is to say that there are two sets of things, all the members of the one set constituting the same ship, all the members of the other set constituting the same ship, and no member of the one set constituting the same ship as any member of the other set. And so on, for any number of ships. If, as we are supposing, the AB, BC, FB, and FL of our example all follow the same sailing schedule, then they constitute one ship. CJ, we said, took off on its own. Hence if JH follows the same sailing schedule as did CJ, then the situation will involve at most two ships.

We could put the matter paradoxically, therefore, by saying that counting ships is not the same, merely, as counting objects that happen to *be* ships. But if we speak strictly and philosophically, we may avoid any such appearance of paradox. We may say that ships are "logical constructions." The things that they are constructed upon are things that satisfy Webster's definition of the loose and popular sense of "ship"— they are structures used for transportation in water. We will not say, therefore, that AB, BC, and the other intact structures we discussed *are* ships. We will say, instead, that each of these things constitutes a ship. Given the concept of "x constitutes the same ship as does y," we could define "x constitutes a ship" by saying "x is a member of a set of things all constituting the same ship." The U. S. S. South Dakota, therefore, would be a logical construction upon one such set of things. If we continue to speak strictly and philosophically, we will not say of the two different things, AB and FL, that each of them *is*, on its particular day, the U. S. S. South Dakota. We will say instead that each of them *constitutes*, on its particular day, the U. S. S. South Dakota. The statements we ordinarily use to describe the ship (e.g., "It weighs more now than it did then") will be reducible to statements about the things that constitute it ("the thing that constitutes it now weighs more than the thing that constituted it then").

We now have an obvious interpretation for the first of the theses I have attributed to Bishop Butler—namely, that it is only in a loose and popular sense and not in a strict and philosophical sense that we may speak of the identity of such things as ships through time. He could be construed as telling us, first, that the expression "x constitutes at t the same ship that y constitutes at t' " does *not* imply "x is identical with y"; and analogously for "constituting the same tree," "constituting the same carriage," and so on. Then he could be construed as telling us, secondly, that if we express the fact that x constitutes at one time the same ship that y constitutes at another time by saying "x is identical with y" or "x is the same as y," then we are speaking only in a loose and popular sense and not in a strict and philosophical sense. And perhaps he could be construed as telling us, finally, that our criteria for x constituting the same ship as y are pretty much in our own hands, after all, and that once we have determined that a given x and y do satisfy our criteria for constituting the same ship, or that they do not, then no possible ground for doubt remains.

But there are points of clarification to be made:

(i) In saying that certain uses of language are "loose and popular" rather than "strict and philosophical," we are not suggesting that those uses are *incorrect*. Indeed, they may be said to be *correct*; for it is the loose and popular interpretation rather than the strict and philosophical one that gives the standard of correctness (at any rate, in the loose and popular sense of "correct").

(ii) I have said that it is only in a loose and popular sense that the thing which makes up the U. S. S. South Dakota on Thursday may be said to be identical with, or the same as, the thing which made up the U. S. S. South Dakota on Monday. But this is *not* to say, of that nonintactly persisting four dimensional temporal object depicted by the stem and the left fork of our upside down Y, that *it* is identical with *itself* only in a loose and popular sense; for that object, like any other, is identical with itself in a strict and philosophical sense. So, too, therefore, for that object made up of the stem and the right fork of the Y, as well as for that object (if our metaphysician was right in assuming that there *is* such an object) made up of the stem plus the right *and* left forks of the Y. Our account of the U. S. S. South Dakota, therefore, should not be taken to imply that there are no such four dimensional objects, or that, if there are such, they are not strictly self-identical.

If we could formulate an adequate set of criteria for applying the expression "x constitutes the same ship as does y" (the one cited above, of course, was only schematic), and if we found that these criteria were satisfied, say, by the original intact object of Monday and the left intact object of Tuesday, then, for the ship that is thus constituted ("AB and FL both constitute the U. S. S. South Dakota"), there would be exactly one nonintact temporal object (namely, the stem and the left fork of the Y). Therefore an alternative to saying that the U. S. S. South Dakota is a logical construction upon a set of things all constituting the same ship would be to say that the U. S. S. South Dakota is a nonintact temporal object having as its parts at different times the members of a set of things all constituting the same ship. In this case, we could say that the U. S. S. South Dakota *is* the stem and the left fork of the Y.

If we speak in this way, then the point that I have attributed to Bishop Butler will be even more obvious. He would now be telling us that the expression "x is a part of the same ship at t that y is a part of at t'" does not imply "x is identical with y"; hence if we use the expression "x is the same as y" or "x is identical with y" merely to express the fact that "x is a part of the same ship that y is a part of," then we are speaking in a loose and popular sense and not in a strict and philosophical sense.[7]

We should remind ourselves, moreover, that merely by referring to AB and FL as "temporal parts" of one and the same temporal object, we do not thereby answer the question we had put originally as "Does FL constitute the same ship as did AB?" and that we might now put alternatively as "Is FL a temporal part of the same ship as was AB?" To simplify the problem even further, consider just two ships, X and Y, and two days, Monday and Tuesday, through which both ships persist. Let us assume for the moment that there is one set of parts that make up the ship on Monday and another, entirely different set of parts that make up the ship on Tuesday. We may refer to the parts that make up X on Mondays as "the Monday parts of X" and to the parts that make up X on Tuesday as "the Tuesday parts of X." We may now distinguish four pairs of successive aggregates of parts: (1) the Monday parts of X and the Tuesday parts of X; (2) the Monday parts of Y and the Tuesday parts of Y; (3) the Monday parts of X and the Tuesday parts of Y; and (4) the Monday parts of Y and the Tuesday parts of X. We must therefore choose between two courses. We may say (a) that these four pairs of successive aggregates of parts constitute *four* temporal objects; or we may say (b) that only the first two pairs constitute genuine temporal objects and hence there are only *two* such objects. If we take the first course and say that there are four temporal objects, we will need a criterion for deciding *which* such temporal objects are to be counted as ships; for we would be left with our problem if we said that the third and fourth objects on the list are ships—that the Monday parts of X and the Tuesday parts of Y make up one ship, and that the Monday parts of Y and the Tuesday parts of X make up another ship. If we take the second course and say that only the first two pairs of objects on our list are "genuine" temporal objects, then we will need to know what is required for successive temporal parts to be parts of one and the same temporal object.[8]

(iii) Finding an acceptable definition of "x is a ship" is a problem for dictionary makers. Finding an acceptable definition of "x constitutes the same ship as does y" is more likely to be a problem for jurists. It should be noted that we may be in agreement with respect to the proper interpretation of one of those expressions and in disagreement with respect to the proper interpretation of the other; or we may be rigid with respect to the one and latitudinarian with respect to the other.

Assuming we have agreed upon our interpretation of "x is a ship," consider the latitude that yet remains with respect to the interpretation of "x constitutes the same ship as does y." According to the particular criterion of constituting the same ship that was satisfied by our example of the U. S. S. South Dakota, today's object and tomorrow's object "constitute the same ship" provided, among other things, that every object that evolves out of today's object and tomorrow's is a ship. And for there to be such evolution, each object, we said, must have some part in common with the object from which it directly evolved. We could say, quoting Hume, that with each step it is "in a manner requisite, that the change of parts be not . . . entire"; [9] but it is very possible that we will find it convenient to relax these criteria. Thus it may be useful to be able to say, on occasion, that a certain object of last year constitutes the same ship as does a certain object of this year even though one of the objects, into which last year's object evolved and out of which this year's object evolved, was itself not a ship. Perhaps the ship was partially dismantled and used for a while as a tool shed or as a restaurant; yet, when it was reconverted, we found it convenient, and pleasing to count the result as the same ship that we had before.[10] We may even find it convenient to say on occasion that though a certain object of last year constitutes the same ship as does a certain object of this year, there was no evolution as defined—the change of parts at one stage was entire. Switching for the moment from ships to rivers, consider this situation: We swim in the upper Rio Grande in the early spring; the river dries up in the summer; new waters then flow in and we swim there once again in the fall. Surely we will want our criterion of "x constitutes the same river as does y" to allow us to say that we swam in the same river twice.

(iv) The expression "x constitutes the same ship as does y," like "x is a ship," allows for borderline cases. We can readily imagine situations in which the only appropriate answer to the question "Is that a ship?" is "Yes and no"—or, better, situations in which "Yes" is no better an answer than "No," and "No" is no better an answer than "Yes." [11] A hydrofoil that is also a hovercraft may serve as an example. We can readily imagine situations in which to the question "Is this the same ship as that?", i.e., "Does this constitute the same ship that that did?", the only answer is "Yes and no."

It may well happen that when we encounter such a borderline case, we must have an answer other than "Yes and no." The captain, as we have seen, may well need a more definite answer, and we may need a definite answer to the question, "Is the combination hydrofoil and hovercraft a ship?", for it may be necessary to decide whether such things are to be subject to the regulations that govern ships or to the regulations that govern aircraft. Similarly, for the question "Does this constitute the same ship that that did?"

When the existence of such a borderline case does thus require us to make a choice between "Yes" and "No" the decision is entirely a pragmatic one, simply a matter of convenience. Which ship is to be called "the Ship of Theseus"—the one that evolved step by step from the original ship, or the one that was assembled from the discarded planks of the original ship? Here we have such a borderline question. The question calls for a convention with respect to the interpretation of "constituting the same ship" (or of "is the same ship as," in its loose and popular sense). We can have it pretty much as we wish, provided we agree. Which ship should the captain go down with? Here, too, we have a borderline question. Perhaps you and I cannot decide, but the courts, or the ships' courts, can decide. If the captain has agreed to go down with the U. S. S. South Dakota, and if the court decides that the aluminum ship and not the wooden one is the one that constitutes the U. S. S. South Dakota, then down with the aluminum ship he ought to go. Or down with it he ought to go unless the authorities decide subsequently (and in time) to "defeat" the convention they have adopted—for any such convention is defeasible and may be altered or defeated if unexpected circumstances show that it will turn out to be inconvenient. The important thing here is this: The convention of the courts, or of the proper authorities will settle the matter. You and I may object to their decision on the ground that some other decision would have been more convenient. But it would make no sense for us to say: Well, it just might be, you know, that they are mistaken. It just might be that, unknown to them, the wooden ship and not the aluminum one is the U. S. S. South Dakota.

(v) There is also a philosophical point to make about our treatment of the problems of the Ship of Theseus and the U. S. S. South Dakota.

Speaking of identity or persistence through time, Bishop Butler said: "In a strict and philosophical manner of speech, no man, no being, no mode of being, no anything, can be the same with that with which it hath indeed nothing the same." [12] We may be certain of at least this much: If there is an individual thing x which is such that, through a certain period of time, everything that is part of x at any given moment of that time is also a part of x at any other moment of that time, then what constitutes x at any moment of that time may be said to be identical in the strict and philosophical sense with what constitutes x at any other moment of that time. In such a case, x would satisfy the concept of *intact persistence* that was introduced above. For it was suggested that an individual thing x could be said to *persist intactly* through a given period of time, provided that, at any subperiod of that time, x has the same parts that x has at any other subperiod of that time. In other words, an individual x persists intactly through a given period of time, provided that, for every z, if z is part of x during any subperiod of that time, then z is part of x during every subperiod of that time.[13] Thus we may say that if just one part of our ship is removed or replaced at a certain time, then other parts of the ship, unlike the ship itself, persist intactly through that time.

We formulated above one possible criterion for saying, of different objects at different times, that they constitute one and the same ship. This criterion, it should be noted, presupposes intact persistence, though not intact persistence of the ship; for if the criterion is applicable in the case of a given ship, then, with each step of evolution, some part of the ship remains behind, for the change of parts is "not entire." Hence, with each step, some part persists intactly; some part will be such that it keeps all of *its* parts. But though the evolution of our ship from Monday through Thursday involved intact persistence of some part of the ship at some time during each change that took place, it does not presuppose intact persistence of any part of the ship from Monday through Thursday. We are thus more liberal in our interpretation of "x constitutes the same ship as does y" than we are, say, in our interpretation of "x constitutes the same bar of metal, or the same piece of wood, or the same hunk of clay as does y." For we are not likely to say of x that it constitutes the same bar of metal, or the same piece of wood, or the same hunk of clay as does y, unless we think that, throughout the changes from x to y most of the parts have persisted intactly. But "x constitutes the same body of water as does y" need not imply that most of the parts have thus persisted intactly. Indeed it need not even imply that the body of water has undergone the type of evolution we described in the case of the ship. Thus, as we have noted, a body of water x may constitute in the spring the same river that a body of water y constitutes in the fall, even though the river has dried up in the summer and y, therefore, has not evolved in the requisite sense from x.[14] We might say what St. Thomas said of the river Seine: ". . . the Seine river is not 'this particular river' because of 'this flowing water,' but because of 'this source' and 'this bed,' and hence is always called the same river, although there may be other water flowing down it." [15] Suppose, then, we say that the river of the spring is the same river as the river of the fall in virtue of the fact that the river of the spring flows through *the same river bed* as does the river of the fall. What, then, would be our criterion for saying that something x in the spring is the same river bed as something y in the fall? It might be the fact that the river bed in the fall has evolved in the manner I have attempted to describe from the river bed in the spring. Or it might be that the material that constitutes the river bed in the spring is found *the same river banks* as is the material that constitutes the river bed in the fall. We might then say that x in the spring constitutes the same river bank as does y in the fall if, once again, y has evolved from x in the manner I have described.[16]

In other words, persistence, in the loose and popular sense, through time would seem to presuppose such evolution; and such evolution, in turn, presupposes persistence, in the strict and philosophical sense, through time. For it presupposes what I have called intact persistence. It is not implausible to say, therefore, that if there is anything that persists, in the loose and popular sense, through any given period of time, then there is something (perhaps not the same thing) that persists intactly through some subperiod of that time.

What now of Bishop Butler's second thesis—the thesis according to which, when we say of a *person* existing at one time that he is identical with a person existing at another time, we are likely to be using "identical" in a strict and philosophical sense and not merely in a loose and popular sense?

I have suggested a possible interpretation of the expression "loose and popular sense of the *same.*" Putting the point schematically, we may say that "x is the same F as y" is used in a loose and popular sense if it is used in such a way that it does not imply "x is identical with y." (The expression "x constitutes the same F as does y" would thus be less misleading for such a use.) I have also suggested that when "x is the same F as y" is used in this loose and popular sense, then it is possible to imagine conditions under which a question of the form "Is x the same F as y?" has no definite answer—conditions under which we may say both "Yes" and "No," for "Yes" will be as good an answer as "No," and "No" will be as good an answer as "Yes."

Such an interpretation of the expression "loose and popular sense of *same*" suggests at once a possible interpretation of the expression "strict and philosophical sense of *same*." For example, we are using the expression "x is the same person as y" in a strict and philosophical sense if we are using it in such a way that it implies "x is identical with y." In this case "x is the same person as y" will be logically equivalent to "x is a person and x is identical with y." I wish to suggest that "x is the same person as y," where the expression in the place of "x" is taken to designate a certain person at existing at one time and where the expression in the place of "y" is taken to designate a certain person existing at a different time, does have this strict and philosophical use.

When we use "the same person" in this strict way, then, although cases may well arise in which we have no way of *deciding* whether the person x is the same person as the person y, nevertheless the question "Is x the same person as y?" will *have* an answer and that answer will be either "Yes" or "No." If we know that x is a person and if we also know that y is a person, then it is not possible to imagine circumstances under which the question "Is x the same person as y?" is a borderline question —a question admitting only of a "Yes and no" answer.

The latter point may be illustrated in the following way. If x knows, with respect to some set of properties, that there is or will be a person y who will have these properties at some future date, then x may ask himself "*Will I be he?*" and to that question the answer must be "Yes" or "No." For either x is identical with y or x is not identical with y.

If it is clear that if x is a person and y is a person, then we cannot answer the question "Is x the same person as y?" merely by deciding what would be practically convenient. To be sure, if we lack sufficient evidence for making a decision, it may yet be necessary for the courts to *rule* that x is the same person as y, or that he is not. Perhaps the ruling will have to be based upon practical considerations and conceivably such considerations may lead the court later to "defeat" their ruling. But if Bishop Butler, as I have interpreted him, is right, then one may always ask of any such ruling "But is it *correct*, or *true*?" For a ruling to the effect that x is the same person as y will be correct, or true, only if x is identical with y.

Here, then, we have one possible interpretation of the thesis that, in one of its important uses, the expression "x is the same person as y" must be interpreted in a strict and philosophical sense. It seems clear to me that "x is the same person as y" does have this use. Whenever a person x asks himself, with respect to some person y, "Will I be he?" or "Was that person I?" then the answer to his question, if put in the form "x is the same person as y," or "x is not the same person as y," must be taken in the strict and philosophical sense.

We should remind ourselves, however, that the expression "x is the same person as y" also has a use which is not this strict and philosophical one. Thus there are circumstances in which one might say: "Mr. Jones is not at all the same person he used to be. You will be disappointed. He is not the person that you remember." We would not say this sort of thing if Mr. Jones had changed only slightly. We would say it only if he had undergone changes that were quite basic and thoroughgoing—the kind of changes that might be produced by psychoanalysis, or by a lobotomy, or by a series of personal tragedies. But just *how* basic and thoroughgoing must these changes be if we are to say of Mr. Jones that he is a different person? The proper answer would seem to be: As basic and thoroughgoing as you would like. It's just a matter of convention. It all depends upon how widely it is convenient for you to construe the expression "He's the same person he used to be." Insofar as the rules of language are in your own hands, you may have it any way you would like. (Compare "Jones is not himself today" or "Jones was not himself when he said that.")

This, however, is only a "loose and popular" sense of identity. When we say, in this sense, "Jones is no longer the person he used to be," we do not mean that there is, or was, a certain entity such that Jones was formerly identical with that entity and is no longer so. We do not mean to imply that there are (or have been) certain entities, x and y, such that at one time x is, or was, identical with y, and at another time x is not identical with y. For this, I believe, is incoherent, but "Jones is no longer the person he used to be" is not.

Nor do we mean, when we say "Jones is no longer the person he used to be," that there *was* a certain entity, the old Jones, which no longer exists, and that there is a certain *different* entity, the new Jones, which somehow has taken his place. We are not describing the kind of change that takes place when one President succeeds another. In the latter case, there is a clear answer to the question "What happened to the old one?" The answer might be "He was shot" or "He retired to Gettysburg." But when we decide to call Jones a new person, we are not confronted with such questions as: What happened, then, to the old Jones? Did he die, or was he annihilated, or disassembled, or did he retire to some other place?

The old Jones did not die; he was not annihilated or disassembled;

and he did not retire to any other place. He *became* the new Jones. To say that he "became" the new Jones is *not* to say that he "became identical" with something he hadn't been identical with before; for it is only when a thing comes into being that it may be said to become identical with something it hadn't been identical with before. To say that our man "became the new Jones" is to say only that he, Jones, *altered* in a significant way, taking on certain interesting properties he had not had before. (Hence we should contrast the "became" of "Jones then became a married man," said when Jones ceased to be a bachelor, with that of "The President then became a Democrat," said when President Eisenhower retired.) When we say of a thing that *it* has properties that *it* did not have before, we are saying that there is an x such that x formerly had such-and-such properties and x presently has such-and-such properties. But to say that there is an x, at least one x, such that x was now this and x is now that, would seem to presuppose the identity of x through time, in *some* sense of the term "identity." Is the sense of identity that is presupposed merely that in which we can say of any temporal object, intact or nonintact, that it is identical with itself? Or are we also presupposing that, in the strict and philosophical sense, whatever goes to make up that person now is identical with whatever went to make him up at the earlier time? [17]

One may well ask: But *need* we presuppose this? Need we presuppose the persistence of a single subject of change when, as we say, the man becomes "a new person?" To appreciate the situation, it may be necessary to imagine that the person in question is oneself. Suppose, then, that you were such a person—that you had undergone basic and thoroughgoing changes and that your friends and acquaintances were in agreement that you are no longer the same person that you were. What, then, if you *remember* all of the relevant facts—that *you* had formerly been a person of such-and-such a sort, that you had undergone certain shattering experiences, and that these then led to a transformation in your personality, with the result that you are not the person that *you* formerly were?

Let us imagine, however, that your friends and acquaintances say to you: "But you are such a *very* different person now that henceforth we are going to treat you like one. We will call you "Smith" instead of "Jones." We will make certain that you are free from all the obligations that Jones incurred. And if you feel guilty about some of the wicked things that Jones did, you need no longer have such feelings, for we can get the highest courts to lay it down that you are two quite different people. Something, surely, is wrong here.

Some people, I have found, see at once that something is wrong and others do not. For those who do not, let me propose that we look in a different direction. What would we think of such talk if we were to hear it *before* rather than after the transformation of our personality?

It will be instructive to elaborate upon an example that C. S. Peirce suggests.[18] Let us assume that you are about to undergo an operation and that you still have a decision to make. The utilities involved are, first, financial—you wish to avoid any needless expense—and, secondly, the avoidance of pain, the avoidance, however, just of *your* pain, for pain that is other than yours, let us assume, is of no concern whatever to you. The doctor proposes two operating procedures—one a very expensive procedure in which you will be subjected to total anaesthesia and no pain will be felt at all, and the other of a rather different sort. The second operation will be very inexpensive indeed; there will be no anaesthesia at all and therefore there will be excruciating pain. But the doctor will give you two drugs: first, a drug just before the operation which will induce complete amnesia, so that while you are on the table you will have no memory whatever of your present life; and, secondly, just after the agony is over, a drug that will make you completely forget everything that happened on the table. The question is: Given the utilities involved, namely the avoidance of needless expense and the avoidance of pain that *you* will feel, other pains not mattering, is it reasonable for you to opt for the less expensive operation?

My own belief is that it would *not* be reasonable, even if you could be completely certain that both amnesia injections would be successful. I think that *you* are the one who would undergo that pain, even though you, Jones, would not know at the time that it is Jones who is undergoing it, and even though you would never remember it. Consider after all, the hypothesis that it would *not* be you. What would be your status, in such a case, during the time of the operation? Would you be waiting in the wings somewhere for the second injection, and if so, where? Or would you have passed away? That is to say, would you have *ceased to be,* but with the guarantee that you—you, yourself—would come into being once again when the *agony* was over? [19] And what about the person who *would* be feeling the pain? Who would he be?

I can appreciate that these things might not seem obvious to you as you ponder your decision. You may wonder: "I would certainly like to save that money. Will it really be *I* who feels that pain? How can it be if I won't know that it's I?" Perhaps you would have some ground for hesitation. But there is one point, I think, that ought to be obvious.

Suppose that others come to you—friends, relatives, judges, clergymen—and they offer the following advice and assurance. "Have no fear," they will say, "Take the cheaper operation and we will take care of everything. We will lay it down that the man on the table is not you, Jones, but is Smith. We will not allow this occasion to be mentioned in your biography. And during the time that you lie there on the table— excuse us (they will interject), we mean to say, during the time that *Smith* lies there on the table—we will say, 'poor Smith' and we will not say, even in our hearts, 'poor Jones.' " What *ought* to be obvious to you, it seems to me, is that the laying down of this convention should have no effect at all upon your decision. For you may still ask, "But won't that person be I?" and, it seems to me, the question has an answer.

Suppose you know that your body, like that of an amoeba, would one day undergo fission and that you would go off, so to speak, in two different directions. Suppose you also know, somehow, that the one who went off to the left would experience the most wretched of lives and that the one who went off to the right would experience a life of great happiness and value. If I am right in saying that one's question "Will that person be I?" or "Will I be he?" always has a definite answer, then, I think, we may draw these conclusions. There is no possibility whatever that *you* would be *both* the person on the right and the person on the left. Moreover, there *is* a possibility that you would be one or the other of those two persons. And, finally, *you* could be one of those persons and yet have no memory at all of your present existence.[20] It follows that it would be reasonable of you, if you are concerned with *your* future pleasures and pains, to hope that you will be the one on the right and not the one on the left—also that it would be reasonable of you, given such self-concern, to have this hope even if you know that the one on the right would have no memory of your present existence. Indeed it would be reasonable of you to have it even if you know that the one on the *left* thought he remembered the facts of your present existence.[21] And it seems to me to be absolutely certain that no fears that you might have, about being the half on the left, could reasonably be allayed by the adoption of a convention, or by the formulation of a criterion, even if our procedure were endorsed by the highest authorities.

NOTES

1. Presented in part as "On the Loose and Popular and the Strict and Philosophical Senses of Identity," as the second of three Carus Lectures entitled "Some Metaphysical Questions about the Self," at the Pacific Division of the American Philosophical Association, Berkeley, California, December 29, 1967. I am indebted to John Wisdom, Sydney Shoemaker, and Fred Feldman for criticisms of earlier versions of this paper. Certain paragraphs have been adapted from my

"The Loose and Popular and the Strict and Philosophical Senses of Identity," in Norman S. Care and Robert H. Grimm, eds., *Perception and Personal Identity*, by permission of Case Western Reserve Press.

2. "Of Personal Identity," Dissertation I, in *The Whole Works of Joseph Butler, LL. D.* (London: Thomas Tegg, 1839), pp. 263–270. The dissertation is reprinted in Antony Flew, ed., *Body, Mind and Death* (New York: Macmillan, 1964), pp. 166–172.

3. Thomas Hobbes, *Concerning Body*, Chapter XI ("Of Identity and Difference"), Section 7.

4. But a nonintactly persisting temporal object should be distinguished from what I shall call an "Edwardian" temporal object (after Jonathan Edwards). An Edwardian temporal object would be a temporal object which is such that, for each moment during which it exists, there is a set of parts which are what make up that object at that moment and which exist only at that moment. Hence if x is an Edwardian temporal object, then for any two times, t and t' at which x exists, there is one set of objects which make up x at t, and another set of objects which make up x at t', and no member of the first set has any part in common with any member of the second set. If, as some philosophers have supposed, all temporal objects are Edwardian, then no object which persists through a period of time could be said to persist intactly, as this term was defined by our metaphysician above; for no object would be such that it has the same parts at any moment of its existence that it has at any other moment of its existence. This extreme Edwardian view was defended by J. H. Woodger in *The Axiomatic Method in Biology* (Cambridge: The University Press, 1937) and by Rudolf Carnap in *Introduction to Symbolic Logic* (New York: Dover Publications, 1958), see pp. 213–216. Jonathan Edwards took this extreme view to be implied by "God's upholding created substance, or causing its existence in each successive moment." For, he reasoned, "if the existence of created *substance*, in each successive moment, be wholly the effect of God's immediate power, in *that* moment, without any dependence on prior existence, as much as the first creation out of *nothing*, then what exists at this moment, by this power, is a *new effect*, and simply and absolutely considered, not the same with any past existence . . ." From this he was able to deduce that it is as reasonable and just to impute Adam's original sin to me now as it is to impute any sin which I may seem to remember having committed myself. (See the *Doctrine of Original Sin Defended*, Part IV, Chapter 2.) But this extreme view, when considered separately from the doctrine of divine re-creation, has at least the disadvantage of multiplying entities beyond necessity. (Compare: "John is kind toward Mary and unkind toward Alice; therefore there is something, namely John-toward-Mary, that is kind, and there is something, namely John-toward-Alice, that is unkind, and these two different things go to make up John.") It should not be attributed to our metaphysician above.

5. See Locke's *Essay*, Book II, Chapter 27, Sections 5, 6, and 8. The point made above does not, of course, imply the more extreme thesis, according to which a statement of the form, "x is identical with y," is always elliptical for one of the form, "x is the same F as y."

6. These concepts might be defined as follows: x *evolves directly* from y, provided: either x is identical with y, or there is no time at which x and y both exist but there is a z such that z is part of y at one time and z is part of x at a later time. (Possibly we should add that, during any subperiod between the earlier and the later time, z has the same parts that it has during any other such subperiod.) And, more generally, x *evolves* from y, provided: x is a member of every class C such that (i) y is a member of C and (ii) whatever directly evolves from anything that is a member of C is also a member of C. (If the definition of "evolves directly" were intended to explicate the ordinary use of this expression, it would doubtless be too broad; but it is not so intended.)

7. We should take care not to misinterpret Butler at this point. In saying

that "this is the same ship as that" is to be understood only in a loose and popular sense and not in a strict and philosophical sense, he is taking the "this" and the "that" to refer to the particular objects that, on their respective days, constitute (or serve as the parts of) the ship in question on those days; he is not using "this" or "that" to refer to the set of things that constitute the ship, or to the nonintact temporal object of which those things may be construed as parts. This is clear, I think, from the following passage: "For when a man swears to the same tree as having stood fifty years in the same place, he means only the same as to all the purposes of property and uses of common life, and not that the tree has been all that time the same in the strict and philosophical sense of the word. For he does not know whether any one particle of the present tree be the same with any one particle of the tree which stood in the same place fifty years ago."

8. Our example involves just four pairs of objects. Consider the number of ostensible temporal objects, or ostensible ships, we would have to choose among, if we added just one more ship and one more day to our example. Or the objects that would be involved if all temporal objects were "Edwardian," as this term was defined in footnote 3 above. (The account that I have given of the history of the U. S. S. South Dakota presupposes that there are some intactly persisting temporal objects, and therefore it is inconsistent with the view that all temporal objects are Edwardian.)

9. *Treatise*, Book I, Part IV, Section vi.

10. An Aristotelian who took ships seriously might say that in such a case two "substantial changes" had occurred.

11. I owe this way of putting the matter to Professor John Wisdom who criticized an earlier version of this paper at Lewis and Clark College in October, 1967.

12. "Of Personal Identity," in Flew, *op. cit.*, p. 265.

13. What if the parts of a thing are "simply re-arranged"—say, from ABC to CAB? If we take the term "part" in its ordinary sense, as I propose that we do, then we must say that the thing will not have persisted intactly, for it will have lost some parts. If the thing changes from ABC to CAB, then it will lose BC, as well as that part that consists of the right half of B and the left half of C.

If we could say, however, that compound things are composed of "ultimate particles" which are not themselves composed of parts, then we could formulate a definition of "intact persistence" which would allow us to say that a thing may persist intactly through rearrangement of its parts. For we could say that a thing persists intactly through a given period of time if, at any subperiod of that time, it has the same "ultimate particles" that it has at any other period of that time. Thus Locke said that, so long as any group of "atoms" (ultimate particles) "exist united together, the mass, consisting of the same atoms, must be the same mass, or the same body, let the parts be ever so differently jumbled. But if one of these atoms be taken away, or one now one added, it is no longer the same mass or the same body." (*Essay*, Book II, Chapter 27, Section 4. This use of "same," I am sure he would have agreed, is strict and philosophical and not loose and popular.)

14. For further possibilities, see Helen M. Cartwright, "Heraclitus and the Bath Water," *Philosophical Review*, Vol. LXXIV (1965), pp. 466–484.

15. *De Spiritualibus Creaturis*, Article IX, ad. 16; translated as "On Spiritual Creatures," by M. C. Fitzpatrick and J. J. Wollmuth (Milwaukee, Marquette University Press, 1949). See page 109 of the translation.

16. One might be tempted to define sameness of river bank or of river bed, say, in terms of *sameness of place*. If sameness of place is not then defined in terms of a relation to things that are said to exist in space, such a definition would seem to presuppose intact persistence of substantival space through time. (It may be noted, incidentally, that our account of "evolving" allows us to say that a thing at a later date evolves from a thing at an earlier date even though there has been no change of parts.)

17. It should be noted that, although the loose and popular use in question is one in which "*x* is *not* the same person as *y*" is consistent with "*x* *is* identical with *y*," it is not a use in which "*x* *is* the same person as *y*" is consistent with "*x* is *not* identical with *y*." It is difficult to think of any actual examples of the latter type of use. Perhaps those who take roles more seriously than they do persons might say such things as "Elizabeth is the same monarch as Victoria was" while aware of the falsehood of the corresponding identity statement. But such uses, fortunately, are not ordinary.

18. " 'If the power to remember dies with the material body, has the question of any single person's future life after death any particular interest for him?' As you put the question, it is not whether the matter ought rationally to have an interest but whether as a fact it has; and perhaps this is the proper question, trusting as it seems to do rather to instinct than to reason. Now if we had a drug which would abolish memory for a while, and you were going to be cut for the stone, suppose the surgeon were to say, 'You will suffer damnably, but I will administer this drug so that you will during that suffering lose all memory of your previous life. Now you have, of course, no particular interest in your suffering as long as you will not remember your present and past life, you know, have you?' " *Collected Papers* (Cambridge, Harvard University Press, 1935), Vol. V, p. 355.

19. See Locke's *Essay*, Book II, Ch. xxvii, Sec. i: "One thing cannot have two beginnings of existence." Compare Thomas Reid, *Essays on the Intellectual Powers of Man*, Essay III, Chapter 4.

20. In this case, there might well be no *criterion* by means of which you or anyone else could decide which of the two halves was in fact yourself. I would agree with Shoemaker's contention that "our ability to know first-person psychological statements to be true, or the fact that we make them (for the most part) only when they are true, cannot possibly be explained on the supposition that we make them on the basis of criteria": Sydney Shoemaker, *Self-Knowledge and Self-Identity* (Ithaca: Cornell University Press, 1963), p. 214. One consequence of this fact, I suggest, is the following: it makes sense to suppose in connection with the above example that you are in fact the half that goes off to the left and not the one that goes off to the right even though there is no criterion at all by means of which anyone could decide the matter. I would disagree, incidentally, with what Shoemaker says (*op. cit.*, p. 236 ff.) about the relationship between criteria and necessary truths—at least, if "necessary" is taken to mean the same as "logically necessary." My own views on this question may be suggested by Chapter IV ("The Problem of the Criterion") in my *Theory of Knowledge* (Englewood Cliffs, N.J., Prentice-Hall Inc., 1966).

21. I would endorse, therefore, the following observation that Bayle makes in his article on Lucretius (see Note Q of "Lucretius," in Pierre Bayle, *A General Dictionary, Historical and Critical*): "The same atoms which compose water, are in ice, in vapours, in clouds, in hail and snow; those which compose wheat, are in the meal, in the bread, the blood, the flesh, the bones etc. Were they unhappy under the figure or form of water, and under that of ice, it would be the same numerical substance that would be unhappy in those two conditions; and consequently all the calamities which are to be dreaded, under the form of meal, concern the atoms which form corn; and nothing ought to concern itself so much about the state or lot of the meal, as the atoms which form the wheat, though they are not to suffer these calamities, under the form of wheat." Bayle concludes that "there are but two methods a man can employ to calm, in a rational manner, the fears of another life. One is, to promise himself the felicities of Paradise; the other, to be firmly persuaded that he shall be deprived of sensations of every kind."

CHISHOLM ON IDENTITY THROUGH TIME

(A RESPONSE)

P. F. Strawson

I have to confess that I have not fully understood Professor Chisholm's notion of "strict and philosophical identity." I have, I think, understood it in part. That is to say, I have, I think, understood the sense he gives to this notion in connection with such things as ships. But for a reason I shall try to make clear this does not help me to understand his application of the notion to the case of the identity of persons. Let me begin by making this reason clear.

1. The church my daughter was married in yesterday is, let us say, the very church I myself was married in twenty-five years ago. The ship I crossed the Atlantic in this year is the same ship as I came over in five years ago. The tree we contemplate in my garden this afternoon is the tree we sat under three years ago. None of these identity-propositions expresses, in Professor Chisholm's sense, a strict and philosophical identity. For the proposition that the church my daughter was married in yesterday is the church I was married in twenty-five years ago does not entail the proposition that all the *parts* of the church, as it was when I was married in it 25 years ago, are the same as the parts of the church as it was when my daughter was married in it yesterday, these parts having all persisted intact throughout that time. Indeed it is in the highest degree improbable that this latter proposition is true. Similarly for the ship and the tree. And for these reasons none of the identity-propositions I have listed expresses a strict identity or is a strict identity-proposition.

Professor Chisholm holds that in contrast with such identity-propositions as these propositions about ships, churches, or trees, propositions asserting *personal* identity over time *do* express strict identities. But I think it must be immediately clear why the examples of the church, the ship, and the tree do not help us in the least to understand in what

183

sense statements of personal identity express strict identities. Consider the statement that the person who has just read us a paper on "Identity through Time" is the same person as the person who published an article on "Counterfactual Conditionals" in *Mind* in 1946. I think Professor Chisholm would allow this to stand as an example of the sort of statement he is concerned with. But it is surely quite clear that this statement does not entail the proposition that the parts of this person, as he was when he published the article, are the same as the parts of this person, as he was when he just now read the paper, these parts having persisted intact throughout this period of time. It is quite clear not only that the entailment does not hold, but also that Professor Chisholm does not think it does. So the examples we began with, of identity-propositions which are *not* strict identities, do not at all help us to understand the sense in which Professor Chisholm holds that statements of *personal* identity *do* express strict identities.

2. Professional Chisholm offers us another contrast which, unfortunately, I find no more helpful in trying to understand this sense than the contrasts we have just considered. He points out that we sometimes say things like "Jones is not the person he was" or "He is not the same man at all as he was in the war/ at Harvard/etc." He also points out quite correctly—and indeed it is something that the very *grammar* of the sentence shows—that, in saying this sort of thing, so far from denying numerical identity of person, we *presuppose* numerical identity of person. For the reference of the personal pronoun in the subordinate clause is to the same person as the reference of the name or pronoun in the main clause. But then he goes on to say that this very fact shows that when we say this sort of thing, the kind of identity we are presupposing is "strict and philosophical" identity. And this perplexes me *in the extreme.* Of course the presupposed numerical identity is *personal* identity. But surely we are all familiar with the fact that, just as we can say "Jones is not the person he used to be—he is not the same man at all" etc., so, as we contemplate the tree in the garden, half-rotten, bearing no fruit etc., we can sadly say "That tree is not the tree it used to be, not the same tree at all" or, of the run-down, ill-disciplined ship, "It's not the ship it used to be, not the same ship at all"; and so on. In these cases too, when we say this sort of thing, so far from denying numerical identity of ship or tree, we *presuppose* numerical identity of ship or tree. But Professor Chisholm would not say in *these* cases that the presupposed numerical identity—of ship or tree—is strict identity. He would say, in *these* cases, that it was loose or popular identity. In the case of persons, on the other hand, he takes over the expression "loose and popular identity" for use in connection with these (certainly very

loose) locutions about Jones not being the man he was etc.; and he ignores altogether the existence of parallel locutions in the case of trees
and ships. He gives no reason at all for proceeding in this discriminating
way. Perhaps it doesn't matter very much in itself that he does this. The
important point is that reference to these certainly very loose locutions
throws absolutely no light on the sense in which statements of personal
identity, as opposed to identity-statements about ships, trees, and
churches, are supposed to express strict identities.

3. I turn now to the two fables which Professor Chisholm invites
us to consider. One of them is perfectly intelligible in itself but again
fails to provide enlightenment on the problematic notion of strict personal identity. Stripped to its essentials, it comes to this. It is perfectly
intelligible to suppose that at a time, t_1, a person should completely
lose all memory of his previous life, and that at a later time, t_2, he
should recover his memory of his previous life up to t_1, but have no
memory at all of what happened to him between t_1 and t_2. There is
complete memory-discontinuity in this person's life at both ends of the
period, t_1 to t_2. We may call this the hypothesis of a *total memory gap*
in a person's life; and I think this hypothesis is indeed perfectly intelligible. As the story is imagined, there would be no discontinuity at all in
the existence of the living human body of the person in question. And
in the absence of extremely strong countervailing reasons, this consideration would provide quite a sufficient reason for holding that the story is
a story about one and the same person throughout. The moral of the
story is, then, simply that the hypothesized total memory gap would
not provide a countervailing reason of sufficient strength to challenge
this consideration. But since it has already become clear that Professor
Chisholm does not equate strict personal identity with the identity of a
living human body, we are still quite in the dark as to what he means
by strict personal identity, and his fable goes no way to showing that
there is any such concept. Professor Chisholm embellishes his story with
the question whether someone motivated by self-interest would or
would not, or should or should not, think it reasonable to *choose* a
pain-filled total memory gap in his future history in preference to the
sacrifice of something highly valued, e.g. money. I have, out of curiosity,
tried this question on various people and received conflicting answers.
The answers may throw some light on the mental make-up—e.g. degree
or kind of imaginativeness—of the answerers; but they surely throw
none on the philosophical question. For identity of the person throughout the memory gap is conceded in any case. But the concession does
nothing to establish, or even to help us to understand, the relevant concept of strict identity.

As regards Professor Chisholm's other fable, the fable of fission, the situation is rather different. Let us speak of the two emergent persons as Lefty and Righty. Lefty and Righty are *two* persons, hence not identical with each other, hence, by transitivity of identity, the original person cannot be identical with both. Professor Chisholm says that it is quite possible, however, that the original person might be identical with one or the other, i.e. strictly identical with Lefty or strictly identical with Righty. He gives us no reason to think that either of the emergent living human bodies would have a better claim than the other to be regarded as a "continuator" of the original human body; and in any case we have already seen that such considerations seem to have little to do with the notion of strict personal identity. He says that the original person *might* be identical with Lefty and not with Righty even though Lefty had no memories at all of the original person's previous life while Righty seemed (to himself and others) to have just such memories. He mentions no other considerations at all—e.g. continuity of character, temperament, taste, and talent between Lefty and the original person— as considerations which might have more bearing on strict identity than considerations relating to memory or putative memory; and indeed it seems quite clear that he would not regard such considerations in this light. Indeed the essence of his position seems to be that such a strict identity *might* hold even if there was no reason whatever to believe that it held and even if such reasons as there were for making any identification in the case favoured the opposite identification. As far as I can see, Professor Chisholm produces no argument whatever in support of this view. He refers, indeed, in a footnote, to the fact which can be expressed, in our current jargon, by saying that first-person ascriptions of some psychological *states* are not made on the basis of criteria. But to conclude from this that there is such a thing as strict *criterionless personal identity through time* would simply be an enormous non sequitur —a point of which Kant, for example, was fully aware.

I began by saying that I did not really understand what Professor Chisholm meant by the notion of strict identity as applied to persons. But, of course, what he says awakens echoes: echoes, for example, of Locke's individual immaterial soul-substance, an entity which Locke succeeded simultaneously in believing in and in demonstrating the utter irrelevance of to our concern with personal identity. Perhaps I should say, not that I do not understand Professor Chisholm's notion of strict personal identity, but rather, that I understand it well enough to think there can be no such thing.

REPLY TO STRAWSON'S COMMENTS

Roderick M. Chisholm

First, a minor point about terminology. I used the expression "the loose and popular and the strict and philosophical senses of identity." Perhaps it would have been better to have said "the loose and popular and the strict and philosophical uses of the expression 'is identical with.'" Mr. Strawson, in referring to my views, uses the shorter expressions "loose identity" and "strict identity." I would like to note that these might be misleading. For I do not wish to say that, whereas some things are strictly identical with themselves, other things are only loosely identical with themselves—as though there might be *degrees* of identity. For everything that there is, whether it be a person or a nonperson, whether it be an individual or a nonindividual, is identical with itself in the strict and philosophical sense of the expression "is identical with"—and, I should like to add, necessarily identical with itself.

Secondly, there is at least one point of misunderstanding. I think Mr. Strawson does not realize how far I might be willing to go with respect to these matters. Or perhaps he suspects it but cannot quite bring himself to believe it. Thus he suggests that I would agree with him in asserting this—that the parts I had when I wrote a certain article back in 1946 are not the same, at least in their entirety, as the parts that I have now. Such a proposition would be true, of course, if being a part of my body is to be equated, strictly, with being a part of me. But this presupposition—that being a part of my body is the same as being a part of me—seems to me to be problematic. Indeed part of the point of my paper was to suggest this very fact—that such a presupposition *is* problematic.

I agree that some of the things I said—things that would be of some philosophical significance if true—were not supported by any arguments. In itself, of course, this is not to be deplored. After all, Mr.

Strawson, too, affirmed certain things last night—certain fundamental theses about the asymmetries of individuals and general characters—and conceded in the discussion that followed that he could not give any *arguments* for what he said. I believe it would not be inaccurate to say that these were certain principles which he—and I—simply saw, on reflection, to be true. More accurately, perhaps, they are principles which we saw to be true after having contemplated certain instances of them.

The two fables I introduced—the one about what Mr. Strawson calls the memory gap and the one he refers to as the fable about Lefty and Righty—were offered as examples which, I had hoped, might help us to see certain general principles which at least *seem* to me on reflection to be true. They seem to me to be worthy of being taken, at least provisionally, as data in our philosophical inquiries about the person; in other words, we should affirm them until we have very good reason for rejecting them.

Let me re-affirm certain of these principles in connection with Lefty and Righty. And let me urge you to try to contemplate in your own case the kind of fission that I attempted to describe in mine. The result of such fission was that there will be two persons, Lefty and Righty, one going off to the left and the other going off to the right. Suppose now we ask ourselves the questions "Will Lefty be I?" and "Will Righty be I?" I wish to say that when I contemplate these questions, I see the following things clearly and distinctly to be true. (And I wish to suggest that you, too, would see them clearly and distinctly to be true—provided you really contemplate the questions themselves and not merely certain related philosophical theses you brought with you to these investigations.) One of these things, then, is this: that if Lefty and Righty clearly *are* persons, as we are imagining, then the questions "Will I be Lefty?" and "Will I be Righty?" have entirely definite answers. The answers will be simply "Yes" or "No." It will *not* be to the point to say "Well, it all depends" or "Well, 'Yes and No' is the best we can do." What I want to insist upon—I concede I cannot give you an argument—is that this will be the case even if all our normal criteria for personal identity should break down. Thus even if Lefty has half my fundamental personality traits and Righty the other half, even if Lefty has half the cells of my present nervous system and Righty the other half, even if Lefty thinks he remembers having done just the things I did on the even-numbered days and Righty thinks he remembers having done just the things I did on the odd-numbered days, and so even if there is no procedure or criterion whatever by means of which anyone could reasonably decide whether one or the other will be I, none the less, the questions "Will I be Lefty?" and "Will I be Righty?" do have definite answers. In the case of each of us, the answer will be simply "Yes" or it will be simply "No." And what I also see clearly and distinctly to be true is that, even under the perplexing conditions I have just described, there is no possibility whatever that the answer to both questions will be "Yes." But, as I say, I cannot argue these points. The most I can do is ask you sometime really to contemplate such questions.

THE CONCEPT OF THE WORLD

Milton K. Munitz

I

The Field of Metaphysics

Contemporary writings in the field of metaphysics cluster around two major views as to what that discipline is about. One takes metaphysics to be a study of *categories*, the other thinks of it as a study of *Being*. The first type of view may, in turn, be further subdivided as between those, on the one hand, for whom the analysis of categories assumes primarily an epistemological character, and those, on the other hand, for whom the field to be investigated is rather to be approached in primarily ontological terms. For the first of these groups as thus subdivided, metaphysics becomes an examination of the fundamental ways which human thought has for organizing its experience. Strawson's conception of descriptive metaphysics may be taken as a clear example of this approach. In a way that has evident continuity with Kant (who is ordinarily thought of as giving priority to epistemological over ontological inquiries), Strawson looks for the relatively unchanging necessities of thought, the "massive central core of human thinking," as he puts it— "the categories and concepts which, in their most fundamental character, change not at all. . . . It is with these, their interconnections, and the structure that they form, that a descriptive metaphysics will be primarily concerned." [1] Those, however, who take the search for categories as essentially "ontological" rather than "epistemological" will be found to give different formulations as to how this is to be construed, and what such categories amount to. Two main subdivisions of this approach may be briefly alluded to here. Thus, for some, categories have to do with the basic *features* of whatever exists, their generic traits and structures. Operating in a predominantly Aristotelian rather than Kantian tradition, these philosophers conceive of metaphysics as an inquiry into the basic traits that apply to whatever exists. J. H. Randall Jr., for example, in describing the Aristotelian conception of first philosophy (a conception which he himself shares), says that it "disregards the diversities of things and examines their most comprehensive and general characters. It analyzes the "generic traits" manifested by existences of any kind; the distinctions sure to turn up in any universe of discourse drawn from existence, those traits exhibited in any *ousiai* or existential subject matter, the fundamental and pervasive distinctions in terms of which any existential subject matter may be understood, as they are found within any such subject matter." [2] For still others, categories are not descriptions of generic *features* of whatever exists, but, rather, are basic *kinds* or *classes* of things. For these philosophers, the main problem of ontology is to determine *"what there is"*—the basic types of reality we have to acknowledge. Do these include, for example, material objects, minds, universals, sense data, nonnatural moral values?

In the conceptions thus far identified, metaphysics is concerned with the analysis of categories to be used in the description of a subject matter that is essentially *pluralistic* and *diversified*. Contrasted with such views there is an altogether different conception in which metaphysics is concerned with the character of *Being* as such. For this approach to metaphysics the views of Heidegger and Tillich, in our own day, are paradigmatic. Tillich, for example, formulates his conception of metaphysics as follows: "The ontological question is: What is being itself? What is that which is not a special being or a group of beings, not something concrete or something abstract, but rather something which is always thought implicitly, and sometimes explicitly, if something is said to *be?* Philosophy asks the question of being as being. It investigates the character of everything that is insofar as it is. . . . This is its basic task, and the answer it provides determines the analysis of all special forms of being." [3]

There is a certain ambiguity and vacillation in this latter conception of metaphysics which comes out even in the foregoing brief characterization by Tillich, and which would be confirmed by a more extensive and careful examination of his own writings, as well as those of Heidegger and others who use the terminology of Being. On the one hand, this tradition, in its concern to contrast Being with beings, the one with the many—to point to the fundamental "ontological difference" as Heidegger puts it—is evidently setting itself a wholly different task from those who conceive of metaphysics as a search for the basic categories that apply to or classify whatever exists; for in focusing its attention on Being rather than on beings, on Being as an undifferentiated whole rather than on the properties or basic kinds that hold for the multiplicity of entities or beings, metaphysics is in no way interested in the basic types of existences, or in what such entities share, or in the properties of entities, even when this property is that of existence. Metaphysics as the study of Being attempts to discover, if it can, what Being is; but it cannot do so by studying the properties, however generic and widely shared these may be, of the multiplicity of entities or beings, the individual things or events that experience discloses. At the same time, Tillich slips into talking of metaphysics as a study of such entities themselves, even though the emphasis is upon their sharing the character of being. He says that "it investigates the character of everything that is insofar as it is." And here we are no longer dealing with Being qua Being. We are treating being as a property that is shared by beings. And this is an altogether different matter from dealing with Being qua Being. This shift has occurred because in fact, those who use such Being-talk are mixing three different enterprises:

(1) They are, in the first place, interested in the problem of answering the question, why particular things exist, or, more accurately, why the world conceived as the totality of such individual things exists. This is the problem of creation. It is a problem they share with the theistic tradition. And in a manner reminiscent of the theistic solution, they typically handle it by deriving beings from Being, by treating Being as the *ground* of beings.

(2) They are also concerned with the problem of descriptive intelligibility, of predication, and not simply with the problem of derivation or of the explanation of existence. And insofar as they cater to this interest, they will talk of the way in which entities or beings share in being, the way in which everything that *is*, has the property of being.

(3) Finally, they are also concerned with Being itself, quite apart from the question of the explanation or description of the multiplicity of beings. And it is only this last concern, the study of Being qua Being, which sufficiently differentiates this conception of metaphysics from the one discussed earlier, namely the study of categories. Though, to be sure, stress on this conception of Being itself is frequently found in the writings of Heidegger and Tillich, it is muddled and interspersed with discussions of these other matters. The terminology of "being" encourages or perhaps makes inevitable the resulting confusion and keeps this last conception of metaphysics from being the clear and univocal thing it might be.

It is therefore in the interest of clearly identifying what, in the tradition of Being-talk, is called the study of Being qua Being, or the study of Being itself, that it perhaps would be best to drop the terminology of "being" altogether, because of its unwanted associations and entanglements, and to choose some other term instead. It seems to me the same interest which philosophies of Being express in this matter can be restated with greater clarity as an interest in understanding the nature of *the world*. Metaphysics construed in this way will ask its questions about *the world* rather than about *Being*. And in what follows, I shall, in fact, adopt this substitution of the term "the world" for the term "Being," and turn shortly to an examination of what consequences this has for our understanding of the scope of metaphysics.

I have thus far distinguished two main forms of interest in metaphysics, or two largely distinct ways of conceiving what metaphysics is about. It would, however, be an oversimplification to say that these are mutually exclusive classes. It is true, of course, that there are many writers, who, in adopting the view that metaphysics is a study of categories, are prone to reject the attempt to give metaphysics an additional interest in determining the properties of something denominated "Being" or "the world." On the other hand, those for whom metaphysics is fundamentally a study of Being are not necessarily or generally averse to conceiving of metaphysics as also concerned with the problem of categories, of determining what can be said in a general way about the plurality of existences or about our basic conceptual ways of dealing with these. But they will generally maintain that the problem of categories cannot adequately be handled without relating it to the primary task of metaphysics, where this is taken to be one of determining the character of Being as such. In any case, there are still other metaphysicians who would not undertake to make any choice of priority or of relative importance as between the study of categories and the study of what I have thus far simply referred to as the study of "Being" or "the world," but who would say instead that these are simply two equally important directions of inquiry that metaphysics might take. A good example of this last point of view is to be found in McTaggart's *The Nature of Existence*. He tells us at the very outset of this work that he proposes "to consider what can be determined as to the characteristics which belong to all that exists or, again, which belong to Existence as a whole." [4] However, in quoting here from McTaggart I do not mean to suggest that when he conceives one of the interests of metaphysics to consist in determining the properties of existence as a whole (what he elsewhere calls "the universe") that this is to be understood exactly in the same way in which, for example, Heidegger or Tillich understand the term "Being," for there will, indeed, be great differences among these philosophers. All I mean to bring out by this reference is that it suggests we do well to recognize a family of doctrines that seems to agree in recognizing something more to the study of metaphysics than simply an examination of categories belonging to, to be predicated of, or to be used in the classification and description of the multiple entities within the world. This "something more" is indicated by saying that it has to do with a distinctive subject matter and that this subject matter is to be labeled "Being," "existence as a whole," or "the world."

In what follows I should like to select for critical examination the view in which metaphysics is concerned with the second of the main interests I have thus far discriminated—an interest that is variously described as a study of "Being qua Being" or, again, as a study of "the world," or in McTaggart's phrase of "existence as a whole." My reasons for this selection are the following: While the conception of metaphysics as a study of categories surely has connected with it innumerable profound and difficult problems, these are, generally speaking, of a fairly straightforward sort and of a kind that we might reasonably hope will gradually yield to patient analysis. The examination of such basic concepts as "individual," "time," "identity," "similarity," "negation," "mind," "material object," and so on, are matters on which much fruitful work has already been done, especially in our own day, and may be expected to continue. The problems here concern details and strategy, ironing out such differences as exist between those who favor one approach or type of analysis and those who favor another. But there is no need to impugn or to call into question the domain of inquiry itself. This is far from being the case, however, with the second line of investigation previously mentioned under the heading of "metaphysics." Here we are confronted at the very outset with a question as to what it is we are being asked to investigate, what the subject matter of our inquiry is; for until we can be satisfied as to this, there is no need to worry about questions of method, of tactics, or of making up our minds which of the various possible views or rival claims about our subject matter we should adopt.

When we are told that metaphysics or ontology has an interest in Being itself, or the world, or existence as a whole, what exactly are we to understand by these terms? It is sometimes said, for example, that the fundamental question of metaphysics is the question "What is Being?" and we also are told that the fundamental task of metaphysics is the study of Being. Of what does such study consist? Of determining its properties? But if we don't already know what this term stands for, how can we undertake to ask any questions about it? And if we do know what the term means, what need is there to ask the question "What is Being?" For reasons already given, I think it would be fruitful in undertaking an analysis of these points to drop the use of the term "Being" and to concentrate our attention instead on the use of the term "the world." And if now we rephrase the fundamental question of metaphysics as consisting of the question "What is the world?" we must ask whether indeed we have a genuine question here or only an interrogatory expression that has only the outward appearance of being a genuine question. What are we asking *for*, and *about* what are we asking what we are asking?

There are, in fact, at least two different sorts of things that might be intended, both of which are conveyed by the same verbal form of the interrogatory expression "What is the world?" (1) In the first place, if the term "the world" has a referring role, our question wants to know to *what* does it refer? Is the term being used as a name or definite descriptive phrase for an individual, or is it a name for a class of some sort, or is it possibly being used in some other way, in some as yet unspecified and wholly unique referring capacity? And how shall we go about identifying that to which reference is being made in one or another of these ways? *What* is it to which we are referring? (2) A second way of interpreting the question looks, not to the referring role which the term "the world" might perform, but instead to the characteristics which may be predicated of it. What properties can we discover concerning the world? In asking the question in the "what" form, the "what" directs our attention to the search for those characteristics we can truthfully predicate of the world. However, it should be noted that, in asking this question, we are already presupposing that the term "the world" can be genuinely used as a referring expression; for if indeed there were no target or referent for the term "the world" we should not be able to ask any questions about it; the question would evaporate for failure to have anything to be about. It would be a non-starter, and the problem of determining predications for the world would not even arise.

Although I have called attention to two ways in which we may interpret the question "What is the world?" there is in fact a point at which these two ways might overlap. Let me indicate what I mean. Where the term "the world" is used as the logical subject of a sentence, it must be able to perform a referring role, for this is indeed what is meant by a logical subject. A necessary condition for a sentence to be capable of being either true or false is that its logical subject must succeed in making reference. Thus, with the use of the phrase "the world" in the subject role we should have to inquire as to what kind of logical subject this is. What type of relation does it bear to its referent? Thus we might assume, to begin with, that it falls under one or another of the familiar types of referring expressions. It might be considered as a proper name, a definite description, an indexical sign, or a common noun. Without undertaking such an analysis of the phrase "the world" at the moment, let us assume that in giving the meaning of this phrase we should be able to provide a verbal as contrasted with an "ostensive" definition. For example, if the world were the name of a class and we gave the defining properties of this class, then in clarifying the meaning of "the world" as a referring expression we should in this case be giving the definition of this term. It follows that if we were to go on to ask what the world is, in the sense in which this has to do with giving the properties to be assigned to that which the logical subject designates, then such properties would in general be of two types. Either the properties (the predicates) merely set out what is already contained in the meaning of the subject term, and the statement is analytic; or else the properties are in addition to those set out in the meaning or definition of the subject, and in this case the statement is synthetic. In the former case, we shall be enumerating certain defining properties. And it is these very defining properties—or some of them, at any rate—which will also make their appearance in the answer to the question "What is the world?" when this looks for a statement of properties in the predicate position of some sentence. And it is for this reason, in this particular situation, that the answer to the question "What is the world?," when this is taken as a request for an analysis of the referring expression, coincides with the request for a statement of its properties as these are to be stated in the predicate position. However, if there are any properties that might be assigned to or predicated of the world that are not contained in its definition, then the second interpretation of our question, namely, "What is the world?," and the answer it might receive, would not coincide with the analysis of the meaning of the term "the world" taken simply as a referring expression. And of course if the term "the world" shows itself to be a term which does not permit of a verbal definition at all, because nothing about it allows it to be assimilated to the character of what we find in common nouns, then the foregoing analysis of the extent to which the first and second interpretation of our questions would come to the same thing, need not apply at all.

These questions and topics for investigation have a peculiar interest for us, since in trying to disentangle how they are to be treated we are preparing the ground for reaching a decision as to whether or not there is something to be called metaphysics which has a distinctive, legitimate, and important subject matter for investigation in Being or the world, and that points in a different direction, therefore, from a purely categoreal investigation.

In conducting our investigation I shall adopt the following procedure. I shall inquire first about the possible ways in which, when we take the phrase "the world" as a referring expression, we may understand this use. As we have seen, one possible interpretation of the question "What is the world?" as the leading question of metaphysics, is that it asks precisely for these clarifications about the use of the expression "the world" as a referring expression. What type of logical subject is it? and how shall we identify that to which reference is being made when one uses this expression in its referring capacity? The analysis of the possible use of the phrase "the world" in its referring capacity has a logical priority over other possible investigations, since in order for it to be possible to have a systematic body of discourse in which we are able to say things *about* the world, it is the world that tacitly or explicitly is the *logical subject* about which various things are said. And unless we can satisfy ourselves that the term does have such a genuine referring use, there would be no way in which we could even get started in setting out our knowledge-claims, for we should not have a subject for such predications to be about. Everything in our present inquiry thus hinges on whether or how we treat the phrase "the world" as a referring expression.

In my discussion I shall concentrate on three main possibilities:

(1) that the phrase "the world" when used referringly, is a term that may be taken to stand for a *totality* of a special, all-inclusive sort;

(2) that the term "the world" functions as a proper name for an *individual*;

(3) that the phrase "the world" when used referringly cannot be described as having reference either to a totality or to an individual and so cannot be assimilated to the ways in which we use either a common noun for a class, or a proper name for an individual.

In conducting this investigation, I shall undertake to argue for the following general thesis: The asking of the question "What is the world?" and the possible "answering" of it turn out to have certain paradoxical qualities associated with them. On the one hand the question "What is the world?" is in some ways the most important and basic question that philosophy can ask; and yet there is no answer to it. One of the reasons there is no answer to it, is that philosophical analysis shows all one might do in "answering" the question is to utter a tautology and say "The world is the world," or else show that the very form of the question, by asking ostensibly for a definition, a description, or an identification, in the use of the "what" form of question, cannot, in the case of the world, be satisfied at all. And so philosophy has as one of its fruitful results the dissolving of the question, and with it the possibility and hope that there can be a body of knowledge about the world that can be set out in a discipline to be called "metaphysics." The paradox, however, is this: that on the one hand, one of the great values of philosophy is to have performed here the kind of analysis which, in forcing us to take apart our initial question, makes us see why it cannot be answered, and why in a certain sense it is an improper question and should not have been asked; at the same time the very same analysis that accomplishes this dissolution of the question, this therapeutic lifting of a false hope and an intellectual snarl, also yields thereby the occasion for a deeper insight into *what the world is*. This insight is not, however, something to be set out in a body of knowledge. Nevertheless, this insight is among the most precious and fundamental that human experience can possess, and far from dissolving it, philosophy leaves it untouched and more entrenched than ever. After all the world exists, whatever our philosophy may say or not say; and any philosophy that denies the existence of the world must be convicted of entertaining an unforgivable absurdity. Yet if pressed to say what the world, whose existence is so undoubted, is, metaphysics or any other form of discourse is unable to do so. What philosophical analysis terminates in, as far as the metaphysical question is concerned, and as phrased in the way I have phrased it, namely, as asking the question "What is the world?" is an insight that shows a certain kinship with religious experience and mysticism. The contribution of philosophy as compared with religious experience or mysticism, however, is that it shows us, step by step, the reasons for this outcome, namely, that we cannot answer the question "What is the world?" though we have an immediate awareness of its existence.

Another way of stating our thesis, more in consonance with the linguistic temper of contemporary analytic philosophy, is this. The metaphysical question can be asked in the form "What does the phrase 'the world' mean?"—that is, "What is the rule of use that tells us how we are to understand this phrase, and what are instances of the actual use, the actual application of this phrase?" Unless we can clarify and make explicit the grammar of the term, "the world," and show some actual instances of its use, we should have to say that the phrase is meaningless and any sentence or body of discourse in which it appears is lacking in meaning as a result of this failure. One of the outcomes of philosophic analysis is, indeed, to show that the question "What is the meaning of the expression 'the world' and what are instances of its application?" cannot be satisfied. The reason for this is that whenever we try to assimilate the expression "the world" to any of our ordinary logical categories or schemes of classification, whether we try to treat it as if it were a name for some individual, a name for a class, a descriptive phrase, or any other such familiar schema, we find that such assimilations will not work: they do not fit precisely what "the world" is. So we are left with this result: Either we must surrender all claim to making this phrase at all intelligible by assimilation to familiar patterns, and admit therefore that it is wholly meaningless, or else we must enter the claim that its role in language is wholly unique, that no assimilation will work and that although it is meaningful, we cannot state what that meaning is, because it is *sui generis*; and the moment we weaken this claim by showing similarities and differences, we have forfeited the claim to its being *sui generis*. Thus, the paradox is that on the one hand, if we accept this analysis, we are forced to admit that by conventional standards the phrase "the world" has no meaning, because we cannot set out by ordinary techniques and by appeal to already well-established criteria and schemes of classification, what the phrase "the world" means; and on the other hand, in the course of making such a survey, we have thereby come upon what is in fact the genuine and ineluctable use of the phrase "the world." Far from having eliminated it completely, we emerge with a more genuine insight into what the "logic" of the phrase "the world" is, although that logic turns out in the end to have nothing to do with the setting out of a body of statements about the world, statements that we can accept as giving us, in any ordinary sense of the term, a true descriptive or explanatory account of the world.

II

The World as a Totality

In our daily commerce with our surroundings, in practical affairs, in the arts, and in the researches of science, men are variously concerned with perceiving, manipulating, producing, transforming, understanding, describing, explaining, predicting, enjoying, avoiding, or using the countless things, objects, phenomena, situations, processes, and events our experience discloses. Insofar as we take a broadly cognitive stance with respect to this vast multiplicity we find that language is the basic tool by which we gain some intellectual dominion and control over these; we identify individuals, we note similarities, we form classes, we make generalizations, we systematize and interrelate in various ways the individuals, or groupings of individuals, thus brought within the range of our understanding, that is, our powers of description and explanation. To dominate intellectually this variegated multiplicity requires the exercise, deployment, and self-reflective critical analysis of the resources of ordinary language and of science, as well as the clarificatory efforts of philosophy, including the metaphysician's concern with categories. But nowhere in all this commerce with things do we encounter the world as such. Or rather, we should not need the concept of "the world" in dealing with this vast multiplicity. We should need, of course, the ways of identifying individuals, of forming classes, laws, and series of various kinds; but for the ordinary purposes of common sense or of science we should not need the concept of "the world." Even the concept of "the physical universe" is but a scientific concept useful in ordering certain ranges of astronomical data. The universe in this sense, however, like the atom, or the class of mammals, is a concept that carves out some domain of entities for selective consideration. The term "universe" as used by the astronomer and cosmologist is a technical term and has no more nor less relevance to the possible metaphysical use of the term "the world" than anything else. In the sense in which the present day cosmologist uses the term "the universe," this has to do with the large-scale distribution of the galaxies. Given the observed population of the galaxies, and other units of relevant cosmologic interest—for example, the recently discovered quasars—the cosmologist investigates the spatial and temporal properties which may be ascribed to the inclusive material system to which the galaxies belong as constituent units, and where the term "universe" is used to designate this inclusive system of galaxies. As such, the properties of this system insofar as these are determinable empirically by testing various proposed theoretical models of the universe, are as much a study of one system of entities or objects as any other subject matter studied in empirical science. The magnitude of this system to be sure is far vaster in terms of the scale of distances, size, and duration of its constituent members than any other object or systems studied in empirical science, but except in terms of such overarching magnitude, the galaxies and their systematic interrelations have no greater metaphysical significance than any other types of entities. In this sense of the term "universe," what the universe is needs to be treated along with other entities, events, and phenomena, in any effort at determining the meaning to be given to the term "the world." But it has no special preeminence for this purpose. In short, the physical universe as an astronomically far-flung domain is not the world. Whether the physical universe requires a finite or an infinite geometry for the working out of a physical theory to describe the relationships among the galaxies, is of no consequence for a metaphysical concern with the world. For the universe has as much or as little to do with the world as anything else,

whether it be, for example, the structure and development of human in-
stitutions, the structure of the atom, or the anatomy of a frog.

As a first step in our inquiry we must examine the claim that if our
interest is in answering the question "What is the world?" or, alternatively, in saying how we are to understand the use of the phrase "the
world," these questions can in fact be answered. Various answers of
course have or might be given. But since in the formulation of those
that are most frequently encountered we find that the words "totality"
or "whole" figure prominently, I propose to stop and examine these expressions and to ask whether we can achieve a satisfactory account of
what the world is by their use.

The terms "totality" and "whole" are by no means synonymous.
To be "a whole" includes among its several meanings that of being a totality, but the converse does not hold. For a totality is a class, aggregate,
or set, whereas a whole may also be spoken of as applying to an individual or a system of individuals where the emphasis is to be placed on
some organization, systematic interrelationship, or organic structure of
its parts. In the present discussion I shall be concerned only with attempts to define the world as a totality. In order for the world to be a
whole as a structural, systematic, or organic unity, that is, an individual
all of whose parts are ordered in a special way, it would first be necessary
that the world be at the very least a totality, a collection, class, or aggregate consisting of plural parts. And it is into the general feasibility of so
describing the world as such a totality that we shall therefore first inquire, since if it should turn out, as I propose in fact to argue, that there
are serious difficulties in the way of our conceiving of the world as a totality, this will *a fortiori* also cut the ground from under any attempt to
describe the world as a single structured, unified whole. Examples of
characterizations of the world as a totality are Wittgenstein's fundamental thesis of the *Tractatus* that "the world is the totality of facts, not of
things," and Strawson's counterclaim that "the world is a totality of
things not of facts." There are, however, a number of difficulties and
objections to conceiving of the world as a totality of any sort. The difficulty of course is not with the notion of a totality, class, aggregate, or
set, but rather with using any of these locutions to describe or define
what the world is. These difficulties and objections are of different types
and may be summarized as follows:

1) Sometimes, perhaps in its most crude form, the world is
thought of as simply "everything," where in the use of this term, no
special prominence is to be given to the component word "thing" as dif-

ferentiated from "fact" or "event." The term "everything" is simply a place-holder of a quasi-universal sort, since taken by itself it is absolutely unrestricted in scope. And since it is absolutely unrestricted in scope it cannot serve as a logically proper means of designation to be used in referring to or in a statement about some well-defined class. Where we do legitimately and meaningfully use "everything" as a universal quantifier, we do so in connection with some range of individuals that belong to some specifiable class, and therefore within some limited universe of discourse. Within the universe of discourse of living creatures, for example, we can make reference to or make asssertions about *everything that is a vertebrate.* The universal quantifier as well as the existential quantifier is employable only in connection with some more or less well-defined class. Taken without such a class the term "everything" is simply another way of using the logician's variable "x" and such a variable cannot stand on its own so to speak, and be used to refer to anything. Until it is put into harness with another term that specifies some domain, or some descriptively selected and marked-out subject matter, the term "everything" by itself does not designate anything, any more than the symbol "x" does. But given some specified and delimited domain of discourse, we can then use the universal quantifier (just as we can use the word "everything") in specifying the range—in this case the universal range—of entities belonging to some class or combination of classes within a universe of discourse. One way of summing up this point then is to say that we need to recognize an important difference between a totality in the sense of a class and the term "everything" as a pure variable. A totality or class can be defined by specifying certain characteristics that apply to its members or constituents, or by a rule for forming a conjunction of its members, or by actually providing such a conjunction of members (if it is a finite class), but the term "everything" is not a class formed in any of the foregoing ways. Its meaning is not provided by a definition but by indicating its use as a quantifier; and such use, to be effective, requires that the quantifier be used in conjunction with a class or totality of some sort, since it has no independent meaning of its own. As a pure variable the term "everything" is not restricted as to type, whereas a totality or class, when spelled out and properly formed, is defined by some predicate or rule of formation by which membership in the class can be determined. If the world is a totality in some sense, the character of this totality cannot be brought out by simply using the term "everything" in an unqualified way and as supposedly self-sufficiently intelligible, for the meaning of what it is to be a totality and the rule of the term "everything" are quite different in character; the latter does not serve to analyze or define the former.

2) In the light of the foregoing, our next step must be to investigate some representative attempts to characterize the world as a totality, where the term "totality" is properly used as designating a class, and where such a class can in some way be discriminated by an effective rule or set of predicates. Here various alternative possibilities open up, in the light of well known attempts in the history of thought to characterize the world as a very special type of totality, to be contrasted with other classes, and where to signalize this contrast and difference such terms as "absolute," "infinite," or "all-comprehensive" frequently come into play. Let us for the moment, however, dispense with these adjectival characterizations of the totality which the world allegedly is and consider some typical examples of attempts to give the defining characteristics of the world as a totality.

(a) One such attempt might be to say that the world is the totality of whatever exists, or, since the term "entity" may be used to replace the phrase "that which exists" we might also say "The world is the totality of entities." Such a description or definition, however, suffers from the well known difficulties that arise from treating "existence" as a predicate. For to say that something exists without otherwise qualifying it is to make use of a second-order concept, a way of saying with respect to some first-order concept that it applies or has some instances. The meaning of "exist" is here conveyed by the use of the existential quantifier "there is." To say that something exists is to say that there is something that has the descriptive property ø for example. To say "dogs exist," is to say there is something to which the term "dog" applies or for which it serves as a term of description or classification. To say "dragons exist" is to say there are cases to which we can apply the term "dragon." To say that irrational numbers exist is to say there are instances of constructions to which we can apply the term "irrational number," and so on. In this sense of "exist," we are using the term tenselessly and as not having anything to do with present actuality, for example, as contrasted with what belongs to the past or to the future; nor are we using the term "existence" as a proxy for some other term such as "living" (as applied to human beings) or for that which has causal efficacy, power, or that which has some specific space-time locus, or the like. Nor does the term "existence" in the foregoing sense have anything to do with the sense which the term might be said to have when this is used as a synonym for the term "the world" itself. In this latter use of the term "the world" however, we are no longer thinking of the world as a totality, but as something *sui generis* and undifferentiated, and where indeed the verbal noun "existence" serves simply as an analytic explication for what term "the world" itself designates. In the present case, however, we are considering the use of the term "the world" as a name for a totality, and we are considering the feasibility of characterizing this totality as one which consists of all those things that have existence. The difficulty with this approach is that there is no such class, for we cannot form a class of those things which "there are." Aristotle put this long ago by pointing out that "being is not a genus, it is not the essence of anything"; or, as this may also be rendered, "There is nothing whose essence is that there is such a thing, for there is no such kind of things as *things that there are.*" [5] We do not pick out a distinctive class—not even an all-inclusive or comprehensive class—when we try to form such a class of all the things that there are. In other words, when we consider what the various cases of "being an instance of," or "being describable by a class term" have in common, we do not form a new class of objects; we have done nothing more than bring out what it means to say that a term can be used descriptively or to classify something or other. But in bringing out what the meaning is of "application of descriptive terms to instances" or what it means to say "there is a such and such" (that is, the meaning of the existential operator) we have not thereby done anything to set up a new class, a totality, to which we might assign the name "the world." To turn the matter around, what if anything we mean by "the world" is not to be satisfactorily explicated by saying that it consists in the clarification of an expression such as "exists," where this is understood as having the meaning of "there is" or the existential operator, and so as having to do with something about how language functions. The use of the term "the world" is not explicated when we clarify the manner in which we use classificatory and descriptive terms and assert, in particular cases, that these can be correctly employed.

(b) Closely related to the attempt to characterize the world as a totality of entities, or as a totality of whatever exists, are those attempts which describe the world as "a totality of facts," or again as "a totality of things (or objects)." In contemporary discussion the term "fact" has come into prominence as a result of the special status Wittgenstein assigns to it in the *Tractatus*, where, as we have already remarked, he defines the world as "a totality of facts." For Wittgenstein, a fact is the counterpart of a true proposition; it is that to which a true proposition refers and with which it shares a common structure. Facts are in the world; they are that about which propositions have to do and with which they correspond when they are true. And facts, for Wittgenstein, are to be differentiated from "objects" or "things." An object is an irreducible simple. The totality of objects fills all of what he calls "logical space" and would be common to all worlds—both our actual world and all possible worlds. However it is only the specific arrangement or structure of such objects—that is, facts and the particular concatenation of such facts—that uniquely identifies our world. A fact in this sense is something contingent: it is the way in which objects happen to be organized and related to one another. And for him all facts divide into atomic facts, that is to say, the irreducible minimal structures that cannot be further subdivided into any further facts (the counterparts of atomic propositions), and compound or complex facts that have these atomic facts as their constituents. He defines the world as being the totality of all such facts, whether atomic or compound.

There have been many critics for whom the attempt to characterize the world as a totality of facts is wholly unacceptable, but who, without surrendering the attempt to characterize the world as a totality, have fastened instead on some other choice by which to define this class. For some critics the choice is better made when one takes the term "thing" or "object" rather than the term "fact." And still others would reject both "facts" and "things" and fasten upon "processes" or "events" as the true basic constituents of the world. In what follows, however, I do not propose to examine the details of these controversies, nor to attempt any comparative evaluation of the merits of speaking of the world as a totality of facts, as a totality of things, or as a totality of events. I shall be little concerned to examine the internal claims and counterclaims of each of these competing accounts, since there is one type of criticism, which if valid, undercuts and makes unacceptable any such attempt to characterize the world as a totality, whether it be of facts, things, or events. Strangely enough the tools for this criticism are to be found in the very *Tractatus* of Wittgenstein from which I earlier quoted his thesis that the world is the totality of facts. And unless I radically misunderstand the import of what Wittgenstein himself says in the section in which he furnishes the tools for this analysis, once we take seriously what he has to say there, it not only renders nugatory the attempts of others to characterize the world in such terms as a "totality of objects," or a "totality of events," but it also reflects upon his own characterization of the world as a "totality of facts," and gives us the basis for rejecting this statement as well.

Wittgenstein, building on a point introduced by Frege, points out that it is necessary to distinguish what he calls "formal concepts" (or sometimes also "pseudo-concepts") from ordinary or "proper" concepts. An ordinary or proper concept, such as "cat" or "star," can be represented by means of a function, that is, by means of a set of descriptive predicates. When we apply a proper or ordinary concept to something and say of it that it is a such and such, say a cat or a star, we are saying something informative, and what we are saying is either true or false; it either fits or does not fit that to which we are applying this concept. In contrast with such concepts, however, Wittgenstein calls attention to what he calls "formal concepts"; these concepts cannot be represented by means of a function or a set of predicates. Nor can they be used informatively about something. They have to do rather with the way in which certain signs are used. Thus for Wittgenstein the concepts "thing," "object," "fact," "concept," "function," "number," "complex," are all formal concepts. They have to do with special types of variables and the way in which these are used in our language. The way of characterizing a formal concept is to show its distinctive use, that which distinguishes it from other formal concepts. The term "formal concept" is used by Wittgenstein in the broad sense to include as species of such concepts not only "concepts" in the narrow sense, i.e. the kind of role performed by a predicate variable ("property"), but also by, for example, "proper name," "number," "proposition," "fact," etc. I shall use the term "formal concept" in what follows in this broad sense. Thus, the way in which the formal concept "property" is used in different from the way in which the formal concept "object" is used. We can bring out the special style of variable involved in the use of a particular formal concept by pointing out its distinctive use.[6] Wittgenstein goes on to point out the consequences of failing to recognize the special status of formal concepts and to illustrate this in the case of the formal concept "object" ("thing").

Thus the variable name 'x' is a proper sign for the pseudo-concept *object*. Wherever the word 'object' ('thing,' etc.) is correctly used, it is expressed in conceptual notation by a variable name. For example, in the proposition, 'There are 2 objects which . . . ', it is expressed by '$(\exists x,y)$ . . . '. Wherever it is used in a different way, that is as a proper concept-word, nonsensical pseudo-propositions are the result. So one cannot say, for example, 'There are objects,' as one might say, 'There are books.' And it is just as impossible to say. 'There are 100 objects,' or 'There are $\aleph_0$ objects.' And it is nonsensical to speak of the *total number of objects*. The same applies to the words 'complex,' 'fact,' 'function,' 'number,' etc. They all signify formal concepts, and are represented in conceptual notation by variables, not by functions or classes (as Frege and Russell believed). (4.1272.)

When we apply the above point to "facts" it would follow that it obviously makes as little sense to say that there is a total number of facts, as it would be to say there is a total number of objects; for facts do not form any kind of *class* or totality, and neither does it make any sense to apply a numerical predicate to this alleged class. For "fact" like "object" does not mark out a class defined by a set of descriptive predicates. Therefore, we cannot form a totality of facts any more than we can form a totality or class of objects or events. The term "fact" like the term "object," for Wittgenstein, is a variable, a place-holder in some statement; its use is exhibited in the specific way in which signs can be employed in informative statements. The world as something that exists, therefore, and about which all our language has to do when it purports to give us information, is not constituted of facts in this sense. Facts do not make up the world any more than, strictly speaking, objects do. What does make up the world are the counterparts of that to which true elementary or compound statements refer when these are expressed by means of *proper* concepts. It is only when we make use of *actual instances of proper concepts* that we have to do with that which is in the world. In the course of talking about the world by means of actual propositions that employ proper concepts, we shall implicitly use and exhibit formal concepts; for example, we shall exhibit the use of the formal concept "object" insofar as we make use of particular proper names, or "fact" insofar as we affirm a structural relation among particular objects.

What then are we to make of Wittgenstein's claim that the world is the totality of facts? Of course, one simple way of saving him from the charge of inconsistency is to say that this thesis is but a summary way of speaking of the actual instances or values of the use of *proper* concepts. The statement "The world is the totality of facts" is to be understood as an elliptical and foreshortened way of saying that the world is constituted of all those individual counterparts of true elementary propositions, each of which by means of proper concepts says something about some actual particular situation that exists in the world. On this interpretation the world cannot possibly be constituted of a totality of facts in any literal sense since the term "fact" has to do with a formal concept and therefore with something about the way in which language is used when set out in logically perspicuous form. However, the world is something which exists whether we talk about it or not and is therefore not to be thought of as literally made up of such formal concepts or any number of instances of the use in language of such formal concepts. If, though, we do take Wittgenstein to mean that the world is constituted of actual individual *instances* of fact, as that which is pointed to by the use of propositions making use of proper concepts and specific *values* for these concepts, then the question arises, In what way can we justify the claim that we can form a *totality or class* of these instances? As we shall see shortly, there are a number of strong objections to this line of thought as well.

Before turning to this fresh point, however, there is a brief matter that calls for some attention. It might be objected to the foregoing account that it radically misinterprets Wittgenstein's views by taking "fact" to be a formal concept and therefore as having to do principally with language and its uses. On the contrary, it may be said, Wittgenstein is concerned to point out the relation, indeed the identity of form, holding between language and the world in the case of true propositions. For him, therefore, there are facts in the world as much or as little as they are in language. And this point is sound enough. Wittgenstein does maintain that there are facts in the world and that one species of such facts are found in language in the symbolism it employs. But the essential point I wish to make by way of criticism of Wittgenstein's views—or at any rate by way of elucidating the consequences of his views—is that, strictly speaking, there are no facts in the world any more than there are in language. Facts are exhibited in the use of variables in language, in the way, for example, names are concatenated. We cannot say that an actual proposition *consists* in such a fact, but rather that it *exemplifies* this formal concept. In like manner, we cannot say that there are any facts in the world or that the world is composed of facts. Rather it is composed of the correlates of particular names concatenated in particular ways. In so far as there are such particular concatenations, they exemplify or exhibit the form of a fact, this time, as we may say, in an ontological or world setting rather than in a linguistic setting. In any case, what makes up such individual concatenations are actual individuals and their particular structural relations. There is, however, as little warrant in this ontological view, as there was in the linguistic approach, to say that the world is *constituted* of facts; for what we mean by "facts" is still formal, and cannot be the matter of the world. To have such matter we need actual individuals and actual connections among these individuals. And if, therefore, we are to define the world as a totality we should need to know something more than the general definition of what it is to be a fact, since the latter, being only formal, cannot tell us anything about what the world is as far as its *content* is concerned. If, then, we are to define or describe the world as a totality it cannot be as a totality of facts, for we cannot define or describe such a totality merely in formal terms. We should need some way of specifying the actual content, and for this the definition of what it is to be a fact is inadequate. This is so whether we take "fact" in its linguistic role as exemplified in the use of variables of various types, or in its ontological dimension as that to which language is correlated, or which is being mirrored by language. The world, therefore, cannot be said to be a totality of facts.

3) Our attempts thus far to characterize the world as a totality have ended in failure. To summarize, we have thus far considered two kinds of reasons for this failure. The first was brought out in connection with

the analysis of the word "everything." We showed that we fail to define the kind of totality the world supposedly is, unless we specify certain of its defining characteristics in addition to using the quantifier "everything"; the quantifier, if taken in an absolutely unrestricted way, does not by itself specify a class. Our next move was to see whether we could in fact succeed in defining this class by using as our defining criteria certain formal marks. Here we once again met with failure. Neither the term "existence" in the sense of the tenseless existential quantifier "there is," nor terms such as "fact" or "thing" are able to serve the purpose of such defining characteristics. What we need are descriptive predicates and not formal ones.

Our next step therefore must be to see whether we meet with any greater success by characterizing the world as a totality by nonformal means. Here we find that there are, broadly speaking, two possible alternatives. To define these alternatives I shall fall back on a distinction made by—among others—W. E. Johnson and J. M. McTaggart. Johnson pointed out the difference between what he called "enumerations" and "classes," and McTaggart pointed to an analogous difference between what he called "groups" and "classes." We have thus far used the term "totality" indiscriminately without taking advantage of making the foregoing distinction and it is time now to introduce it. Let me quote McTaggart's account of this distinction.

A group must be distinguished from a class. A class is determined by a class-concept. This concept consists of one or more qualities, and everything which possesses these qualities is a member of that class. Thus the quality 'to be a member of the class P,' can be defined, the definition being 'to possess the qualities of X, Y, and Z.' And by means of this definition we can determine whether any particular thing is a member of the class. But the members of a group are determined by denotation. L is the group which consists of A, B, and C. Thus we cannot determine by a definition what are the members of a particular group. It is true that the quality of being a member of L may be defined as the quality of possessing either the qualities RST, or the qualities UVW, or the qualities XYZ, where these qualities form sufficient descriptions of A, B, and C, respectively. But we cannot know this definition until we know what the members of the group are, and therefore we cannot determine what they are by means of this definition.[7]

To bring out the force of this distinction let us consider the following simple illustration. The class designated by the phrase "President of the United States" is for example a different class from the class designated by the phrase "Prime Minister of England." The class designated by the phrase "President of the United States" is defined by specifying those characteristics which serve to characterize all those who belong to this class, a list of characteristics which would include, for example, a listing of the powers of this office as given in the Constitution of the United States. One can define this class without referring to any individual members. According to this usage a class is specified by setting out a rule for determining whatever is to be considered a member of this class. Thus a class may or may not have any actual members. As it happens Washington, Jefferson, and so forth, are members of the class "President of the United States." And we may apply this class designation to them; but it is possible to define a class even though it does not have any actual members. This might have been the case, for example, if there had only been a drafting of our Constitution but no person had ever been elected first President of the United States. Of course the classes that empirical science is interested in, and that we are concerned with if we are to think of the world as a class, would be the kind of class that in fact has members, those for which the class designation has successful application. When zoologists establish the class "Rhesus monkey," for example, it is because they encounter *in experience* a number of individual creatures among whom they find certain striking resemblances, and state in a class-defining formula what the characteristic marks of this class are. In general, a class is determined by specifying a list of characteristics by means of a rule or definition.

By a *group* as contrasted with a class, however, is meant a collection that can be specified only by means of a list of the individuals, constituents, or members of the *group*. And the giving of such a list—which can be as arbitrary as one pleases—is all that is required in determining the group. In specifying the group one must make use of proper names, definite descriptions, or existential statements affirming that there are members of some particular class or kind. (In this last case, such existential statements may be taken as surrogates for the use of statements containing proper names or definite descriptions for the constituent individual members of the given class.) Thus we can form a group (to use McTaggart's illustration) of "the table at which I am writing, the oldest rabbit now in Australia and the last medicine taken by Louis XV." Therefore in order for a group to be designated there must be actual members and these must be referred to by some identifying process. Moreover, any combination of individuals or groups is itself a group. To specify a group all that is necessary is the use of the enumerative "and" in a statement, all of whose conjuncts can be themselves identified. The groups so formed vary of course in interest so that the group we should form, for example, by enumerating each of the Presidents of the United States by name (viz., Washington, Adams, etc.) is a group we should normally have more interest in than, say, the group previously mentioned, namely, "the table I am now writting on, the oldest rabbit in Australia and the last medicine taken by Louis XV." However, according to present terminology the collection formed by enumerating the Presidents of the United States by name, would be a group; what determines them as belonging to this group is the fact that they have been so enumerated. If one should, for some reason, add Napoleon to this previously enumerated group (of Washington, Jefferson, etc.) this would simply change the character of the group; it would be a different group, some of whose members overlapped with the members of the first group, but it would be a group nonetheless.

When we apply these distinctions in determining to what extent we may describe the world as a totality, the first point that emerges is that the world cannot be said to be a class, if by a class is meant simply the specification of a set of characteristics which may or may not be exemplified. If the world were a class it would be essential to what we mean by "the world" to insist that there be actual instances of this class, cases that would exemplify its defining characteristics. The world would have to be a class with actual members and not simply a logical possibility: it would make no sense to say that the extension of this class is zero. In the remainder of this section, I shall consider, in turn, the feasibility of considering the world as a totality, when treated, first, as a group, and second as a class where, in this latter case, the defining characteristics are taken to be "entities having space-time location."

(a) It is an essential requirement of a group that it can only be specified by an enumeration of its constituent members, and if there were no way of enumerating these (or denoting them, to use McTaggart's term), then we should not be able to specify the group. The enumeration of the individuals or constituents is all that we have for setting up the group; and whatever be the connections, common properties, or interrelations we may subsequently find among the members of this group, we must presuppose that we have known these constituents to be in fact members of the group. Thus the fact that we characterize the world as a group leaves open the possibility that some systematic interrelations may be increasingly discovered among its constituents. And as such systematic interconnections come to be established, it becomes increasingly possible to speak of the totality as a "whole" as a "unity," and not simply as a "group." If, therefore, the world is to be said to be such a unity or whole, this would have to be argued for separately and in addition to the claim that it is a totality. But the minimum, it appears, that we might argue for now is that the world is a totality and that the type of totality it is, is a group specified by giving a list of its constituent members. Let us then consider what the specification of the world-totality would come to if we followed this procedure.

We see immediately, however, that there is no obvious way in which we can satisfactorily apply the notion of a "group" to characterize the world. The basic reason why the enumerative "and" and the notion of a group as formed of actually identifiable or empirically specifiable constituents cannot serve to give us a rule for defining the world is that it is essentially incapable of completion. To indicate what I mean by this let me first take once more the case of a normal, empirically definable class; we mark out such a class K by means of characteristics a,b,c, and we identify, for example, some particular object as a K because it has a,b,c or sufficiently resembles or comes close to its having a,b,c, for us to classify it as such. "This" we say (as we point to some object in front of us) "is a table." Or again, given the class marks a,b,c, we are able to say, "There are in fact many instances of K; we have found many things which have a,b,c," although with respect to a vast number of such classes we are unable to say how many there are or might be that have the characteristic a,b,c. Here we can say that the *membership* is essentially incomplete, since we cannot say, for example, how many objects there are or might be to which the term "table" might be applied. In this situation the defining characteristics of the class are kept constant and we say the membership is open-ended. But in the case of specifying a group, we are not concerned with keeping any set of characteristics constant; for what determines a group is not some set of characteristics, but only the membership itself as enumerated in some enumerative rule. Hence, the moment there is a change in the composition of this rule, in the list of conjuncts, there is thereby a change in the group itself. Thus, suppose we form a group consisting of empirically existent classes (each of which may be open-ended), the group consisting of the classes "dogs," "cats," "monkeys"; this will be a different group from the group, "dogs," "cats," "monkeys," "horses." If our interest is in specifying by means of a group-statement what the world is, we should find that *no list we could give would be adequate*. We cannot give such a conjunctive enumeration because there is no way of establishing that the list we would be tempted to give is complete. "Well," it might be said, "what if it weren't complete?" The reply to this is that the moment we are able to add any item to any list, we should thereby have changed our definition of the world, since it would now be specified by a different—even if only partially different—series of conjunct members. It follows that anytime, for example, a new type of object is discovered (I leave out controversial classes or those whose logical status may be open to dispute) we shall have changed our definition of "the world." Today quasars are known to exist; ten years ago they were not known; does it follow that we have changed our conception of the world? It *would* follow if we take the notion of group as the device by which to give a characterization of the totality which the world is. But clearly we have no way of saying at any time that some new class of individuals might not come to be discovered; we cannot say that we are ever able to draw up a final and complete list of individuals or classes. And since we cannot draw up a list which exhaustively states every kind of thing there is, we cannot say that we are able ever to give an adequate rule for specifying what the world is as a totality. It seems a reasonable presumption that fresh discoveries will continue, indefinitely, to be made: hence no definition of the world which rested on the claim that an exhaustive survey can already be made, even of its basic "classes" or "kinds" of things, is to be taken seriously. It follows from these considerations that we should not reach the world by a process of summation. For all such efforts at reaching a philosophically viable concept of the world start, in a sense, with the wrong end. They start, that is, with the multiplicity of entities and try to reach some unifying whole in which all these multiplicities will somehow be subsumed, included, incorporated. But we would not succeed in getting at the world in this way.

(b) There is, however, another line of investigation—another attempt belonging to the general view that the world can be defined as a totality—which we have yet to consider before venturing any general conclusion that the world is not definable as a totality. Would it not be possible to define the world as a totality, in the sense of being a class, rather than a group, a class moreover not only with actual members, but whose defining characteristics unlike our previous efforts at specifying these, can be given through descriptive predicates? We must turn, finally, to this last possibility, and to a major effort in this direction that seems at first glance perhaps more promising (and is indeed one that finds wider acceptance) than any of the other routes of analysis we have followed thus far.

If asked to give some account of what they understand by the term "the world" some philosophers would reply by saying: "I mean by "the world" the totality of objects in time and space." By way of amplification of this brief formula they might go on to say something like the following: "By "totality" I mean, in general, the entire extension of some class, and in the present case I mean the entire extension of the class of objects in space and time. For specific purposes it may be necessary or convenient to refer to the membership of this extension distributively or collectively, but whichever is done, it is the fact that this class has an extension consisting of the actual, particular objects in space and time that makes possible such reference. When reference to the extension of this class is made in the distributive mode, we commonly use the expression "each and every" and when we wish to refer to the extension taken collectively we use the expression "all." (Since the term "all" is itself ambiguous, meaning sometimes "each and every" and sometimes "all" in the collective sense, we could, if necessary, make it clear that the latter sense is intended—"all" in the sense of a "collective totality.")

Further, in describing the world as a "totality of objects in space and time," it is not necessary for us to be able to say whether the magnitude of this totality is finite or infinite. Whether it is one or the other is something on which we need not be able to make some conclusive pronouncement, or about which we should be able to give convincing reasons in the present stage of our knowledge; indeed, it might even be the case that we should never be able to get adequate knowledge by which this determination can be effectively made; or as a still further possibility, it may be that this is something not calling for discovery of a matter of fact and therefore of knowledge, but rather for a *decision* or stipulation. We may leave this question altogether open, as something on which further factual inquiry and/or discussion of a conceptual sort may properly be undertaken and sought for. In any case, whatever the outcome, it does not hinder us from saying that the world is a totality, even though we are not prepared now, or perhaps ever will be, to specify whether it is an infinite or finite totality. So much for a brief account of what I mean by the term "totality" in the phrase "totality of objects in space and time." "

"As for the other key expression in this formula, I should wish to use the expression "object in space and time" as a descriptive expression. To indicate in a general and rough way what I mean by this phrase, let me first say what I do not mean. I do not mean that we are to think of space and time as some kind of all-inclusive containers in which objects are literally located or situated. Certain uses of the terms "space" and "time" may lend themselves to this imagery, particularly the conception of space as a vast void or vacuum, as among the ancient atomists, or the conception of absolute space as in Newton; but I do not share these views. Furthermore, the term "time" is likewise used by various writers as referring to something that is itself a vast process or flux moving relentlessly from a remote and perhaps infinite past to an equally remote and perhaps infinite future, in which all individual objects are somehow caught up and carried along. Once again there are plentiful instances of this sort of talk, perhaps intended only half playfully as in some mythologies and poetic conceptions, but in any case taken more seriously by a number of metaphysical writers from Heraclitus down to the present. In rejecting this sort of talk, I prefer to think of space and time as compressed ways of referring to two great families of terms and measuring devices by which we are able to assign locations and extensions to objects. In one group we use terms such as "now," "yesterday," "four minutes," "past," "a thousand years hence"; in the other group of expressions we use such terms as "here," "one mile long," "to the left of," "spherical," and so on."

"To say that an object is "in space and time" is to be understood as meaning no more than that in describing the object, whatever other predicates may be employed (for example, that it is blue, or that it is made up of sodium molecules in a gaseous state, or that it costs one hundred dollars, or that it inspires us with awe or gives us pleasure), we shall need to make use of some one or a combination of the battery of terms that we collect under the headings "space" and "time." In some cases I may wish to use just spatial terms, in other cases just temporal terms, in still other cases a combination of terms taken from both categories. I may say, for example, "This table top is two feet square," or "The concert will take place tomorrow afternoon at three o'clock," or "There was a fire that lasted two hours in the building at 42nd Street and Broadway in New York City, yesterday," and so on. To assign spatial or temporal predicates can very generally be found to consist in doing one or both of two sorts of things, namely, either to give a *location* to something—that is, to show in what manner it is situated *vis a vis* other objects—or to say what its *extent* is. In the case of space, extent includes such predicates as shape and size, in the case of time, extent has to do with duration, i.e., how long a stretch some happening or activity in which the object was involved amounted to. Of these, perhaps the matter of assigning locations is the more basic operation, since "extent" can be defined by reference to a series of specific locations of the parts of the object. For spatial locations of objects, we need some standard of reference. In specifying such a standard we shall need at some point to make use of an agreed-upon "origin of coordinates." For this purpose, some would claim we need an indexical sign such as "here" or a demonstrative such as "this" that points to some particular object and that either serves itself as "origin of coordinates" or to which some more convenient, preferred origin of coordinates may be related. The way in which the spatial location of an object is achieved, whether in relatively simply ways or through the sophisticated devices of science, is to be able to specify the particular place in some unified and agreed-upon framework that is occupied by a particular object."

"In specifying such a place, the notion of distance or measured length plays a crucial role. Distances may be given either crudely and qualitatively, or with precision and refinement through the combined use of mathematical and technologic resources. Similarly, in assigning a temporal location to some object—to say *when* something occurred in which the object was involved, we shall need once more some standard of reference, some temporal origin of coordinates, and perhaps also—although this is a matter we could leave open for present purposes—some indexical or demonstrative device, including the use of the term "now," which itself can serve as origin of coordinates or to which some other preferred one could be related. A unified and agreed-upon temporal framework is one in which some particular occurrence can be located *vis a vis* some agreed-upon temporal origin of coordinates. The duration of some event can be given by identifying its boundaries (its beginning and end) and by determining the size of the interval with respect to some standard for measuring this duration. Further, the entire duration can be temporally located within some temporal framework with its agreed-upon origin of coordinates."

"Clearly, the matters here being broached in connection with the analysis of space and time are of wide ramifications and open to many differences of opinion, and it is not intended that what has been said thus far is in any way sufficient as a full dress analysis of this important topic. But perhaps enough has been said for our present purposes and by the way of a hint at the direction analysis might take. If carried out successfully, it could give satisfaction at a deeper level of what is intended by the use of the phrase "object in space and time." "

"As a further point in clarification of what I mean by the formula "The world is the totality of objects in space and time," let us consider briefly the question of existence. Of course in the formula "The world *is* the totality of objects in space and time," the word "is" as used here is the "is" of definitional identity or substitutability. One way of reading this (as a syntactic matter) is to say that the term "the world" is to be regarded as having the *same meaning as,* and therefore as one that can be used as a replacement for the phrase "the totality of objects in space and time." Another way of reading this (in the semantic mode) is to say that when used referentially, the phrase "the world" and the phrase "the totality of objects in space and time" are to be understood as having identically *the same referent.* Let us, however, now consider what existence comes to when we ask what it means, if anything, to say that *some particular object in space and time exists,* or further, what it would mean, if anything, to say that *the world* (in the sense of "the totality of objects in space and time") *exists.* Here, as we know from current discussions of the concept of existence, there are two principal alternatives favored by analytic philosophers, represented on one side by writers such as Russell and Quine and, on the other, by Strawson, for example. Those who take the approach pointed to by the original Russellian theory of definite descriptions will take existence not as a descriptive predicate but rather as something to be handled through the use of quantificational devices when a statement is put in canonical form. For Strawson, however, who would stress the referring role performed by specific terms in sentences used to make assertions, the matter of existence is not to be handled through the appeal to quantificational devices. For him, rather, existence is bound up with the way in which we go about establishing the truth of a *presupposition*, the presupposition, namely, that what the subject term of our proposition refers to, can in fact be found. Paradigm cases of such confirmed and confirmable presuppositions, are to be found wherever we accomplish the *identification* of a particular material object. To be able to say that a particular material object has been identified in any fundamental way is to give its location in a unified spatio-temporal framework in such a way that this can be accomplished noncontroversially. Once again, in connection with this bare summary there are many matters that would call for much fuller discussion in any adequate treatment of this topic. However, for our present purposes, we may perhaps be allowed to leave the particular way of analyzing existence as a matter to be further explored, as between the two lines we have indicated, and to say simply that when we assert that a particular object in space and time exists, this can be handled in one or another of the two ways mentioned. This results in the following. If we were to adopt the Russell-Quine terminology, to say a particular object exists in space and time is to say no more than that *there is* an object having such and such spatial and temporal predicates, and that this statement can be established as true. On the Strawsonian analysis, to say that a particular object in space and time exists, is to say, in effect, that we can successfully *identify* and reidentify a material object as having a particular location in a unified spatio-temporal framework."

"What now of the statement "The world exists"? If this is to be given any meaning at all, we must proceed by reminding ourselves of the point made at the outset, namely that the primitive idea with which we must start is the idea of a particular object in space and time. We were then able to characterize the world as the totality of such objects in space and time. If then we are to understand what it means to say that the world exists, we must show how such a statement is to be understood in the light of the analysis just given of what it means to say that an object in space and time exists. For the existence of the world comes to nothing more than the totality of the individual existences of particular objects in space and time. To say that the world exists is tantamount to saying that *each and every member* of the class or totality that we take the world to be, itself exists. The extension of the class of objects in space and time consists of objects which, *taken distributively*, exist. This, as we have seen, can be read—following Russell—as saying: "There is such and such an object with such and such spatio-temporal predicates, and there is such and such an object with such and such spatio-temporal predicates and so on, and so on." If we were to give the analysis that adopts Strawson's approach, this would come to saying that each and every member of the class of objects in space and time can be correctly and noncontroversially identified as having its own unique and distinctive location in a unified spatio-temporal framework. In short, to say "The world exists" is to say no more than that each and every member of the extension of the class "object in space and time" can be correctly identified in its space-time location, or can be referred to by means of a confirmed or confirmable existential statement."

The account I have just given, it must be confessed, is not based on the views of any single writer that I happen to know; it is, rather, a brief composite picture, hopefully not a caricature, made up of various bits and pieces, various strands of doctrine that, it is assumed, have been put together in a coherent way. The account I have given is, to be sure, one that different thinkers would wish to fill out in one direction or another by giving special emphases or particular analyses. At the same time it is also one which, as a schematic summary, may be recognized as sufficiently lifelike and viable to be accepted as a description of a point of view widely shared at the present time.

There is clearly much that makes sense in the above summarized position, and I, for one, should not wish to dismiss it in its entirety, though it seems to me that there is something radically at fault and missing in it. Moreover, whatever is sound in it, it seems to me, could be salvaged and appropriated for a more adequately stated theory.

To go to the heart of the matter as quickly and briefly as possible, I should like to suggest that the chief difficulty with the account I have just summarized is that it takes as its sole primitive idea the notion of a particular object in space and time, and, in so doing, overlooks the need to recognize in any acceptable account of the world that the concept of the world is itself a primitive idea. On the view previously summarized, the world is defined as "the totality of objects in space and time"; and as so defined it is therefore replaceable by the idea of "a totality of objects in space and time." Moreover, in analyzing the use of the term "existence" in connection with this totality, we have seen that this reduces to the use of the term "existence" distributively in connection with each member of the extension of the totality. But in taking this line of analysis, we altogether overlook the need to do justice to the existence of the totality of objects in space and time as a *collective totality*. To say that the world is a primitive idea is brought out by saying that the sense in which we affirm or recognize *that there is* a totality of objects in space and time, when this totality is taken collectively is a unique one; it is to affirm or recognize that this "there is" is not reducible to the sense in which the "there is" is used distributively in connection with each member of the extension of the class or totality of objects in space and time. The sense in which the totality as a collective totality exists is a wholly different and unique sense of "existence"; and, I am now suggesting, it is to deal with this unique, irreducible, and primitive idea that we do well to use the term "the world." In short, there is no need to impugn the analysis, of the kind previously given, of what it is to be an object in space and time, or what it means to say that an object exists. Nor, indeed, is there any reason to deny that for certain purposes it might even be useful to form a class or totality of these objects and to be able to refer to this class distributively. But what is being challenged here is the claim that this takes care of all that we should take note of in dealing with ontological matters. To acknowledge, on the other hand, that there is an irreducible and primitive sense of the term "the world" which cannot be constructed out of the single primitive idea of "an object in space and time" is to take a long additional step in the working out of an acceptable ontology.

Once we accept the claim or proposal that *the existence* of the totality of objects in space and time is something we can treat as a distinct and primitive idea, to be distinguished from *the totality of objects in space and time*, and that we are going to designate *the existence* of the totality of objects in space and time as "the world," then, of course, it is no longer possible to continue to use the term "the world" to *mean* the same as "the totality of objects in space and time." On the view being proposed, namely, that "the world" is a primitive and undefined concept, we should either have to find another term to replace the phrase "the totality of objects in space and time," if we wished to have such an abbreviated term to serve as its replacement, or else simply do with the phrase, "the totality of objects in space and time." Let us, for the present, adopt the latter alternative. The question we now face with respect to our use of the term "the world" is basically this: What consequences for our philosophy follow from taking "the world" as a primitive concept? One way of summing these up, as I shall try to show, is to say that we cannot treat the term "the world" in our present sense as any kind of referring expression, or descriptive expression. The *existence* of the totality of objects in space and time is not itself a totality or an individual, or indeed any other normal or familiar type of concept. Another way of expressing this is to say that the world is *transcendent*. And in saying this we are reminded of the fact that *some* of the things traditional theology says about God, and *some* of the things certain traditions in philosophy say about Being (as distinct from beings) are precisely applicable to what we should want to say about the world. Also, if we make suitable adjustments in terminology, we should find that we are able to get at the sense of Wittgenstein's well-known remark: "It is not *how* things are in the world that is mystical, but *that* it exists."

The presupposition that if something exists it must yield to some positive description, that it must be possible to assimilate it in some fashion to what we already know, to that which in some way is already familiar, is one that we commonly employ in our everyday dealing with objects, persons, events, and situations. It is a presupposition that is deeply embedded in our use of language, and in the processes of thought that such language serves to express. We inevitably use general terms in giving descriptions, whether, for example, these consist of definitions of the properties of a class, or definite descriptions of individuals. General terms by their very nature are founded in their meaning and use on the possibility of establishing resemblances of some degree or other among individuals we encounter in our experience, whether these individuals are things, occurrences, persons, or situations. However distinctive any individual is, there is always some respect in which we find it comparable to some other individual; and the fact of such resemblance-associations is the basis of our varied efforts to assimilate, that is, to classify and describe anything whatsoever by reference to other cases with which it is compared, and with which it is brought into connection. It follows therefore that if anything were absolutely unique, that is, wholly incomparable and incapable of assimilation to resemblance-classes of one sort or another, we should not be able to give a description of it, since we should not be able to use general terms at all. All we could do if there were such an "entity" would be to say over and over again, "not this," "not that." Our account would be completely negative, and this of course would raise the question, whether under these conditions we could be said to have given an "account" at all, since in our normal use of this term we mean our ability to say something positive about whatever it is to which we are referring; and such positive descriptions are always available or possible because, as we have pointed out, some resemblance-classes, and hence the use of general terms are always feasible and available. If something were absolutely and wholly unique, however, it would not be possible to say anything positive at all about it because it could not be brought into comparison with, or possess some degree of resemblance to anything else; we should not be able to assign it to any kind or class whatever, since it would not be *like* anything else whatever.

To face, now, our present problem in connection with the world: may it not be that in the case of the world our "account" (so-called for the moment) must always be of this negative sort, because the world, being absolutely unique, cannot be assimilated to anything else? This, at any rate, is the hypothesis that we would do well to explore. If the world is absolutely unique, then we should be equally misled to want to describe it by assimilating it to anything else, as we should be misled in applying to the "use" of this expression any of the standard linguistic criteria that we readily bring into play with other expressions and concepts. To consider, for example, that the term "the world" must be capable of a referring use or a descriptive use, in the way in which other concepts are so used would be to do violence to its nature. If, however, no assimilations will work, can we even speak of this as a meaningful concept at all since the criteria of meaningfulness or of use are wholly inapplicable to it? There are, broadly, two alternatives that face us here. One is to eliminate the phrase "the world" altogether, if it cannot measure up to the criteria we normally employ: if it cannot be made to submit to the logic of our other concepts. We should, under these conditions, find that having eliminated the concept "the world" altogether, we can get along perfectly well with other concepts that are more tractable and normal, and everything we should want to say can be said without recourse to the concept of "the world." The other possibility is to say that in our intellectual economy we must be prepared to leave room for such a term as "the world," although its "logic" is so unique that none of our ordinary criteria will apply to it; that nevertheless this is precisely its character. And to signalize this special status of the term or concept "the world," we shall say that what it "means" or "refers to" or what its "use" has to do with is *transcendent*. It is this second alternative that is to be examined here.

III

The World as Individual

As a further step in our analysis, and before turning finally to the suggestion that the world is transcendent, let us consider the suggestion that the term "the world" can be used to refer to an individual in the sense that *the* world is an instance of the type or class term "world." If the phrase "the world" functions in its referring capacity to an individual, we need not abandon our efforts at giving a positive description of it, since *the* world means *this* world in which we find ourselves, and it is therefore something that can be described after all, namely as a case of being *a* world, since we know what it is to be a world in general. *Our* world, or *this* world, or *the* world is one instance of what it is to be *a* world. To the question, therefore, What is the world?, when this is interpreted as a request for identification or classification of the use of this expression as a referring expression, we must now examine the answer that would consist in saying that the expression "the world" refers to an individual..

The temptation to think of the world as an individual is so great that it undoubtedly dominates or lies in the background of the popular use of the term, and makes its influence felt as well in some more sophisticated and technical versions that one finds in many well-known metaphysical systems of traditional philosophy. Among popular conceptions, undoubtedly, the influence of traditional theism with its central reliance on the model of creation of the world by a transcendent Deity, feeds on the model of the relation of a craftsman to his handiwork, as that in terms of which to explain the existence of the world. Just as when confronted with an artifact, such as a watch or a statue, we explain its existence and its character by reference to the creative capacities and skill of its maker, so too the world, regarded as a complex and all-inclusive individual thing, is that for whose existence and character an explanation is sought, and such an explanation is then found in the doctrine of divine creation.

The temptation to think of the world as a particular thing finds its reverberations, aside from theistic conceptions of God's relation to the the world (as modelled on that of the relation of a craftsman to his handiwork), in other ways of talking as well. Thus the contrast that is frequently drawn in metaphysics, by Leibniz or Wittgenstein for example, between the *actual* world and *possible* worlds, is evidence of such an assimilation of the world to the creational model, though at a considerable distance from, and as a result of radical transformations in that model. The term "world" serves as a class name for all possible worlds within which the actual world, *the* world in the sense of *this* world— this contingent, existent world—is one instance.

While it would be rash and undiscriminating to offer a wholesale condemnation of the use of this model of the world as an individual thing or whole, since there may be a certain imaginative value in this way of talking regardless of its truth-value, there are nevertheless a number of critical difficulties that stand in the way of our using this conception of the world if intended seriously and literally in the construction of a metaphysical theory, or as a valid explication of the term "the world."

The general logical difficulty with the creational model, and the contrast that some philosophers draw between this actual world and all possible worlds, is that in treating the world as a particular or individual thing, it misapplies the term "individual thing" in the sense that we should normally give to this term. To apply the term "individual thing" to the world is, to borrow a term from Ryle, to commit a category mistake, although, in committing this error in the present case, we are not strictly speaking, shifting from one *category* to another *category* and applying what holds for one to another, since "the world" is not itself a category. Nevertheless, there is a philosophical mistake in taking the category of what it is to be an individual thing in its ordinary meaning, and applying this to the world. For to be an individual thing is, in its paradigm meaning, to be a particular that we are able to pick out and identify in various ways from among a plurality of other things, and that stands to it in varying degrees of resemblance or similarity.

The world, however, cannot be identified if by "identification" we mean the sort of thing we do when we pick out or refer to some individual by such means as the use of personal pronouns, demonstratives, indexical signs, definite descriptions, proper names and, most effectively of all (as Strawson has so well brought out), by location of the individual within a unified spatial and temporal framework. In such a framework the individual is related to other individuals and found to have its own unique and distinctive place. None of this is possible for the world, for the world is not anything that can be located within a spatial or temporal framework. At best we might say that individual things and events are found "within" the world, and therewith too, the use of spatial and temporal frameworks by which to uniquely identify or locate such individuals; but neither what it is to be an individual nor what it is to be a spatio-temporal framework applies to the world itself. To say that both individuals or spatio-temporal frameworks (or even a single unified spatio-temporal framework) are to be found "within" the world is however, it should be noted, to make use of a spatial metaphor. For the world is not an all-inclusive container within which literally all such entities or patterns are located. Whether we can expect to find any description of the "relation" between what, again, we metaphorically refer to as the "contents" of the world and the world itself, a description that is, that is not metaphorical but literal is a fundamental question we shall not at this point undertake to examine.

It is clear that in the sense in which we ordinarily use the term "individual thing" to mean a selected object from a surrounding context of actual things, the world is not a thing in this sense. Our world is not a particular world to be found within a class of worlds, all of which in some way either coexist at the present, and are available for inspection, or that existed sequentially over a period of time, and of which our world is the currently existent instance. That there are no coexisting worlds or even sequentially existing worlds is not something that calls for empirical determination; it is not something that can be established as true or rejected as false on the basis of some observational, theoretical, or inferential process. For all we need to say is that if we do choose to label something "a world" in the sense in which this is a single individual member of a class that can be observed at the present time or whose members other than the present ones are inferentially established as instances that existed in the past, or will exist in the future, that we should no longer be talking of "the world" in the sense which is of relevance to our present metaphysical interest. "World" in this sense would now have an astronomical or physico-cosmological meaning, which would make all such "worlds" parts or elements of some wider series or collection, and at best (although there are difficulties here, too) it is this wider series or collection that is to be thought of as "the world" rather than any single member, instance, or element in it.

The other possible alternative in which we might try to think of the world as a particular thing is to revert to the controlling image of the creational model and its faint reverberations in the contrast that some philosophers draw between the actual world and possible worlds. Here we are not dealing, as in the model just considered, with what it is to be an individual in the sense that such an individual belongs to a class, all of whose members are actual individuals, that is to say in which the other members of the class, along with the present one which is being selected, coexist, or already have existed prior to the present one, or will exist in the future after the present one goes out of existence. Rather, the contrast between the actual and possible individual worlds has to do with the actual world which uniquely exists, and possible worlds which never have or ever will exist: no other world than the actual world either coexists at the present time, or has ever existed in the past or will ever exist in the future. There is, on this view, only one world: the actual one. Nevertheless, it may be contrasted with possible worlds, those that might have been, but which are forever relegated to the status of being merely possible and that will never descend to the level of becoming actual. Such a way of talking about the actual world, *this* world, figures in the language of the creational theist, who, whether crude or sophisticated, contrasts the world that God actually created, with the worlds that he might have created, with these which though possible were not in fact created, were not made actual. In the creational model, God's relation to the world is analogized to the relation of a craftsman to his work of art. The Divine Craftsman might have made any number of possible imagined worlds, but for one reason or another he rejects them all with one exception and actually creates this particular world. (This model, too, would need more careful discussion than I can give to it here, since there are various ways in which even the paradigm cases of artistic creation would need to be considered, as not always involving a stage in which a number of alternatives are already fully thought out, blue-prints as it were, in which all details are spelled out and from which the particular one that serves as the design for the actual work is selected. For, as is well known, in the case of crafts, technologies, and the creation of works of fine arts, the creational process may rather consist in a far more complicated process of *continual modification and remaking,* in which *at different stages,* various alternatives are considered and tried.[8] It is sufficient for my purpose to acknowledge that however we do construe the process of artful creation, on the model we are now considering the actual world would ordinarily be contrasted with other possible worlds which resemble the finally created world in varying degrees.) Where the creational imagery is presumably abandoned, as, for example, in the constrast that some philosophers draw between the actual, contingently existent world and logically possible worlds, the selection process is one not to be attributed to the designful purpose and choices that God made in his creation, but is something for which perhaps no adequate explanation is ever to be found, either because there is no such explanation at all, or because we, as human beings, are unable to provide any such adequate explanation. Yet even for such a view it presumably makes sense to pick out the actual world, the world that contingently exists, from a wider class of possible worlds, and where, as some philosophers would maintain, it is indeed possible to determine some of the features of these possible worlds as a matter of logical necessity.

It seems to me that there are a number of serious objections to this way of talking about the world as an individual. In the first place, as far as the creational model either in its crude or more sophisticated forms is concerned, I think it is sufficient to call attention to the fact that such a view, resting as it does on the use of an analogy of the world to a thing

made, begs the question, or is viciously circular. We are here considering the feasibility of saying that the world is an individual thing. The
creational model presupposes that it *is* a thing and that it *can* be compared, as in the domain of art generally, to that which is actually made
as contrasted with works that might have been but were not created.
Our question, however, has to do with the acceptability of treating the
world, to begin with, as an individual. The creational model in assuming
that we *can* treat it as such, is presupposing the answer to the very question we should need to thrash out and establish on its own merits. And
it surely will not do to appeal to the creational image of God as a Divine Craftsman in support of this, because it is simply a building-out of
this very analogy, and it is the analogy itself that is here being questioned. The question at issue is whether we can treat the world on the
analogy of an individual thing. The creational model cannot itself constitute such evidence or consist of such an argument. It rests on the use
of this analogy, but it doesn't warrant it.

Further, as far as the kind of language is concerned that some philosophers use in contrasting the actual, contingent world with the class
of possible worlds, I think that very often one can trace a fairly clear
connection historically between such talk and the use of the creational
imagery of traditional theism; and insofar as implicitly there is such reliance on creational imagery these philosophic views are subject to the
critical difficulty previously mentioned. But even where such links with
the creational imagery of traditional theology may be wholly lacking,
and one chooses instead to talk of those features of possible worlds that
may be established as a matter of logical necessity rather than as a result
of divine design or thought, it seems to me that there is the further difficulty that we are given no sound reasons why it would be desirable to
speak of that which is being described in the formal language of logic or
mathematics—the language in which presumably one gets at the features of such logically necessary aspects or structures of all possible
worlds—as a language in which one is describing *possible worlds*. I
should not deny, of course, that there are calculi of various sorts, mathematical and logical, with their own syntax, postulate sets, and so on. But
it seems to me far preferable to consider these calculi simply as *constructed languages or systems of symbolic notation* rather than as means
by which we are somehow given blueprints of *possible worlds*. Why is
the terminology of "worlds" at all relevant and fruitful here? One can of
course see in certain philosophers, notably in Leibniz, the connection
between such talk of mathematical possibilities, and a theological interest in and affinity for creational imagery. But why, apart from such theological motivations or affinities, is it at all necessary to talk of these lan-

guages as dealing with possible worlds? There are logicians and mathematicians and the calculi, the syntactical systems, they create. These calculi, like other creations of the human mind, are particular entities along with other particular entities. They are as we might say— though this is language we shall have to re-examine on another occasion —*within* the world just as are shoes and sealing wax, people talking English or Hungarian, and the blueprints drawn by ship designers. They are not, however, the ground-plans of worlds. These languages are particular entities "within" the world, the unique world, not means of access to or insight into other possible worlds.

Another quite different way of expressing the general point I have been making about the concept of the world is to stress the basic differences, in this connection, that separate the concept of the world from all other concepts. For whereas in connection with other concepts it is important to distinguish the specification of the meaning of the concept by some linguistic rule, and the instances to which it applies, this distinction, familiar and important as it is for all ordinary concepts, does not apply to the concept of the world; for to pin down in some fashion or other what the world is by some conceptual or quasi-conceptual "understanding" is thereby to have also, by the same act of awareness, come into contact with that which is the unique existent exemplification of that concept. We cannot have the concept of a world apart from the concept of the world as actual. What meaning, if any, can be given to the concept of possible worlds (and I have been suggesting that this is a dubious extension to and extrapolation of the concept "the world") feeds indeed on the prior and ineliminable concept of the world as actual. Indeed to speak of the world as actual or existent is a pleonasm. There cannot be a world which is not actual—at any rate the world we know and start from is the actual world, that which exists, and within which we come to construct, among other concepts, for whatever they are worth the notion of "possible worlds." In the case of the world, then, existence and essence are one, and we cannot drive a wedge between them as we do for other concepts. If there is any warrant for the notion of necessary existence it is to be found here, in the concept of the world. The world necessarily exists, not in the sense that we must be able to give a *reason* for its existence, but rather in the sense that to deny existence to the world is self-contradictory. It makes no sense to say that the existence of possible exemplifications of the world is a contingent matter, as we should normally say this sort of thing for other concepts. To have the concept of the world at all is already to have the concept of something that does exist and in this sense cannot not exist. Whatever be the difficulties with the Anselmian ontological argument as applied to the necessary existence of a Being that transcends the world, the Anselmian "argument" (so called) is perfectly valid when applied to the world itself. And insofar as the world does have in this sense necessary existence, we can say that for this very reason the concept of the world transcends all other concepts. That to which it applies, the world, is transcendent because it does not lend itself to description by other concepts, by concepts, that is to say, that may at best only successfully apply to classes, objects, or entities "within" the world but that do not apply to the world itself.

IV

The World as Transcendent

I have thus far dwelt on the reasons why it would be an error to determine what the world is by considering it as a putative referring term whose meaning is to be given by assimilating it to the way in which we should think of a class or totality, or to the way in which we identify an individual. But there is a deeper objection to our procedure altogether that should make it wholly futile to think of "the world" as a term that might function as a referring phrase; and the reason is that whenever we use a referring phrase we do so normally in a context in which we wish to *say* something about that which is so being referred to. And even where, as in abortive cases of making a statement—that is, where we manage to pick out something but do not go on to say anything about what is thus picked out—we have at least managed with some degree of success, for example through the use of indexical signs, demonstratives, or proper names to mention or to point to something about which we might have gone on to say something. However, the term "the world" functions in none of these ways; for the world is not anything that can be described or picked out. It can neither be defined as a class nor identified as an individual. And for this reason we face a wholly different situation from what we ordinarily face when asked to give the meaning of a term. We come armed, as it were, with criteria of meaningful reference and meaningful descriptions that are appropriate to all those individuals or classes of individuals with which we ordinarily have commerce. All our ordinary language and the logic that specifies the criteria for the effective use of this language, have to do with these normal uses. When we seek to apply these criteria, however, to the world, we should find that they are wholly inappropriate. Strictly speaking, therefore, what the phrase "the world" signifies is not a concept or a name at all. We should be obliged to give altogether negative accounts of it if pressed, or else resort to synonyms that are just as unenlightening as the term "the world" itself.

The first point then that we need to stress in connection with the use of the term "the world" is that its use is not to be found in a propositional context. We are not to look at it as, for example, a referring expression that might occupy the subject role in a proposition. Nor indeed could it fruitfully serve in a predicate role; for to what could such a putative predicate apply except to the world itself? And in this case we should have been obliged to have as our legitimate *subject* the term "the world," thereby emerging with nothing more than a trivial identity, or what in this case is a degenerate proposition. For the term "the world" functions neither as a subject nor as a predicate. It is thus perhaps best to think of it not as a term in a proposition at all; and so if by a "concept" we mean that which can or must be able to function in one or the other of these ways, it is not a concept at all. "The world" is a "term" only in an extended and special sense whose role, if it has one at all, is not to be found in any part of a propositional assertion.

One way of pointing to this difference is to say that whereas all ordinary concepts are *used* in one way or another in discourse, the concept of the world is not used at all; at best we can say it is a concept that is *had*. But then we have the option either of stretching the term "concept" so that it includes those concepts that are had as well as those that are used, thereby making room for the concept of the world; or else we could insist that all concepts if they are genuine must be concepts that can have their use made manifest, their role in discourse shown to conform to one or another of the conventional and familiar types. And under these conditions, one should have to admit that "the world" is not a concept at all. It is something we might then wish to call a "pseudo-concept" or a "quasi-concept." It makes relatively little difference which procedure we adopt, since the important point is that what the phrase "the world" has to do with is completely different from what any other concept or name has to do with.

It follows from this that metaphysics in the sense of a body of propositional discourse purporting to give us some reasoned conclusions about the world as the subject of our knowledge is impossible. For not only is there no such thing as metaphysical argumentation about the world whether of a rigorously demonstrative kind or even of a more loosely probabilistic sort, there are not, even more stringently, single metaphysical propositions at all, let alone propositions that form parts of more complex argument-structures. For to have a metaphysical proposition is to be able to say something about something. And if the subject of our would-be metaphysical assertion is the world, what is there we can say about it? Anything we can say about the world, if it is to be taken literally, would be a tautology such as "The world is the world," or "The world exists." Any other statement would be at best metaphorical, borrowing its terms of description from some segmental domain of the world, yet not literally applicable to the world itself.

In connection with this last point, it is worth noting that terms such as "existence" or "Being" if taken as synonyms for the term "the world" are not explications of the meaning of the latter but simply alternative expressions that may be used to replace the former term. No doubt the terms "existence" and "Being," as we have ourselves already had occasion to note, are themselves used in a variety of ways, some of which have little to do with the sense in which we are at present considering them as substitutes for the term "the world." Thus the term "exists" as used in the meaning of the existential operator is one such normal, though for our present purpose, irrelevant use; or again the sense in which the term "Being" is used by some ontologists as a name for that which is the Ground for the world (God), that which explains the existence of the latter, is again irrelevant to our present use. We come closer to the way in which both the terms "existence" and "Being" may be used as synonyms for "the world" if we take them as verbal nouns. Thus if we take the world as engaged in an "activity" unique to itself, we might say "the world worlds," or "the world carries on as a world," or simply "the world exists," where "exists" now is the verb that simply points to the very same "fact" to which the term "the world" does, and "existence" becomes the verbal noun, the nominalized version of the verb "to exist" as used to describe that which the world "does." Just as we might paraphrase the statement, "Tom runs" by the nominalized expression "the running of Tom," so we can replace the statement "The world exists" by "the existence of the world" or simply "existence." The difference of course between Tom and the world is that Tom can do various other things besides run; running is not of his essence; in the case of the world, however, all that it can do is to exist, and to say that it exists, is to give, if you will, its essence. In so stating its essence, we have simply given a nominalized re-expression in verb form of the term "the world." Instead of speaking of the "worlding" of the world, we speak of its "existence," and therefore in using the term "existence" as a synonym for "the world" we are not advancing our insight into what the world is, nor giving any analysis of the meaning of this term. To one who fails to understand the use of the term "the world," the term "existence" or "Being" in the sense in which these are substitutable for "the world" are not any more revealing or enlightening; whereas to one who already has some grasp of what the term "the world" points to, the terms "existence" or "Being" are usable substitutions, but neither better nor worse than the term "the world" itself.

I have myself just now used the expression, "points to" and spoke of the term "the world" as "pointing to" something. But is not the notion of "pointing to" or "referring" in the light of our earlier analysis something that the term "the world" or any of its synonyms cannot do? And is not therefore this terminology interdicted by our own earlier discussion?

Once more we are confronted with a point that has begun to emerge thus far, namely that such criticisms and objections, if pressed on the basis of the criteria we normally employ, are perfectly sound. They have the value of forcing us to recognize that only if we are willing to stretch our accustomed categories to accommodate the unique fact encountered in our experience of the world can we make use of such standard locutions at all. Thus should we want to say that it is by a form of "awareness" or "experience" that we identify the world, we should not be able to find any of the familiar modes or types of awareness or experience fitting what is involved. It is not, for example, a sensory awareness to be found in the use of one or a combination of our senses of sight, hearing, touch, and so on. When I use my eyes for example, I can see a pair of shoes or a star, but I can never see the world. I can hear a cow mooing, or an orchestra playing, but I can never hear the world, and so on for any of the senses, taken singly or in conjunction. Their targets are always specific objects, events, persons, situations, however complex; but among such objects, events, persons, and situations I never encounter the world, nor in any combination of these. Nor is the experience of the world an esthetic experience such as one enjoys in the heightened and intensified exercise of our senses or in having our imagination engaged in conjunction with such sensuous excitement. Nor is it something involving thought, if by "thought" is meant the use of concepts, ordered in statements and arguments. Nor is it even an emotional experience, whether of awe, dread, astonishment, and the like, in their ordinary meanings. Take the term "astonishment" by way of example. It does not mean in the present context, the emotion of being surprised, as we are, for example, in seeing something which we did not *expect* to see, for surely expectations here are completely out of the question; they play no role whatsoever. We come closer to what "astonishment" might mean here when we think of the term "wonder"—but again not in the sense of asking a question such as "*Why* is there a world?". Wonder or astonishment in the sense we are at present interested in it, is one of the springs of philosophy, as Plato and Aristotle long ago noted.[9] At best therefore, with respect to each of these cases of the use of such terms as "astonishment," "wonder," "awe," and the like, we should have to say repeatedly it is not this, not that: or else in each case, we should have to stretch each of these terms to include the unique and distinctive sort of things involved in "knowing" the world (where again "knowing" is used here, too, in a special and unique sense), or else we must lapse into silence. For after all, each of these terms—"awareness," "thought," "emotion," "identification," and the like—is a term that comes to be employed to describe a family or group of related or resembling human activities: however, nowhere in the familiar range of activities do we find the sort of thing that is involved in "knowing" the world as such. All that we can do therefore is either content ourselves with a negative description, that is to deny that it is describable by any of the familiar types of human experience for which we already have a particular word (e.g. "sensation," "awareness," "thought," "knowledge," "concept," "emotion," and the like), or in each case stretch the term to make room for what is involved in the case of knowing the world. But none of these terms as stretched will do anything to further elucidate the other terms as stretched, for each is equally indescribable in positive terms—terms, that is, that are borrowed from its own related family of uses. And so we wind up with a collection of negative terms, or stretched terms, but no one of them can be used in any ordinary sense. All of which is simply another way of saying that the world as "experienced" is wholly unique, and cannot therefore in any ordinary sense be verbalized or conceptualized at all. To be aware of the world is to be aware of the world and is not reducible to any other types of experience. The term "the world" is used "to point to" or to "remind" us of that of which we have an unmistakable and unique awareness. We do not start with the term "the world" and attempt to give it a definition, either verbal or ostensive, for no such ordinary definitional techniques are possible. It is rather the other way around. We have an awareness or experience of the world, and we call that of which we have this experience "the world."

I have dwelt thus far on the examination of the concept of the world in order to bring out some of the distinctive logical features it possesses in contrast to ordinary concepts. Among such logically distinctive properties we have called attention to the following: (1) It is not an expression that can readily be assimilated to any of the standard and familiar ways we have of classifying terms as, for example, a name for a class, a proper name for an individual, a definite descriptive phrase, and so on. (2) Unlike other concepts, there is no valid distinction between the meaning of the concept and its application. (3) The term "the world" is not used, it is had; it does not function in a propositional context either as a subject or as a predicate; and therefore is not part of an argument-chain in which we can undertake to set out knowledge-claims of a metaphysical sort about the world. One way of summing up the results of our discussion thus far is to say that since the world is unique, and our experience of the world qua world is also unique and not assimilable to other types of experience, the world is itself *transcendent* and our coming to "know" of the world is an act of *transcendence*. However, to say that *the world is transcendent* is not to give a positive description of the world, but only to employ a second-order term to express the fact that no first-order descriptive terms we should wish to apply to the world in attempting to give a satisfactory account of the world will in fact serve. To say that the world is transcendent is thus not to give a property of the world. And to say that by performing an *act of transcendence* man knows the world in a way which is wholly different from any other form of knowing or awareness is simply again to call attention by such terminology to the aspect of absolute uniqueness with which we are concerned in dealing with the world.

I have been dealing in the foregoing with what Heidegger calls the *Seinsfrage*, the question of Being. Since I have chosen, for reasons given earlier, to use the term "the world" rather than the term "Being," we may regard the *Seinsfrage* as a question about the world's existence. However, it is important not to be misled here by this terminology—or to confuse this with another topic that, though close to the matter I have been discussing, is nevertheless distinct from it. Thus in one sense of this phrase to raise "the question of the world's existence", to ask for example, "Why is there a world at all?" is to raise a question about the world that I should wish to argue we come ultimately to recognize as an unanswerable question, and so a mystery. This mystery about the world's existence takes many forms. Suffice it here to remark that one way of expressing this mystery, this question about the world, is to employ a pseudo- or quasi-concept, that we can express by a hypothetical expression "reason-for-the-world's-existence"; this is a reason which unlike any use of the term "reason" in its usual employments (as purpose, evidence, or causal explanation) would be so distinctive that *if* it existed, it would hold only for the world as such and for nothing else.[10] To raise the question about the world's existence that proves to be ultimately unanswerable by any rational means (and so a mystery), is to ask whether there is a reason-for-the-world's-existence. And insofar as this question is unanswerable or a mystery, it is a further way of expressing the point that everything having to do with the world as such is wholly other from our dealings with any other subject matter. For to say there is an ultimate mystery here is to say that our desire to explain the existence of the world is incapable of satisfaction. The principle of sufficient reason may be taken as a perfectly valid regulative or metaphysical principle when applied to phenomena "within" the world, but there is no way in which we can satisfy ourselves that this principle and the demand for explanation which it supports, *must* apply to the existence of the world itself. There may be a distinctive reason-for-the-existence-of-the-world, but there is no necessity that there must be such; and whether there is or not we have no way of proving by rational means: hence the ineluctable mystery. The mystery of the world's existence is one aspect therefore of the *transcendence* of the concept of the world. We cannot bring to bear the kinds of normal demands, criteria, and rules we ordinarily do in connection with more restricted subject matters.

My principal aim, however, has not been to explore in depth the matter of the mystery of the world's existence. It has been rather to give reasons for saying that anything we wish to ask or say about the world as such must be hemmed in and, in a sense, frustrated by the fact that we are dealing with an absolutely unique subject matter. And this uniqueness is what I have signalized by the use of the term "transcendence" and described by saying that the world is transcendent.

NOTES

1. Strawson, P. F., *Individuals* (London: Methuen, 1959), p. 10.
2. Randall, J. H. Jr., *Nature and Historical Experience* (New York: Columbia Press, 1958), pp. 124–5.
3. Tillich, P., *Systematic Theology* (Chicago: University of Chicago Press, 1951), p. 163.
4. McTaggart, J. M., *The Nature of Existence* (Cambridge: Cambridge University Press, 1921) Vol. I, 3.
5. Aristotle, *Analytic Post*, 92 b 13–4; cf. G. E. L. Owen, "Aristotle on the Snares of Ontology" in Bambrough, R. (ed.) *New Essays on Plato and Aristotle* (London: Routledge and Kegan Paul, 1965); Anscombe, E. and Geach, P., *Three Philosophers* (Oxford: B. Blackwell, 1961) 89, 159–210.
6. Cf. Anscombe, E., *Introduction to Wittgenstein's Tractatus* (London: Hutchinson 1959), p. 123. Miss Anscombe states the matter as follows: "If any proposition 'ϕ A' contains a symbol 'A' for something falling under a formal concept, then we may introduce the appropriate style of variable into the two blanks of '(E___) ϕ___' or 'For some ___, ϕ___' Thus 'Socrates is snub-nosed and X is bald.' 'For some X, X is snub-nosed and X is bald.' 'Socrates is bald and Plato is not', 'For some f, Socrates is f and Plato is not f'. 'Ten men mowed the meadows' —'For some n, n men mowed the meadow.' Thus, 'along with an object falling under a formal concept, that concept is itself already given: (4.12721); The concept

object is given by using 'Socrates', the concept *property* by using 'bald', the concept *number* by using 'ten', and in each case the formal concept is to be symbolically expressed by a style of variable (4.1272)."

7. McTaggart, J. M., *Nature of Existence*, I, 130.

8. Cf. Gombrich, E. H., *Art and Illusion* (New York: Pantheon Books, 1960).

9. "For this is especially the *pathos* (emotion) of the philosopher," Plato says in the Theatetus (155d) "to be astonished. For there is no other beginning of philosophia than this." And Aristotle concurs: "For through astonishment men have begun to philosophize both in our times and at the beginning." (*Met.* A 2,982 b 12)

10. Cf. Munitz, M. K., *The Mystery of Existence* (New York: Appleton-Century-Crofts, 1965).

NOTES ON CONTRIBUTORS

W. V. QUINE   Professor of Philosophy, Harvard University. Publications include: *Elementary Logic, Mathematical Logic, Methods of Logic, From a Logical Point of View, Word and Object, Set Theory and Its Logic, The Ways of Paradox,* and *Ontological Relativity and Other Essays.*

MAX BLACK   Susan Linn Sage Professor of Philosophy, Cornell University. Publications include: *The Nature of Mathematics, Problems of Analysis, Models and Metaphors,* and *A Companion to Wittgenstein's Tractatus.*

PAUL ZIFF   Professor of Philosophy, University of Illinois at Chicago Circle. Author of *Semantic Analysis* and *Philosophic Turnings.*

HILARY PUTNAM   Professor of Philosophy, Harvard University. Co-editor (with Paul Benacerraf) of *Philosophy of Mathematics;* contributor to various philosophical periodicals.

PAUL G. MORRISON   Professor of Philosophy, State University College, Brockport, New York. Contributor to various philosophical periodicals.

P. F. STRAWSON   Professor of Philosophy, University of Oxford. Publications include: *Introduction to Logical Theory, Individuals,* and *The Bounds of Sense.*

RODERICK M. CHISHOLM   Romeo Elton Professor of Natural Theology and Professor of Philosophy, Brown University. Author of *Perceiving: A Philosophical Study*, *Realism and the Background of Phenomenology*, and *Theory of Knowledge*.

BERNARD WILLIAMS   Professor of Philosophy, University of Cambridge. Coeditor (with Alan Montefiore) of *British Analytical Philosophy*; contributor to various philosophical periodicals.

JUSTUS HARTNACK   Professor of Philosophy, State University College, Brockport. Author of *Philosophical Problems*, *Philosophical Essays*, *Wittgenstein and Modern Philosophy*, and *Kant's Theory of Knowledge*.

ARTHUR C. DANTO   Professor of Philosophy, Columbia University. Author of *Analytic Philosophy of History*, *What is Philosophy?*, and *Nietzsche as Philosopher*.

GERTRUDE EZORSKY   Associate Professor of Philosophy, Brooklyn College of the City University of New York. Contributor to various philosophical periodicals.

WILFRID SELLARS   Professor of Philosophy, University of Pittsburgh. Author of *Science, Perception and Reality*; *Science and Metaphysics*; and *Philosophical Perspectives*.

MILTON K. MUNITZ   Professor of Philosophy, New York University. Publications include: *The Moral Philosophy of Santayana*; *Space, Time and Creation*; and *The Mystery of Existence*.

Date Due

228083